CW00419270

The Valley of the
Upper Thames

The Valley of the Upper Thames

H.W. JOHN CUSS

ROBERT HALE · LONDON

© *H.W. John Cuss* 1998
First published in Great Britain 1998

ISBN 0 7090 5908 6

Robert Hale Limited
Clerkenwell House
Clerkenwell Green
London EC1R 0HT

The right of H.W. John Cuss to be identified as
author of this work has been asserted by him
in accordance with the Copyright, Designs and
Patents Act 1988.

2 4 6 8 10 9 7 5 3 1

Photoset in North Wales by
Derek Doyle & Associates, Mold, Flintshire.
Printed in Great Britain by
St Edmundsbury Press Limited, Bury St Edmunds
and bound by
WBC Book Manufacturers Limited, Bridgend

Contents

Acknowledgements   7
Introduction   11

1   A Land Divided: From Earliest Times to the End
     of the Civil War   15
2   A Changing Countryside   23
3   The Canals   31
4   Change is Inevitable   42
5   Administration   49
6   The Upper Reaches   57
7   Life Beneath Thames Waters   67
8   Kemble, Gloucestershire   72
9   Ewen, Gloucestershire   80
10   Poole Keynes, Gloucestershire   86
11   Somerford Keynes, Gloucestershire   94
12   Ashton Keynes, Wiltshire   104
13   South Cerney, Gloucestershire   114
14   Cricklade, Wiltshire   124
15   Cricklade – Religious Foundations   135
16   Cricklade – Topography   148
17   A Strange, Eventful History   157
18   Petrie's Cricklade Case   166
19   Latton, Wiltshire   174
20   Down Ampney, Gloucestershire   181
21   Eisey and Watereaton, Wiltshire   191
22   Castle Eaton, Wiltshire   198
23   Kempsford, Gloucestershire   207
24   Inglesham, Wiltshire   218
25   Lechlade, Gloucestershire   224
26   Lechlade – Churches and Manor   234

Appendix   246
Bibliography   250
Index   253

Dedicated to my parents

Acknowledgements

In the 1940s the late Dr T.R. Thomson was responsible for the formation of The Cricklade Historical Society of which I was a founder member. I am greatly indebted to his widow, Mrs Janet Thomson, for her ready and willing permission to reproduce numerous passages from *Materials for a History of Cricklade*, the greater part of which was researched and written by Dr Thomson and which he edited for the society. In conveying my gratitude I also acknowledge all those contributors to his work including my distant cousin, the late Cecil Taylor Cuss, who was responsible for chapter three. My thanks are also due to the following:

Mr T.T. Ramsden-Binks, the Society's Museum Curator in Cricklade for giving me details of the attempt by the Inland Waterways Association to arouse local interest in the Thames and Severn Canal revival scheme, and for his early assistance and advice on sundry matters pertaining to this book; to Audrey Tomlin for her kind permission to reproduce her sketches in the Castle Eaton chapter and of the early church at Eisey; to the Wiltshire Archaeological Society for the use of articles in the society's annual magazines.

It would be impossible to forget the help given by my elder sister Mrs Phyllis Hammond and her husband Ray in answering my numerous requests over the telephone to 'cast their minds back'. To my younger sister, Mrs Stella Humphries, go my heartfelt thanks for all her care in checking the first draft. I have to thank Mrs Lynn Thomson for her professional advice, so freely and generously given, and last but by no means least for the artist Eddie Taylor's reproduction for the jacket of the book. With the help of them all, this book has been possible.

I should like to offer my thanks for the ready permission to quote freely from the delightful little booklet, *Glimpses of*

Victorian South Cerney published by the South Cerney Trust, through their kindly and helpful Secretary Dr M.H. Bride, and their Chairman, Professor A.M. Oakeshott. I am also most grateful for the ready permission kindly granted by the Oxford Archaeological Unit to quote freely from their preliminary findings in the Anglo-Saxon cemetery in Lechlade's Butler's Field. These are published under the title, *Invested in Mother Earth* – a fitting acknowledgement to the past.

Illustration Credits

Cricklade Museum: pp. 40, 126, 127, 129, 137 & 140. Audrey Tomlin: p. 201. Oxford Archaeological Unit: pp. 243–4.

All other illustrations by the author.

The Brook

I come from haunts of coot and hern,
    I make a sudden sally
And sparkle out among the fern,
    To bicker down a valley.

By thirty hills I hurry down,
    Or slip between the ridges
By twenty thorpes; a little town
    And half a hundred bridges

'Till last by Philip's farm I flow
    To join the brimming river,
For men may come and men may go,
    But I go on for ever.

I chatter over stony ways
    In little sharps and trebles,
I bubble into eddying bays,
    I babble on the pebbles

With many a curve my banks I fret
    By many a field and fallow,
And many a fairy foreland set
    With willow weed and mallow.

I wind about and in and out
    With here a blossom sailing,
And here and there a lusty trout
    And here and there a grayling

And here and there a foamy flake
    Upon me as I travel,
And many a silvery water break
    Above the golden gravel.

And draw them all along and flow
    To join the brimming river
For men may come and men may go
    But I go on for ever.

I murmur under moon and stars
    In brambly wildernesses,
I linger round my shingly bars
    I loiter by my cresses.

I steal by lawns and grassy plots
    I slide 'neath hazel covers,
And move the sweet forget-me-nots,
    That grow for happy lovers.

I slip, I slide, I gloom, I glance
    Beneath my skimming swallows
And make the netted sunbeams dance
    Along my sandy shallows

Then out again I curve and flow
    To join the brimming river
For men may come and men may go
    But I go on for ever.

Alfred, Lord Tennyson (1809–92)

Introduction

Tennyson's words portray so well this lovely valley of the Upper Thames with its major tributary, the Churn. Here, undoubtedly, is a unique part of England, not only because it is the beginning of England's most important river but, as the Revd W.H. Hutton wrote: 'It may be truly said that there are not many districts in England more characteristically English, more pastorally beautiful, or more full of associations with great names in literature than the "Upper River".' Through prehistory and the mists of time, there have been variations in its course, but the soul of this ancient waterway has remained immutable. Some of the changes have come about simply through the course of nature, a particularly noticeable example being the ox-bows between Watereaton and Castle Eaton. There have, of course, been many changes made by man for his commercial advantage as in the case of the water-mills, one of the earliest of which was built at Ewen, almost within sight of the source itself. Again, there are changes which have come about as a means of defence against the most enduring enemy, fellow-man himself. The Dobuni tribe belonged to the late Iron Age and wandered across Europe, as did a score of others, eventually to find, at last, this fertile partially wooded valley in which to settle down.

Here, then, I have tried to portray a few of the historic events that have taken place in and around the two important towns of Cricklade and Lechlade, together with a brief history of the villages whose life-blood in earlier times has been the river itself. Cricklade was a town of considerable importance, dominating the area for fifteen hundred years. It is the highest navigable point of a river of which every drop has been described as 'liquid history'! The early establishment of Christianity is discussed briefly, together with something of the great families who established themselves along

11

the banks following the Norman Conquest and the consequent effects on the existing communities.

The story would be incomplete without some mention of the coming of its two canals, the Thames and Severn and the North Wilts, and of the railways, the Great Western and the Midland and South Western Junction with the cumulative effect both canals and railways had on the wildlife of the area. Neither could I have passed over the life beneath the waters of the Thames, nor the richness of its birdlife.

Few historical narratives exist that take in a broad sphere of this little scrap of England that is the Upper Thames Valley. The River Thames itself might conveniently be divided into three parts, consisting of the upper, middle and lower river. Although the upper river has been defined as ending at Oxford, I prefer to call it the upper Thames as far down as Lechlade only, for it is to this town that navigation can be virtually guaranteed at any time of the year. Above it, at least in the past two centuries, navigation has generally been regarded as 'all labour and sorrow'!

Some historians have defined that, by the time of the Norman conquest, the river from Wallingford to its source was probably the most peaceful, prosperous and civilized part of England. However, it must be remembered that the accuracy of such assertions can seldom, if ever, be fully relied upon. Thus it is that we see in every historical work such interpolations as 'circa', 'It is thought that', 'It is reasonable to suppose', 'The most likely place', 'I believe that', 'Circumstances might suggest', and so on. Ancient history is full of anomalies and never quite definitive, but the remote past can lend it credibility. In pre-recorded history the only certainty is uncertainty and the historian is left to co-ordinate the thoughts and writings of those long gone, or, if he or she already has many years behind them, to piece together the more recent past from personal, memory or from the memories of others.

Cricklade is the only Wiltshire town on the River Thames. It has had a dominating influence on the upper river since the Roman Vespasian conquered the area soon after the invasion in AD 43. This market-town has been described as 'the highest navigable point of the river to be reached by flat-bottomed boats' but, as will be seen, this was not the case. It is reasonably certain that navigation took place from here by the Romans to *Londinium*. It is not my intention to dwell at length upon our ancient ancestors, those fierce Dobuni who, more than fifty generations ago, were in occupation of the upper Thames to be ultimately subdued by the Roman invaders. The Romans themselves, and indeed the Anglo-

Saxons who followed in their wake, had a considerable influence on the river and on Cricklade itself. It will be convenient therefore to begin early in this story and to dwell at greater length on what was once a very important town indeed, and to loiter upon matters when the Domesday Survey began looming large on our historical horizon and when England's history is considered by many to have truly begun. That it is my birthplace is purely coincidental.

The veneer of civilization, as perhaps of beauty itself, is surely merely 'skin deep'. The baser traits are seldom revealed in country districts like this Upper Thames Valley. However, when they did appear they certainly caused a sensation! In turbulent times, law suits became as certain to follow one another as the seasons, and often lasted much longer. Many irascible and mindless incidents have been almost lost now in the mists of time. There were the problems of the navigable Thames reaches which in earlier days extended as high as Waterhay Bridge where a wharf is thought to have existed. The town wharf at Cricklade once occupied the site of the playground and part of the local school itself, long since abandoned. There is a question as to which of the two streams Thames and Churn, at their confluence a hundred metres below the Town Bridge, is the true source of the river, sometimes known as the Isis. The historical Thames is the shorter by many miles but its course is the more direct! However, it is doubtful if more than a trickle of water has exuded from this lonely, deserted spot at Thames Head within the memory of our grandparents.

The history of a place is its people. My family name in Cricklade is of merely recent origin by British standards, my ancestors not having settled there until the latter half of the seventeenth century, but practically every village and hamlet in the valley will have some records of this ancient name.

There are, however, many families in Cricklade today whose ancestry can be traced back as far as records go, names like Giles, Little and Kilminster among them. (A full list of these can be found in the Appendix.)

I have pointed out the changes brought about by technical advances and increased leisure time since the two world wars, and of how religious observances in Cricklade, contemporaneous with towns and villages everywhere, have been affected. One outstanding example of this was the reinstatement of Roman Catholicism in St Mary's Church, the home of that ancestral worship in this town. Such an important moral advancement could be helping to offset the sadness in the hearts of thinking men and women at the general regression in the religious outlook of every Christian denomination.

H.W. John Cuss
Cricklade

1 A Land Divided: From Earliest Times to the End of the Civil War

In pre-Roman times the valley of the Upper Thames was largely under the control of a tribe known as the Dobuni who had their capital at Bagendon a few miles north of Cirencester, which some historians believe was Cirencester itself. It later became the Roman town of Corinium. The Dobuni ruled an area from the Welsh border east to Lechlade, north to Worcester and south to Bath. The neighbouring tribe, the Atrebates, had their capital at Silchester with the direct link between the two capitals crossing the River Thames where Cricklade now stands.

The Dobuni had their settlements on the well-drained gravel terraces where most of the hamlets, villages and towns are scattered along the valley to this day. Many such settlements would have been used by their Iron Age predecessors and artefacts of the period have been found over a wide area. There was plentiful water and easily worked agricultural land. Aerial photographs show evidence of round huts within the parishes of Ashton Keynes, Cricklade and Latton. The Uffington White Horse is thought in some quarters to have been a Dobuni tribal symbol.

Romanization of southern England was painfully slow and, with the Dobuni being a tough nut to crack, an offensive strategy may have turned into one of defence or, at least, one that held these troublesome natives for a time in a position of status quo. The possibility, therefore, that Cricklade's defensive ditch and wall were Roman could not for a time be ignored out of hand. The coral rag limestone from which the wall was built came from a 'safe' quarter at Blunsdon to the east from whence the incursion was made.

To those who would have doubts of the feasibility of such

theory, it has to be remembered that the terrain met with by Vespasian upon his descent of Blunsdon Hill was something to which he had hitherto been unused in his westerly advance. Here was the river, and beyond it a wide expanse of swamp and bog to be crossed before his advance could continue. He would have found some form of causeway, little used and impossible to cross in winter and possible only in periods of drought and low rainfall. A permanent substantial crossing had to be made to reach the higher and better drained ground on the neck of gravel at Latton for his extension of what was to become Ermin Street and his western conquest to the Severn. Faced with fierce resistance to his immediate advance the consideration to halt and consolidate would have been very strong. Nowhere more convenient for this purpose existed than the higher ground sloping north and the river itself a line of defence – of which full advantage was yet to be taken by the Anglo-Saxons 500 years later – and his decision to 'dig in' would have been overwhelming.

The late Dr T.R. Thomson, although himself finally concluding that the Cricklade walls were Saxon, would have at some time held lingering doubts for he wrote:

> If a camp was to cover an area the same as that covered by the present wall line at Cricklade, if the inside were dry in all seasons, if the river be touched at this point, if the site were to command the river crossing, and if the layout custom must be rectangular, then the site of the medieval town walls is the only possible site for a marching camp. No other orientation of such a square will satisfy the above conditions. There is a tradition that the walls are Roman.

If the Romans used the Thames for transporting timber or non-perishable foodstuffs from this fertile area to London, mentioned in chapter six, then they would have used Cricklade, 'the highest navigable part of the Thames' as a port for their largest provincial capital Corinium only six miles away.

Whether or not the site of Cricklade was only a Roman 'marching camp', we are forced initially to believe that, with so many artefacts found within being Roman and the relative sparsity of anything Anglo-Saxon, its walls were indeed Roman. However, as we will see from the following outstanding results of excavations, lingering doubts of their origin begin to be dispelled.

Several excavations were made from 1958 to 1963. In 1953–4 great quantities of Roman and Romano-British pottery were found near the town's north-west corner and by comparison the

Anglo-Saxon remains belonged to a much later date than the Roman road – Ermin Street – that passed it within half a mile. Furthermore, the shards are of civil domestic use rather than of a military character. The late R.T. Wainwright tells us that there is abundant evidence 'for settlements in or near Cricklade from the third to the fourth centuries . . .' It has been presumed that these were of village communities all within easy reach of the road.[1]

The lifeline had been cut off from Rome and the Anglo-Saxon rule which was to last until 1066.

> They answered that they were called Angles. 'It is well', he said, 'for they have the faces of angels and such should be the co-heirs of the angels in heaven.'
>
>> Pope Gregory I (540–604) upon seeing some English slaves in the market place in Rome

The history of this period is obscure but we know that from about 550 the West Saxons had established themselves from the Avon in Wiltshire to the Severn at Gloucester. There were endless battles and skirmishes between the newly established tribes and also with the Romano-British. One such incident took place near Kempsford and Castle Eaton where a mounted force of Hwicce, led by Ethelmund, was defeated by the Wiltshire men under Weobstan.

The pre-eminent figure amongst the Anglo-Saxons was, of course, Alfred the Great (849–99) born and commemorated at Wantage. He and his Anglo-Saxon successors continually resisted the Danes until Harold succumbed to William of Normandy. Within a hundred years the system of land holdings had been drastically changed and manors became the most important key to ownership. Farmland was allocated by the crown to the lord of the manor and the monasteries. There are numerous manors still existing along the upper Thames valley which remain much as they were in Norman times. A village could contain more than one manor, as in the case of Down Ampney – the village and its church could be enfolded entirely within the lord of the manor's ownership.

The thirteenth century saw the development of overseas trade with wool and cloth becoming important exports from the Upper Thames. Agriculture was the predominant industry and the valley was particularly famous for its cheeses.

Changes to the well-established manorial system were inevitable with the advent of the Black Death when villeins first began to receive payment in cash rather than in kind. A ship had brought the plague from Calais to Melcombe Regis in Dorset in

1348 and by 1350 it had spread throughout the country. Victims were buried well away from the nearest village in places known as 'black pits'. One such site is near the Upper Thames, a mile outside the village of Siddington.

As mentioned in chapter twenty, Queen Elizabeth I was not a stranger to the Valley of the Upper Thames. When I was very young, legend still remained strong in Cricklade that she slept at Abingdon Court, which is still standing and inhabited today. This may well have been on the night of Friday, 5 September 1592 when she was on her way to meet the Gloucestershire gentry at the Muttleford Stream on Ermin Street on the Gloucestershire–Wiltshire boundary three miles north of Cricklade.

There are numerous accounts of the long years of struggle between king and parliament in all of its three phases, from the decisive Battle of Edgehill October 1642, to that of Worcester September 1651, when the forces of Charles II were finally defeated, but here we will touch only on those parts of it that affected the Upper Thames valley.

Not least among the reasons that brought about the Civil War were the arbitrary enclosures of land, particularly for the creation of parks and disafforestments. This was not new for it had started with Henry III but matters came to a head in revolts in many parts of the country from about 1625 to 1636, during a period that came to be known as 'The Eleven Years Tyranny'. Grazing being seriously inhibited, the commoners who paid amercements for their own and agisted sheep and cattle became jealous of their common rights, and were 'fenced out', resulting in impoverishment and hardship. Of the Forest of Braydon whose most northerly edge bordered the Thames at Cricklade a surveyor wrote:

> [the forest] hath but a small game of deere in yt; for that by reason of the surcharge of cattell, there is no feede for the deere, which growthe by meanes that all the borderers stock their commons adioyninge in the forest with sheepe, and by that means their cattell do wholly feede in the Forest ... sundrie riotous insolances, and great disorders don and committed in the night season by persons unknown, armed with Muskets ... meetings in troops and great multitudes, to pull downe and deface the ditches, gates, mounds and fences lately sett up and erected by his Majesties farmors of his hignes lands.

It looked as if the affair would 'grow to a head' when the arrest of the perpetrators was ordered. In June of that year a farmer's agent reported that they have 'chopped in sunder all the rayles and cut up the high coppice hedges, soe that things is now in common, and they are not contented but they threatened to pull downe the lodge and kill me'. Seven of the offenders were given away by an informant, whose house was pulled down. The consensus of opinion against the enclosures was general and those that would not physically oppose gave help and sustenance to those who did. Sir Neville Poole and Sir Edward Boynton, the deputy lieutenants, failed to call out the trained bands, they being 'none of the best friends and will not wagg but upon sufficient warrant'. The Star Chamber extorted names of some of the participants in the riots at the trial of the twelve arrested men. They came from all walks of life and warrants were issued for their arrest. Among a few of these well-known names were Thomas Lloyd, rector of Wootton Bassett, Richard Bathe a member of a greatly respected family who beat Read, the King's messenger. There were four members of the Maskelyn family, land owners in the district, one of whom, Henry, was described as a gentleman. Women as well as men were involved, and one, Mrs Epaphrodites New, left no doubt as to which cause she would be supporting when the Civil War began eleven years later. Sir Edward Boynton and Sir Neville Poole participated as they had been reluctant to act against the rebels, and in such cases the nature of a person's allegiance was obvious. Indeed, in 1642, they became adherents to parliament.

When the Devizes mayor asked an innkeeper to accompany the force who were intending to march against the levellers at Braydon, he received a refusal. The anger of many not being so much against the King himself, but against the distress and impoverishment the disafforestments were causing. Charles was much loved by the vast majority of his subjects, of which numerous accounts during his reign leave indisputable evidence, particularly during his execution.

Almost six years before the outbreak of the Civil War the uprisings were mostly being suppressed, partly because more land was given than had at first been offered.[2] The mounds at Chelworth were thrown down under cover of darkness some years before the outbreak of the Civil War and were not restored until five years afterwards.

We still have physical reminders of these troubled years where, in many churches, damage was caused by Cromwell's troopers. Again at the riverside of the Thames within our story, the walker will see that there is something abnormal in the unnatural contours of the landscape. It is all that remains of massive earthworks which legend suggests were made by Cromwell as a defence against the army of Prince Rupert. There was one particular occasion in 1643 when the Parliamentary army under Essex spent a night at Cricklade on its return from raising the siege of Gloucester. On 16 September, Sergeant Foster wrote:

> We advanced from Ciceter five miles to a village called LETTON, where our London Brigade was quartered for the night; the Lord Generall, with his army quartered a mile further at a market town called CRICKLET; at the village aforesaid were ten cavaliers, who were sick and lame, and brought thither to be quartered, who when they heard we were marching to this place, found their leggs and run away. Sabbath day, September 17, we marched from Cricklet to a market town called SWINDOWNE, 8 miles.

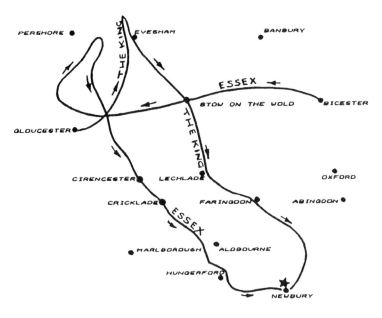

Map showing numerous areas where troop movements took place during the Civil War

Thacker gives us a slightly different version of this incident. Between Cirencester and Cricklade the army is said to have collected a thousand sheep. A spur of the period, found in Paul's Croft at Cricklade, is in the local museum. The horses were probably picketed in St Sampson's Church. This practice was not unusual. Cromwell himself was known to have stabled his horse before the altar in the crypt at Westminster. On 25 November 1645, Colonel Nicholas Devereaux wrote to William Lenthall of '. . . a most malignent man one Lieut-Col. Nott, he, as I am persuaded drew the King's forces into our quarters at Cricklade where we lately lost 10 horse.'

By 1646, the inevitable effect of the war's numerous battles and skirmishes together with a serious outbreak of some form of bubonic plague in the district was beginning to have disastrous consequences. The inhabitants of many towns and villages caught up in the fighting, already precariously balanced on an economic knife-edge, soon began to suffer dreadful hardships. In that year there occurred in the Quarter Sessions Great Rolls for Wiltshire the following:

> The humble petition of the inhabitants of the town and parish of Cricklade Showeth. That although your petitioners are much impoverished both by the unnatural war and also by the late grievous mortality being deprived of all markets and deprived of all benefit of the law made for the relief of infected places and ten months and upward hundred of poor and sick people destitute of bread, destitute of money, destitute of employment, yet nevertheless a weekly sum is demanded of your poor petitioners towards the relief of the town of Highworth. Their humble suit therefore is (the premises considered) that you vouchsafe to order that your petitioners may be exempted for a time takes of this nature and the rather since the days of our affliction we were burdensome to none and the late visitation hath left many widows and orphans to be provided for to our great charge. Signed by William Byrt, bailiff and thirteen others.

With the passing centuries the pattern of life in the Upper Thames Valley could not have changed very much. It was Thomas Hardy in *Far from the Madding Crowd* who reminded us that: 'Five decades hardly modified the cut of a gaitor, the embroidery of a smock-frock, by the breadth of a hair. Ten generations failed to alter the turn of a single phrase.'

Notes

1. In March of 1996 during work on the extension of the Cricklade dual carriage-way (bypassing the village of Latton) many bases of stone walls were discovered which may prove to be a villa neighbouring that of Court Farm nearby.

2. It was at about this time that a charity was devised. The King appointed that one hundred acres of the Braydon Forest area were to go to the poor of Cricklade and Chelworth forever. This was called 'The Hundred Acres Charity'.

2 A Changing Countryside

Oh, to be in England
Now that April's there,
And whoever wakes in England
Sees, some morning, unaware,
That the lowest boughs and the brushwood sheaf
Round the elm-tree bole are in tiny leaf,
While the chaffinch sings on the orchard bough
In England – now!
'Home-Thoughts, from Abroad', Robert Browning (1812–89)

Little altered in the pastoral landscape of the Upper Thames from Roman times until the coming of the canals brought about the first of many changes that were to dramatically influence its ecology. As will be seen, the changes that began with the canal builders, continued with the railways and ended with the valley we know today, have, nevertheless, been beneficial rather than detrimental to its bird life. The chaffinch still sings at the woodland edge and the sweet notes of the robin can still be heard in every cottage garden.

In the spring a livelier iris changes on the burnish'd dove;
In the spring a young man's fancy rightly turns to thoughts of love.
'Locksley Hall', Alfred, Lord Tennyson (1809–92)

Bird study was my greatest pleasure in boyhood and it has remained with me in a long life. I used to wait for the Oxford and Cambridge boat race with the keenest anticipation, for only then the spring equinox – when the day and night are of equal length – would be drawing near and I knew that the house-martins would soon be home again to repair their old nests beneath the eaves of my grandparent's house in the High Street. Soon I would be finding moorhens' nests along the rush-lined banks of the river below Eisey Bridge, and peewits in the great field behind the church on the hilltop and the redshanks would be yodelling all along the meadows by the river.

Without the canal the only means of transporting goods had been by roads that were bad and the pack-horse, an unreliable stage-coach that served only the main routes, and the river. At first, the Thames and Severn Canal, followed by the North Wilts Canal, from Cricklade to Swindon, had but little effect on, for instance, the bird populations until the coming of the railways when their demise seemed assured. Within a few years these waterways, which for two generations became so much a part of the English scene, no longer echoed to the shouts of the bargemen. Silent and neglected, in a few years they were choked with weeds; rush and sedge lined their banks and their tow paths were overgrown with bramble, dog rose and hawthorn. The benefit to the flora and fauna was immense, and little imagination is needed to realize the particular advantages this actually gave to the bird life. The dereliction transformed these waterways into ribbons of damp wilderness for nearly half a century. Earth-moving machinery, after the Second World War, made their back-filling relatively inexpensive and much of the land has been restored to its former use, although short stretches of the old canals can be found. I found my first nest of a red-backed shrike when a boy in the bramble by the towpath of the Thames and Severn at Eisey and in a reed bed by Court Farm, was my first nest of a reed warbler when with suppressed excitement I beheld therein my first egg of a cuckoo. I had a fleeting, but unmistakable, glimpse of the one and only hawfinch I have ever seen in Wiltshire, which flew from a hawthorn growing in the dried out bed of the North Wilts. near its junction with the Thames and Severn at Latton Basin.

Although one might be excused for considering that only a disadvantage to bird life would have resulted by the coming of the railways, the ending of the canal era offset this, if only in a small part. Ballast holes had been excavated to provide spoil for the permanent way. These filled with water and their banks became overgrown. This again was an advantage to nature that can still be seen in many places today. I saw my first sparrow hawk's nest in an old hawthorn that grew on one of their banks, and moorhen, mallard, little grebe and mute swan; the latter can still be seen by some main lines from a passing train. All have taken full advantage of the cover afforded. The present day encouragement to farmers to grow less food, would make it seem likely that these ballast holes, having survived for so long by disused railway tracks, will remain unchanged for the foreseeable future.

In the 1950s hundreds of miles of line were closed down and fell silent and many of these miles of narrow strands of green were left intact and are now used as nature trails, footpaths and bridle ways. Inevitably this has resulted in breeding havens for many hedgerow species, replacing in large measure the hedgerow habitat lost to monocropping during the wartime era of 'grow more food'.

It can already be seen how, since the days of the pack-horse were numbered, this valley of the Upper Thames has had overwhelming benefits for bird life.

Ironically, following over-production of food, farmers are now being recompensed to replant hedgerows. They are being urged to plant mixed woodland for long term investment, and financially compensated for allowing 15 per cent of their arable and grassland to lie fallow over specified periods, all of which is giving further considerable advantages to bird populations.

The other great change in our Upper Thames landscape all along the valley is in the wide open areas of water created by the extraction of gravel pit lakes. Much of this is now a leisure area known as the Cotswold Water Park. The gravel pits, covering several square miles, naturally attract wildfowl in considerable numbers. About forty-five mute swans were seen feeding in a field off the A419 near the entrance to the Water Park recently and a golden oriole and a red-footed falcon have been seen there.

A species that has utilized the gravel pits to a very large extent, is the little ringed plover. Since the first nesting record for Britain at Tring, Hertfordshire, in 1938 the species has bred sparingly in nearly every county in England where suitable habitats have been found. Several pairs now return regularly to breed in such places as these gravel pits, which stretch from Somerford Keynes in the west to Lechlade in the east. The population in 1969 was estimated at only a hundred pairs. The bird has not been slow to exploit the areas of newly exposed gravel, which is so much to its liking. The nest is a hollow scrape lined with small stones, or sparingly with stalks of vegetation, and is in all respects so much like that of its larger cousin the ringed plover when seen at a distance as to be almost indistinguishable from it. However, there are features in the field that place the species apart and although both nest and eggs are similar, the latter are only about the size of those of a song thrush.

So it was with great excitement one afternoon that a birding friend and I went off together to a place where he suspected a pair of these birds might have a nest.

The area of gravel workings at this site, beyond Lechlade, on either side of the A361, was well known to me. Four years previously, when an extension of the gravel excavations threatened an ancient site of early man, I contracted for my firm in a rescue dig for the Ancient Monuments Branch of the Ministry of Works, now the Department of the Environment. The site of the nest was only a mile from Halfpenny Bridge and the River Thames itself.

The gravel workings of the Upper Thames valley have also been of great benefit to sand martins, and breeding colonies can now be found in many places. There was a large, well-established colony at the site created by topsoil and gravel removal at Smerle Farm near the nest site of the little ringed plovers. Suitable breeding sites for these birds in the Upper Thames area were rare before gravel, in quantity, began to be taken.

An unusual nesting site for sand martins existed at the road bridge over the River Key, not far from the last house in Cricklade on the road east, where now the overpass for the new dual carriageway is situated. This consisted of a thin layer of turf laid on the parapet wall of the bridge that formed the road verge, and here a colony of three pairs had successfully established themselves. The horizontal tunnels to the nests that are normally excavated by the birds – some pairs not infrequently adopt drainage holes – were necessarily very shallow. It was at a time when horse-drawn vehicles in the second decade of the century were slowly being replaced by motor cars. The milk carts that delivered the milk to Cricklade Railway Station every afternoon, Model T Fords and Foden steam wagons alike, all lumbered past close to the nests at this remarkable site.

It is not difficult to evaluate how bird life has benefited from the geographical changes, for remarkably enough there are more. Cricklade's population has almost doubled since the Second World War and the field known as Paul's Croft, as well as others, is now unrecognizable. Streets and houses cover land, once virgin fields, cattle pastures and cowsheds, hedges, ditches and cattle ponds. For several years the birds that haunted these fields, hedgerows and farm buildings were driven out, there were a few never to return; of these were the spotted flycatchers, the swallows that nested in the cowsheds, and the grasshopper warblers that built their flimsy nests in the undergrowth of the hedgerow ditches. Sadly no more can the swallows' twittering be heard from the straw-built shed nor the remarkably sustained low-pitched churring of the grasshopper warbler, which has been described as not unlike a fisherman's reel being wound up at speed.

When I was young my first grasshopper warbler's nest was in the side of a ditch within a couple of fields of home, and it was a special day indeed, for their eggs are among the most beautiful of our smaller passerines. Few clutches of any species are more handsome than those of the grasshopper warbler. The *Handbook of British Birds* describes them as thickly spotted with brownish-red on a creamy ground, often forming a zone, and generally with a hair-like streak. My first clutch had the more rare purple-red blotches, which are also described.

These pastures are now built over and dwelling-houses with pleasant gardens, cover all the sites. Apparently since the gardens have matured there are more birds to be seen than ever before. A tiny ash sapling has had the nest of a mistle thrush over many a year past. My son, who lives there still, recently told me that as he was leaving early one morning he heard a piercing 'ke, ke, ke', and looked up in time to watch a 'food pass' between a male and female sparrowhawk above the house. It is not so surprising to hear that a heron often takes goldfish from his pond, and a kingfisher has also been seen there. This bird nests commonly along the Thames beyond the house-covered fields. So it can be observed that, by and large, the birds have found this new environment very much to their liking, with gains in number and variety far exceeding losses.

A bird that seems to have disappeared from the meadows since around the middle of the century, after its spread from grassy uplands with which it was once associated, is the curlew; I have seen their nests a few miles away between Cricklade and Highworth in the east and near Minety to the west. At the north-ernmost tip of North Meadow and the pastures to Hailstone and beyond, were once the nesting grounds of curlew and redshank. A large field beyond North Meadow was much favoured and there was another on the far side of Hailstone Bridge, in the centre of which was a pool of clear water with the largest number of great pond snails I have ever seen. Since gravel has been taken, the field and pond alike are gone and all is water.

North Meadow has gained considerable importance since the rare snakeshead fritillary became rarer still, for here grows 80 per cent of this beautiful flower in Britain. The consequence is that it is now under the aegis of the Nature Conservancy with a warden in charge during the flowering season from April to July. The meadow has been lammas, or common land, for the exclusive benefit of the people of this ancient borough for more than a thousand years.

Brucellosis and certain other infectious diseases in animals, which can be passed to humans, particularly through cows' milk, have resulted in clean water being piped to cattle pastures. Since the 1950s their familiar ponds, so much an integral part of the English countryside, have practically all gone, taking away drinking places that were oases for many species of breeding birds and the insects on which they fed.

The principal losers were probably mallard, moorhen, pied wagtail and robin, but there were others too. In my boyhood I found many a nest of blackbird, song thrush, long-tailed tit and kindred species in the bramble, hawthorn and pollard willows, which crowded so thickly around the banks of ponds. However, we now see that on balance the man-made changes since the inception of the canal era, have, with a few exceptions, been of enormous benefit.

There have been other changes taking place here in the Upper Thames. The loss of the common elm has been keenly felt everywhere. It was a tree synonymous with the shires of England. Tennyson wrote 'The moan of doves in immemorial elms', and Gray 'Beneath those rugged elms, that yew-tree's shade'. Many villages had their own famous tree; the Revd Gilbert White wrote of the great elm of Selborne, where a pair of ravens nested year after year. No rural landscape was quite complete without one or two growing by the church or shading the village green. There were few sights more noble and satisfying than one of these great trees. An exception must have been the famous 'long walk' in Windsor Great Park; beech and lime certainly, and hornbeam and ash but rarely elm. Rooks have been said to desert their ancestral tree when their nests were in danger. The tree's aesthetic qualities and the hard nature of the wood that could serve so many purposes, assured that it continued to flourish until Dutch Elm Disease brought it to near extinction. The older elms presented a knotted and gnarled appearance and lived to great age. Three elms that once grew near the Cricklade railway station were all that remained to show where once the great Braydon Forest had extended down to the Upper Thames. One of them, which was hollow about six foot above the ground, had a girth of such proportions that it held five of us boys sitting comfortably in a circle within. I have calculated the age of these elms – by taking their diameter in inches at arm's height and multiplying the answer by six – as being in the region of 500 years; they would have been mere saplings, struggling to the light in the forest glade in the Middle Ages.

When the predominant hollow elm was no more, jackdaws took

to chimneys in increasing numbers in which to build their nests. These have been found to make an excellent substitute and in districts where the birds are numerous, private dwellings have conspicuous wire balloons placed on the chimney pots to prevent their access.

Other greatly favoured artefact sites for nest building when access was available were, and are still, the belfries of country churches where chicken wire has not been placed over the open latticed stonework emitting the sound of the bells. The first jackdaw's nest I saw was in just one such belfry, in the church at Down Ampney. The poultry-house smell was overpowering, for there was not one nest but four, each on the crown of a great half-cone shaped pile of sticks, sheep's wool, paper, dead grass and rag in the four windows. I have never forgotten the excitement on examining these four nests, each with a full clutch in a deep wool-lined cup. My notes of those days so long ago, tell me that the accumulation of the great mass of sticks and debris would have filled a farm cart. Jackdaws' nests have always had a fascination for country lads.

I have frequently expounded the virtues of Norfolk as a birding county, and had almost made myself believe there was no other to match it for numbers and variety of species, but on reading my notes, virtually unopened since the 1950s, there can be no doubt in my mind that I have been treating Wiltshire and Gloucestershire most shamefully, nowhere more so than this glorious area around the upper river.

In this valley there are one or two country lanes that remind me of a book I had as a child, published by Blackie, and whose title was *By Hedgerow, Mead and Pool*. On the cover was the picture of just one such country lane that I know, a lane that leads to nowhere winding around a bend where brambles were spreading to cover the track, and perched on a bush was a fine cock blackbird. Together with its companion volume, *By Common Pinewood and Bog*, these treasures of long ago must have had a profound influence on my life and love of nature.

Nearly all these lanes, like Norfolk's Peddars Way and Wiltshire's Ridge Way, are the remnants of ancient tracks whose origins are lost in mystery and legend, many like Big Rose Lane, not far from the foot of Blunsdon Hill, and Blind Lane, between Cricklade and Chelworth, have long since been portions of a whole whose beginnings and ends are still unknown. Big Rose Lane, a bridle way running very wide and straight for about half a mile, forms part of a district boundary. The summer choir along this lane and the wood called Watereaton Cover near one end, was unsurpassed in bird song, and of them all the nightingale was the most beautiful.

3   The Canals

An artificial waterway, cut across
land for navigation.

The pack-horse, although sometimes used singly usually worked in numbers known as Pack-horse Trains, both for greater convenience and as a protection against footpads. They would have been a common sight in some villages and towns even after canals had already been built, but were gradually to fall into disuse, as did the canals after them. Those 'dark satanic mills' of the Industrial Revolution wrought great changes in a countryside where the life-line had been the river and the pack-horse. Now something had to be done, internal trade being as vital to England's economy as was its commerce with countries overseas. The effect on country life and the country folk became almost as dramatic with the onset of the canals as that to be created by the railways a century later.

In many places road conditions were worsening rather than improving during much of this period. Their upkeep was a Parish Council's responsibility, and many fell short of their duties, begrudging rates for their upkeep and only maintaining them at their best within the confines of their own village. A directive heading, typical of this period, when road conditions were becoming desperate for Bicknoller in Somerset, reads: 'Composition for the teams, draught or plough, for the Estates, Labourers and other inhabitants of the Parish of Bicknoller, liable to Statute work and duty for the repair of the highways in the said Parish, 1768–1832.'

In the days of Queen Anne, heavy coaches carrying seven people were pulled at a walking pace by six-horse teams. Between 1750 and 1790, 1,660 turnpike companies were formed by Act of Parliament and the roads soon began to improve. The transport using the roads also began to improve. The lightly built stagecoach of about 1760 was pulled by a team of two or four horses and was as yet without springs; it took a day to travel a hundred miles at a cost of about ten shillings (fifty pence) per passenger. It was due to this limited capacity and high costs that it first became logically imperative to make better use of the rivers, particularly for transporting goods in bulk, and many that are today irrelevant and choked with weeds, were cleaned and locks were constructed, the highest of which on the Thames being St John's Lock below Lechlade and just outside the area of our story.

River improvements were soon followed by the construction of canals that were intended to form an integral part of an inland waterways transport system. Although the first canal to be built in Britain was the thirty-miles stretch from the River Lea at Ware to London in the seventeenth century, used mainly as an aqueduct to supply the capital with pure spring water, the most famous was the Worsley, carrying coal from the Duke of Bridgewater's collieries at Worsley to the centre of textile manufacturing in Manchester, a distance of ten miles. After this canal was built the price of transporting the coal was halved. The financial success of this early enterprise had the effect of speeding up canal and barge building, mainly in the north at first, but soon spreading to the south and the south-west.

A simple demonstration of the relative efficiency of waterway transportation is explained, when it is shown that the weight carried by a pack-horse was one eighth of a ton, whereas a horse could draw a wagon weighing one ton. Then again if the wagon was on rails the animal could pull eight tons but the same animal harnessed to a barge could pull fifty tons.

In the south-west an early objective of the canal builders was to join the English Channel and the Bristol Channel by both canal and river, so saving the long, dangerous voyage by sea round Land's End. During the wars with France, French privateers were taking heavy toll of shipping all around the English coastline, and by the turn of the century this speeded up canal building considerably.

The new canal was to have been called the Grand Western. The press reported:

> ... that it was resolved unanimously that among the advantages that could arise from making the canal, appears to be easy communication betwixt the Bristol and English Channel instead of sailing round Land's End, which requires various winds (and both in winter

and war is a tedious and dangerous navigation). That this canal can convey materials for building, also iron, cheese, salt, groceries, hardware, wool etc. It is an object of National importance by the ready conveyance of timber of His Majesty's dockyards from the north of Devon, the counties of Somerset, Gloucester, and particularly of the Forest of Dean, Hereford, Worcester, etc. The general communication between Ireland and Scotland with the western part of England and the Bristol Channel would also be rendered much more easy and safe . . .

So much for the best laid schemes of mice and men. I have no figures of tonnage delivery on the Worsley Canal, but a further idea can be obtained, in monetary terms, of savings made by using the canal, by quoting calculations made for the Chard Canal in Somerset, as it was first known (a part of the Grand Western system). When it was estimated that delivery of coal could be reduced from £1 11s 8d (£1.58) to 14s 2d (71p) per ton by using the canal, the sum of £95,000 share capital was subscribed in one hour. With such glowing estimates and all the stories heard of the success of canals in the north of the country, it was little wonder therefore that the upsurge in canal building became so great during this period around the middle of the eighteenth century.

Financial difficulties plagued many companies. Stretches of some canals were completed, only to soon fall into disuse generally through the spread of the railway network. Many ambitious projects never quite reached fruition.

Here we might add a postscript: the railway companies, whilst certainly having enormous physical obstacles to overcome, nevertheless generally had an advantage over the canal builders. Geological distractions and costs per mile for building in the ground were considerably more than above it, often porous subsoil and rock had to be sealed – as with the building of the Thames and Severn across the Jurassic oolite of the Cotswold limestone. Locks were expensive to build, there were as many as a chain of twenty-nine, in steps on the Kennet and Avon Canal (now almost fully restored) and in the fifty-nine foot fall on the North Wilts. From Swindon to Latton there were eleven in as many miles. Sometimes considerable tunnelling was also necessary, an outstanding example of such being on the Thames and Severn. The Sapperton Tunnel was started at both ends and by sinking shafts at a number of points on the route. A constant supply of water was required and 'feeders' maintained. The railways were virtually unaffected by frost, which in hard winters could close canal traffic entirely, whilst neither flood nor drought could have but little if any effect upon them. Another enormous advantage for the railways was their speed and that they were able to operate for twenty-four hours a day.

The Thames and Severn, that once played such an important part in the economy of the valley down to Lechlade, was joined by the Stroudwater at Walbridge near Stroud, which in turn connected with the Gloucester and Sharpness (formerly the Gloucester and Berkeley), half a mile from Framilode. The Thames and Severn's twenty-nine miles took it through Sapperton Tunnel, which pierces the ridge between two river basins and was once the longest in the country. Work on the canal's complete restoration is well under way to return it to full use, which is the dream of many. Its devious route takes it to the River Thames at Inglesham. It connected with the North Wilts. at Weymoor Bridge near Latton village, where it has been known as The Latton Basin. It fed Cricklade at Latton Wharf a mile to the east.

In my reference to the pumping station near Thames Head (see chapter six) I refer only to its effect on the river as a means of pouring filth from the Great Western Railway (GWR), Swindon works. However, its purpose was also to deliver water to replace that being lost through seepage in the canal. The company used a wind pump in the early stages, which was replaced by a very efficient steam engine by Boulton and Watt in 1792. This pump lasted for more than 50 years and was replaced in turn by a beam engine that could raise 12,000 gallons an hour from a well nearly 90 feet deep.

The Thames and Severn Canal was opened, the Revd W.H. Hutton tells us, 'under very high auspices and golden hopes' in 1799 after taking seven years to build. 'The canal workers', he continues, 'must have been quite a colony in Lechlade, the registers for one year show six deaths and four baptisms amongst them'. The canal was never a complete success and was bought up by the GWR in 1893 – no doubt to extinguish all future hopes of competition. There are great difficulties to be overcome before the revitalized Thames and Severn can come into being; probably the greatest of these will be the crossing of the dual carriageway at the north end of the Cricklade by-pass on Ermin Street. I well remember the humpbacked bridge of red brick that once served this purpose but it was levelled when the canal was filled in during the late 1920s or early 30s; Temple Thurston writes of passing beneath it in 1911 in his hired barge the *Flower of Gloster*. The canal from South Cerney to Latton Basin remains, but much of it from Latton eastwards will have to be re-routed.

One of the last people to navigate the canal, described in his book *The Flower of Gloster*, was E. Temple Thurston, mentioned above. This was before many of its sections had become derelict and unusable. In its twenty-nine miles the Thames and Severn Canal returned to the administration of the former owners but the decline in traffic continued. The highest tonnage recorded was in 1841, with ten barges a day and receipts amounting to £11,330. Perhaps the true death knell of the canals was the introduction of nationalization of all forms of transport in Britain by a Socialist Government when any hopes of a competitive edge, even had there been any, over railway transport was gone for ever, and by the time a Conservative Government had been returned to power and transport was again in private ownership, canal transport was virtually a thing of the past.

Fred Thacker refers to a milestone on the canal near Thames Head. During a visit to Eisey one summer I saw two of these milestones flanking the way over the site where the canal bed ran through the hamlet and where probably the wharf was sited. At least one of these had been removed from its former position; they were of stone with a metal plate attached; one of which stated that Walbridge was 22½ miles distant and Inglesham 6¼. (See chapter twenty-one for illustration.)

Tunnels were the bane of the canal builders and they must have been dreaded by the bargees who had to navigate them. Yard for yard they cost many times that of construction across open country. Seldom, due to cost, was there a towpath built, and the vessel was propelled by the men's feet against the tunnel sides; retractable 'wings' on each side for support aided them in this onerous task. In short tunnels 'shafting' took place by means of poles against the sides and the roof.

Fortunately for the Stroudwater and Thames and Severn Canal Trust, the Sapperton Tunnel remained virtually intact, for otherwise the reality of opening up the old Thames and Severn Canal route might have proved an impossible task because of the high cost.

The ten or so miles of the North Wilts. Canal, from Latton Basin, crossed the Thames a short distance from Latton Basin where it joined the Thames and Severn. It then swung round to run alongside West Mill Lane, at the southern end of which it passed through a tunnel beneath the Cricklade to Bath road and Double Days field. It emerged opposite the entrance to Fiddle Farm; I remember as a child the dark and forbidding entrance with its ivy-covered, crumbling brickwork, the dank, dark green water there, the pond weed, disturbed for more than a generation only by dabchick and moorhen and the steep banks on each side of the canal, which extended to the Cricklade Wharf.

About sixty years after it was built the northern end of the tunnel was bridged by the Midland and South Western Junction Railway west of the railway station. Even if the tunnel could have been filled in and consolidated there must remain some uncertainty of the long-term stability of the post-Second World War housing built above or near its course, in the field known as Little Double Days; Great Double Days and Little Double Days were once Double Days before it was severed in two by the passage of the Midland and South Western Junction Railway.

Objections to the canals came from many quarters. Progress has ever been fettered, as a general rule, by objectors' motives of self interest. Having no vested interests himself, William Cobbett was an exception, but he was not sufficiently far-sighted to realize the enormous benefit the canal would eventually bestow on this rural community; a portion of what he wrote during one of his rural rides is worthy of note. He says: 'While the poor creatures that raise the abundant wheat, barley, cheese, mutton and beef are living on potatoes, an accursed canal comes kindly through the parish to convey all the good food to the tax-eaters in the Wen [his favourite term for London].'[1]

In Cobbett's day the pack-horse was still the only satisfactory means of transporting goods where water was not available. Pack-horse trains must have been a familiar sight in those days. Carriages frequently broke down in deep ruts in marshy ground or on clay subsoils. In spite of this there were objections to the canals on the grounds that those obtaining a living by road transport and pack-horse would be seriously affected; it was envisaged that the coastal trade would be reduced and whole areas of valuable land would be destroyed and so forth. However, there were those who had a different view, and for all William Cobbett's kindly, though minuscule, misgivings and the host of other objections, the canals were to prove of enormous benefit to the conditions of both rich and poor alike. Indeed they can be said to have created the beginnings of the general prosperity enjoyed by so many today. Temple Thurston was to describe the canals as 'those broad and beautiful roads, great highways into the heart of the most glorious country in the world'.

There was never quite the same nostalgia for the canals as that created by the railways, with the enormous power that inspired so much awe in all who saw one of these great locomotives for first time. Nevertheless, its fermentation is exemplified in the existence of the Inland Waterways Association (IWA) formed in 1946. There have also been those worthy characters who have wished to uphold something of the romance and peaceful quality of the waterways of which some would have had special memories. Temple Thurston was one of these and Eric de Mare, who wrote *The Canals of England*, was another; if the IWA had been in existence in de Mare's day he would surely have been a founder member, advocating as he does a scheme for canals to criss-cross the country, needing no locks, at 330 feet above sea level. He theorizes that 'an average waterway can safely accommodate a larger amount of traffic than an average railway, and boats can follow or pass one another closely', and that 'like road transport and unlike rail, water transport can load or unload almost anywhere along the route'. Had he been fortunate enough to see barges on the Mississippi River, passing beneath the road bridge at Memphis, Tennessee, or on the Dutch and Belgian canals, his views on the use of waterways for the transport of goods in bulk would have been even stronger.

A legacy of romance for the canals still lives in the memories of the very few who can still recall the voices of the bargees urging their tired horses to greater efforts as they struggled to keep a timetable, or perhaps had their thoughts on their next meal by a welcoming fire at the next wharfside inn. Nearly all of these old inns along the canalways have gone now, like many of the coaching inns of earlier days although many of these do remain.

Those with a penchant towards canals, might want to read 'Memorandum Presented to the Minister of Transport: The case for canal revival presented'.[2] In his *Lost Canals and Waterways of Britain* it is obvious that R.L. Russell is just one more of those who probably has nostalgic thoughts on canals. He writes very positively on the possibility of restoring the Thames and Severn Canal. He opines that a new cutting will have to be made from Latton near Cricklade to the Thames, virtually from the point I have mentioned where the new dual carriageway of the Cricklade by-pass crosses its original route, before the canal can be restored for navigation and that several new locks would be involved and others resited. As Russell states in his excellent and readable book, one of the failings of the canals was that locks were constructed with unequal falls. He is hopeful that one day before so very long the remarriage, as he puts it, of the rivers Severn and Thames may again be celebrated.

The Stroudwater Canal Society was formed in 1972 to later

become the Stroudwater Thames and Severn Canal Trust, now the Cotswolds Canal Trust, the ultimate objective being to open up these waterways to their full use. Soon transformation began to take place, at first at the western end, and the rot was halted, all as a result of voluntary work plus the Government's job creation scheme, to make a cherished dream come true.

The North Wilts. Canal, which at its inception was to be called the Severn Junction, had a difficult passage through its early planning stages. It was first thought that its economy would mainly depend on coal from the Forest of Dean, supplying it in great quantities for the GWR at Swindon. It was one of three schemes chosen as being the easiest to build and would make use of the Thames and Severn Canal company, already deeply involved in the Forest of Dean coal trade, and a supporter of the project.

The inadequacy of the Upper Thames as a commercial waterway was highlighted when the Thames and Severn Canal Company gave its full support to the North Wilts. project. This gave them the opportunity of bypassing the poor Upper Thames navigation. A Bill was first introduced in the House of Commons for the building of the canal in February 1811 and given its first reading the following month. Meanwhile objections to it had poured in from many quarters. Both the University of Oxford and the Oxford Canal Company were involved in this, the latter because they faced competition in their coal trade from the invasion of coal from the Forest of Dean. The Thames and Severn petitioned in favour and stated: 'the navigation of the Thames is imperfect, precarious and dangerous, and because of it the expectations of this Company have fallen short.' The Bill was withdrawn, but only when it was realized that the Thames and Severn would have to make an application for a further Bill to make the junction with their canal at Latton.

The engineer for the North Wilts. project made his estimate of the cost of the canal at from £60,000 to £62,000 according to where it would terminate. There was a fall from Swindon to Latton of sixty-nine feet, which was to have eleven locks and was planned to follow along at least three miles of road to reduce costs. It was found that the Wilts. and Berks. Canal Company would have to conserve water and so a proposal was made to build a reservoir at Coate for a reserve supply at a cost of £10,000. Edward Loveden, a Thames Commissioner, was expected to put up violent opposition to the scheme for he owned the lock on the Thames at Buscot, with a toll of one shilling for each five tons of cargo that passed through; and this was repeated on the return journey, which was something hitherto unknown. The charge had been made since 1771 and he stood to lose a great deal of money if ever the North Wilts. Canal was built.

Water for the North Wilts. was to be supplied by the Wilts. and Berks. Canal Company and none from any other source. As precaution against this possibility the lock at Latton Basin was to be kept closed if water levels in the canal fell below that of the Thames and Severn. The Wilts. and Berks. was to meet five-twelfths of the cost of the North Wilts. construction, the public four-twelfths and the Thames and Severn the remaining three.

A petition dated 2 January 1813 in support of the North Wilts. Canal Bills contained forty-five signatures of tradespeople and gentlemen in the neighbourhood of Cricklade. The Basin at Latton was marked out in February 1814. Soon work on the construction virtually ceased through lack of funds. However, a loan having been received from the Exchequer's Commissioners, instructions were given for work on the North Wilts to continue.

The Canal was officially opened on the 2 April 1819. In 1840 15,000 tons of Forest of Dean coal passed through the canal for the building of the Great Western Railway Works at Swindon.

Below are rates charged by the Wilts. and Berks. Canal Company and which probably would have also applied to the North Wilts. Canal. Rates charged for tonnage carried on the canal were calculated by a standard method of measurement for all classes of goods and were as follows:

For all Hay, Straw, Dung, Peat and Peat Ashes, Chalk, Marl, Clay, Sand, Lime for Manure, and all other Manure and Materials for roads – ½d per Ton, per Mile

For all Coal, Culm, Coke, Cinders, Charcoal, Iron-stone, Pigiron, Iron-ore, Copper-ore, Lead-ore, Lime, (except for manure) Lime-stone and other Stone, Bricks and Tiles – 1½d per Ton, per Mile

For all Corn and other Grain, Flour, Malt, Meal, Timber, Bar-iron and Lead – 2d per Ton, per Mile

For all other Goods, Wares and Merchandize whatever – 2½d per Ton, per Mile

And in proportion for any greater or less Quantity or Distance; Fractions of a Quarter of a Ton to pay as a Quarter, and any Fraction less than Half a Mile as a Half Mile.

Barges passing any Lock, when the water does not flow over the Waste Weir, with any Goods, first enumerated, on Board to pay One Penny per Ton per Mile in addition to the Half-penny herein before charged. Goods remaining on Wharfs more than Forty-eight Hours, to pay such Rate as may be agreed on.

Fractions of a Quarter of a Ton to pay as a Quarter, and any Boats under Twenty Tons to pay for Twenty Tons when passing a lock.

The Feofees of the Cricklade Waylands Estates sold some two acres in Church Close to the North Wilts. Canal Company in 1814. Commerce on the North Wilts. Canal virtually ceased with the closure of the eastern section of the Thames and Severn in 1927 and the western end in 1933.

Nowadays under the umbrella of the Cotswold Canals Trust, the aim is the preservation of the line of the Cotswold Canals (Stroudwater Navigation and Thames and Severn Canal) and promotion of their use for recreation; to promote the towpath as a long-distance right of way; to promote the restoration of the Thames and Severn from Inglesham to the area of the Cotswold Water Park and the ultimate restoration from Saul Junction to the River Thames.

The great advantage to wildlife by the dereliction of a canal cannot be under-estimated.

The Thames and Severn Canal token with which workmen were paid during its construction. It shows a Severn Canal trow and the eastern portal of the Sapperton Tunnel

Notes

1. Cobbett, William, *Rural Rides*, 2 v. (J.M. Dent, London)
2. Published by the Inland Waterways Association, 11 Gower Street, London WC1 (1947).

4 Change is Inevitable

See how this river comes me cranking in,
and cuts me from the best of all my land;
a huge half moon, a monstrous cantle out.

Henry IV, William Shakespeare

The Upper Thames has not been a stranger to the formation of these 'monstrous cantles' (saddles). 'It is astonishing what a river can do, and all by following gravity in the innocence of its heart.' Nature's changes, complained of so bitterly by Shakespeare, and echoed here by Robert Louis Stevenson, had begun aeons before the Roman invasion of Britain. It was at that time, however, that the man-made changes of which there is ample evidence today along the infant Thames, can be said to have begun. We could be excused for being surprised to learn that man has made any alterations at all, other than minor diversions for the water mills, it having, superficially, so much the appearance of being as nature had intended.

A few deviations in the stream's course were made at the village of Ashton Keynes where it can be seen to flow unnaturally across meadow land to Waterhay Bridge. About a mile before Cricklade the first major deviation was for West Mill at Cricklade. In their order but not necessarily chronologically, the purpose was first commercial, to improve the water supply to West Mill; second, it was defensive, for extra-mural defence of Cricklade to the north; third, for the supply of water for the town at the north-east corner of its defensive walls and last for political reasons further down at Rushy Mead, below Eisey Hill.

From a point on the river half a mile above the site where, not so long ago, Cricklade's West Mill still stood, is the highest practical part of the stream from whence a boat might be launched to explore the river down to Lechlade. Above this point the river has not been used commercially since farm produce was carried down to Lechlade. It is now effectively cut off from the upper reaches, to Waterhay and Ashton Keynes, by an aqueduct formed when the North Wilts. canal was constructed at the dawn of the nineteenth century. A smoothly winding stream on an uncontoured map usually gives a sound indication of the level terrain through which it passes.

One of the first alterations brought about in the upper river changes its course to the site where the last West Mill stood. A mill must have been operated on this site by the Anglo-Saxons, when it was possibly at a lower level than its modern counterpart, and its capacity would have been inadequate for Cricklade's increasing population. It is not known when the direct course of the river was created. This is on a virtually level plane, giving a sluggish flow and holding back a considerable head of water as some insurance against low rainfall, and would have permitted the mill to continue to operate for a limited period. Some historians have suggested that two mills may have been operational on the site.

At The Stank, the boat would have to be portaged across the road and re-launched in the Priory Field. This however, might depend on the water level passing under the low arch of the Town Bridge, accurately described by Dr Thomson as a dam with a hole in it. Its complete inadequacy led to flooding of the North Meadow and the road north out of the town – the ancient causeway that joins the A419 at Cricklade Wharf.

Water levels can vary considerably. In 1928 when the worst flooding ever recorded took place along the Thames, I was able to float the canoe over the barbed wire fences to the south of North Meadow and over the meadow itself. Fourteen people perished at that time through the floods in London.

The Cricklade Town Bridge was rebuilt in 1854, replacing one of which little is known, except that it had 'bays' and 'steps', we're told. It would have been wider and higher to enable barges to sail up to West Mill and beyond, and would have been of timber construction, no doubt built and rebuilt many times through the centuries.

Before we float on too far downstream, so to speak, I should mention the diversion of the River Churn which was made north-west of West Mill to its present course, meeting the Thames below the Town Bridge. The reason for this could have been something to do with the lade feeding Latton's upper and lower mills. However, as it is known that this lade existed before Domesday and that it took the greater part of the Churn from above the weir at Cerney Wick, some other reason may exist for the diversion. It might have brought about the necessity of altering the Thames course above the mill earlier.

By the time the Town Bridge is reached, and beyond, our punt will have been floating on the second diversion of the river's course, from a point at the south-east corner of the North Meadow to just past the mouth of the Churn in Priory Close, the reason for this diversion being the town's extra-mural defences, and the fact that a mill probably existed near the Town Bridge. There are some lingering doubts in the minds of a few historians as to whether the builders of Cricklade's town walls and the extra-mural defences were Roman or Saxon. My personal view is that they must have been Saxon, although some credence has been lent to it being the Romans by the great number of Roman artefacts discovered in the little town. The next of the river's diversions is to the north-east corner of the settlement, bringing a water supply closer to the fortifications. This is borne out when we see the unnaturally direct course thereafter towards the Roman Ermin Street (A419), where it would have rejoined the old course, now a ditch marking the parish boundary at Map Ref: SU086947.

We now have only to move downstream for a very short distance, and once more our boat is in another new course beginning a little below the mouth of its tributary, the River Key. It is found from early records that problems arose over land at Calcutt, known as Rushy Mead, which lay by the river between Calcutt and the Latton tithe lands of Eisey. The dispute arose between Richard de Abingdon, Vicar of St Sampson's, and the Rector of Latton over tithes of hay grown on this fourteen acres. The contention ran on into the fourteenth century. Tithes, by their very nature, have long been the subject of disputes and litigation and, as pointed out by W.C. Tate in his book *The Parish Chest*: 'Keen incumbents saw great possibilities in sheepfolds and grazing meadows.' The history of tithes is not altogether edifying, particularly when the argument, on one side at least, was with men of the cloth. It was the 'great' tithes – corn, hay, wood etc. – that have been the greatest cause of disputes, rather than the 'small' tithes that were usually minor problems between the vicar and one of his poorer parishioners. The latter were generally settled amicably enough.

There now exists a drainage ditch which is likely, of old time, to have been the Thames's true course. The course actually diverted to run where it is found today, around the foot of Eisey Hill, and where once was Latton land became Cricklade land. The points where this diversion began and ended are seen at Map Refs: SU110938 and SU118938. A glance at the map reveals that the confluence of the Ampney Brook is showing an acute angle with the downside of the river, giving credence to this section of the course of the river being man-made. Tributaries, at least on level meadow land, do not naturally enter a parent river at such an angle, and it can here be considered as being extremely unlikely to have done so. A trench excavated on the south side would prove or disprove this conclusively.

By now our boat has been on three quarters of the first two and a half miles and almost a quarter of its journey to Lechlade on a course diverted within the past two millenniums.

Continuing towards Castle Eaton are one or two other interesting features; with a few exceptions in this four miles this river appears to follow any but its natural, slightly winding course across the meadows until leaving the Horse Bridge behind. Near the historic Watereaton House, our boat will pass the first of three oxbow lakes on the east side. My dictionary defines an oxbow thus: 'A horse-shoe bend or loop in a river, leaving only a narrow strip of land at the neck; if this neck is cut through an oxbow lake is formed.' It cannot be known if these necks of land were finally severed with the help of man, or cut through by natural means to form the lakes; nature herself takes away from the one and gives to the other. These 'monstrous cantles' were of little commercial use to the beneficial landowner, but where they were left in their natural state, they have become perfect havens for wildlife and make a wonderful additional attraction to what must have been a riparian landscape of unsurpassed delight.

On the river's west side and nearly opposite the second of the oxbows, is a curious backwater known as Cowneck. Fred S. Thacker[1] thought it may be the ancient bed of a river. The angle of entry into the Thames is right. At its junction with the main river it has been earthed in, about six foot wide as I recall, at a width convenient for a riverside path to continue uninterrupted, and adequate for the bargemen's convenience long ago when the water was low. I visited Cowneck again in recent years when, with my son and daughter we drove to Alec's Farm, to continue along an ancient track, at one point crossing a low humpbacked bridge of an open section of the Thames and Severn Canal, alongside a stone building, its stone-tiled roof intact, where I was told canal horses were once stabled. A walk of about half a mile, following the river bank took us to this mysterious neck of water I had not seen for sixty-two years. It was much as I remembered it, but the narrow strip of water was now joining the neck to the river, possibly done for drainage purposes. A dense bed of reeds at the inner end was inhabited by a large colony of reed warblers. The remnants of another oxbow a hundred or so yards on the Cricklade side came to mind, completely forgotten when I wrote the above. It was exactly as I remembered.

Although I have not discovered any historical reference to this, it will be seen on the OS *Landranger* series that the next likely man-made redirection of the river's course – before our punt reaches Lechlade – is at Castle Eaton where a drainage ditch, likely to be the old natural bed, forms a part of the district boundary, just as it does at Cricklade. The river, diverted in a large loop, now runs close to and past the village church. It seems that this was done to be certain of a water supply nearer at hand in times of stress, although why the village did not spring up nearer the original course has to remain a mystery.

Tributaries all along the Upper Thames are in plenty, from tiny runnels to those as large as the Churn and the Coln. The first, however, of any importance, must be the Swill Brook, longer even than the Thames itself, which rises east of Crudwell to enter the Thames just south of Ashton Keynes; it is itself swollen by Derry Brook, and large enough to be shown on the one-inch OS Map. Together in earlier days, they gave water enough to enable barges to travel beyond Cricklade as high as Waterhay Bridge although how they got past West Mill is something of a puzzle, probably a portage is the only answer, for boats would have been of no great size in these more upper reaches. The second and more likely possibility is that at West Mill products were conveyed the short distance by horse and wagon to and from the Town Bridge wharf; the route taken was a track, most of which has long since been lost but is well documented, that ran direct from West Mill to the High Street. Only the part once known as Gas Lane remains; from there it is only a few hundred yards down to the Town Bridge where the wharf was situated, or conveyance could have been by way of Rectory Lane, which has also been said to have once continued to the mill; its entrance is also on the High Street and considerably closer to the wharf than is Gas Lane.

After the Churn, the River Key, flowing in on the south bank, enters the river where now the Cricklade bypass begins, following the line of Roman Ermin Street to Latton village. It is a small stream, rising under the Purton ridge and draining the clay soils over a limited catchment area.

The next of the Thames's tributaries, within our Upper Thames catchment area is Ampney Brook. This rises in the Cotswold Hills between Cirencester and Ampney Crucis, the first of the three Ampneys, Ampney St Peter and Down Ampney, which is in our valley and mentioned later, being the other two. A short distance downstream on the south bank, the River Ray, that once carried filth from some of New Swindon's industries, enters. In *c.* 1926 its pollutants contaminated the river as far as Castle Eaton and beyond, destroying every living thing in its waters. My kinsman, another John Cuss, when writing about the pumping station near Thames Head taking water to the railway works at Swindon wrote: 'Out of the works came a stream of very dirty water, forming the River Key, which became a muddy stream and eventually re-found the Thames at Calcutt.' His memory failed him a little for it is the River Ray that rose by the GWR Swindon Works at 'Even Swindon' and comes out at Seven Bridges. The Key is of course further upstream.

The last to feed the Upper Thames before we reach Lechlade is the Coln, a famous trout stream. This rises in the Cotswold Hills, near Syreford, a few miles east of the Churn at Seven Springs, tumbles down out of the escarpment to caress beautiful Withington, and then bequeaths its name to Coln St Dennis, Coln Rogers and Coln St Aldwyns. It flows through Bibury, regarded by William Morris as 'the most beautiful village in England', where the trout were so tame they would almost take food from the hand, and Fairford, too, all places that are the very essence of Cotswolds, before it enters the Thames by Inglesham Round House.

From Thames Head to the Nore and the North Sea, no part can be more peaceful, secluded or as lovely as these few miles of upper reaches between Cricklade and the Inglesham Round House; but from there and from Lechlade itself, all that is best of the Thames's upper river is left behind. From Eisey Bridge to Castle Eaton and beyond to Kempsford, one might float downstream for mile after mile, out of earshot and sight of any other living soul, the solitude completely undefiled. The colourful banks come alive in summertime with hemp-agrimony, meadowsweet and coltsfoot; comfrey, willow herb and yellow iris and a hundred lesser plant species concealed in another world. Every bend reveals a scene unchanged by the centuries and as beautiful as it can have ever been 'so that we came nearer to perfection of life there than I was ever sensible of otherwise'.[2]

Within this preamble I touched on Isis as being the alternative name for the Thames. The name appeared in the fourteenth century, derived from Julius Caesar's Tameses, when it was wrongly thought that Thames was a derivation of Thame and Isis and applied only to the river below Dorchester. The map-makers will not allow the alternative to be forgotten.

Notes

1. *The Stripling Thames* (1908)
2. North, The Hon. Roger, *The Lives of the Norths*, 3 vols (1890)

5 Administration

Even the weariest river winds somewhere safe to sea.

Although The National Rivers Authority (NRA), which came into being in September 1989, will already be familiar to all who share a protective love for our rivers and streams, safeguarding the Thames waterway is nothing new. It has, however, been essentially for commerce and a source of power for its mills as well as for the general good of the people dwelling within its influence, rather than for giving any aesthetic pleasure, and has taken place in one form or another during the years covered by this story.

Mills and weirs were the bane of navigation in early times, but mills there had to be; an Act of 1695 states:

> By length of time impositions were laid on the navigation, by Persons, Owners, and Renters of private Weirs, Locks, Bucks, Winches, &c. which were a very great Hardship attending the Navigation, & of Ill Consequence to the Carriage of Goods upon the said River of *Thames*, which Abuses were regulated by an Act made in the 6th & 7th *W*. III which Impowered the Justices to settle the Rates for each Bargeor Vessel passing through; which Act was Temporary, & continued only for Nine years, although during the Continuence thereof, the Navigation of the R. *Thames* was carry'd on with Success, and was at a Certainty.

The first mill at Ewen was still about six miles, as the river flows, above the highest point to which smaller barges could navigate to Waterhay. It was likely to have been a barge wharf for Ashton Keynes, and I suspect that some produce for shipment down-stream would have been carried down in smaller boats from the village to the wharf. Here, it does appear that the stream had at some time in the distant past been straightened across the flat meadowland.

In 1828 the river was navigable to West Mill, Cricklade, for barges of six to seven tons, and there must have been a weir and hatches there, for I remember them when a boy at the termination of the direct course of the river from the aqueduct mentioned in the previous chapter. The three or possibly four hatches were operated separately to a worm and wormwheel system by a large wheel to allow the operator plenty of leverage when water pressure against the paddles was heavy.

In order to allow the North Wilts. Canal to cross, the aqueduct would have been constructed some ten years earlier, by which time there would, long since, have been no further necessity for barges to pass upstream to Waterhay. Conveyance of goods from Ashton Keynes to Cricklade by road, for loading on to barges at Cricklade wharf would, by that time, have proved more economical.

So much has transpired at Cricklade's West Mill in the past seventy years. In whatever period we may live, every generation sees environmental changes that are inevitably regarded with displeasure, and it must be remembered before a nostalgic visit is made to old scenes and places that our worst fears are all too often sadly justified. Such it was with Cricklade's West Mill site when I saw it again after an absence of many years. Once long ago, I recall so well the mill itself, built and rebuilt over nearly two millenniums, only to be destroyed without thought of its historical associations or its ivy-clad beauty. Spared for another generation it would now be a 'listed' building, a delight for all to see. All has now vanished, covered with concrete, and now a cowyard. The deep, mysterious millpond, with its legendary giant pike and its shady elms, is also consigned to history.

In Domesday it is mentioned that four mills existed between Cricklade and Inglesham. Thacker tells us that the first of these was just below Cricklade Bridge, a point of considerable interest to those historians of this ancient borough who believed a second mill existed near the town bridge, albeit above it and not below as Thacker stated – West Mill was of course further up river.

The second mill was at Watereaton where, Thacker tells us, 'under its ancient name of Nun Eaton, the Godstow Priory Settlement probably had a mill; and the fourth at Ham weir, below Hannington Bridge'.

West Mill was bought up by the Thames Conservancy at the turn of the century. The earliest mention of it is in a perambulation of Braydon Forest by Henry III (1216–72).

Thomas Baskerville (1692) on leaving Cricklade wrote:

> So farwel Cricklad, come off ye ground,
> We'el sail in Boats, towards London Town,
> ffor this now is, the highest station,
> By famous Tems for Navigation,
> But when th 'tis joyn'd with Bath Avon
> ffor this now is, the highest station,
> By famous Tems for Navigation,
> But when th 'tis joyn'd with Bath Avon
> Then row your wherries farther on,
> ffor Baskervile, Matthews were Projectors
> Who did conclude, sixty Thousand Pound,
> Would thoroughly open each river ground,
> ffor by power of Lockes, Rains and Ffountains,
> They'l make Boats to dance upon ye mountains,
> But further yet, to ease your mindes
> How these great works, were then designed,
> Here read their Book, there you will see,
> 'Twas possible such things might be.

It was indeed possible such things might be. More than a century later in 1810, the North Wilts. Canal was opened above Cricklade, from Latton to Swindon where it joined the Wilts. and Berks. and from thence to the Kennet and Avon and so to join Bath and Bristol. One estimate for the cost of building the North Wilts. Canal made by the engineer for the project happened – in figures only – to be precisely the same as Baskerville's namely £60,000, if it terminated at Eastcott, Swindon; but if it continued to Swindon Wharf it would cost £62,000.

Little emphasis need be placed on the importance of the rivers for the conveyance of goods in those times, and of the difficulties and hazards in their use. We need only to read of the efforts made to facilitate such traffic by the construction of canals, as *Phillips Inland navigation* (1692) by Joseph Moxton, hydrographer to Charles II, amply demonstrates. Moxton drew a map to show how such a scheme would be practicable.

The Rawlinson manuscript in the Bodleian Library has a note of 1683, believed to be by the father of Thomas Baskerville

> At the head of this stream which mets the Tems at Cricklad, a gentleman of my name, skilled in the arts of conveying water, Mr Thomas Baskervile, who now lives with the Lord Ward at Dursley Castell in Staffordshier, Hee did propose to the lord chancellour Hide a

feasability of uniting the Avon and Temes and so to make good the
Navigation for Boates from Bristoll and Bathe up the river till they
got into the Tems and then downstream to Oxford and London. This
gentleman in [1618] takeing my House in his way from London
homeward, I fell into discourse with him concerning this thing. Hee
told mee there was a possibility of doing it; and that if ever it were
done there would bee such a stock of water in the Dikes that the
River Tems should never want water, but bee supplied from thence
for Navigation in the driest summer.

Thacker writes:

Two or three meadows above Eisey Bridge the Dance Brook enters
upon its southern bank, little deserving its title here . . . . It gives its
name to the Dance Common just outside Cricklade. Now a farm
blocks the way, but if you persevere round you will arrive at a rustic
bridge called Hatchetts, on the outskirts of Cricklade where
baptisms were performed within living memory. Rose Cottage
adjoins it, well known to men who navigate through Cricklade;
above which Taunt marks an old weir site; perhaps the ruinous old
house on the right bank was the weir-keepers; it stands at the head
of the pool and then the walk is barred by the 'nimble-footed Churn'
and I went to my night's rest, back over Hatchetts Bridge and into
Cricklade.

> Here Roughton River Ree
> Joynes with the Tems as you may see
> Thomas Baskerville

The 'Roughton' River was the Ray which, owing to the similarity of
names and their propinquity, Baskerville had confused with the
Key – the Dance Brook.

Although both the Hatchetts Bridge and the Eisey Bridge of the
same design might well have allowed barges with low loads to pass
beneath their central arches, it would appear that they are of
comparatively recent origin, recent that is, in the time span of
which I write and did not exist before the nineteenth century.

Of this bridge Thacker writes:

Eisey trestle Bridge. Not in Baskerville; possibly in his time there
was an ancient ford, 'well known to hunting men', which preceded
the bridge. In February 1878 a complaint reached the Conservancy
that the landowner had driven piles in the River expressly to
obstruct navigation. In March 1882 the Thames Valley Drainage

Commissioners widened the channel here and at Water Eaton just below. In about 1894 the Conservancy again had to order the removal of a chain and posts erected across the River a little above the bridge.

Fallen trees, weeds, shallows created at times of flood water, all were the natural obstacles that had to be overcome when barge traffic made their slow, tortuous journeys to and from the Thames's highest collection and distribution point at Cricklade Wharf. Man-made obstructions appeared, however, to have created far more delays to river traffic than those made by nature herself, and from what we read, it was the small weirs before the institution of lock cuts in the middle of the seventeenth century, that were the most serious problem, causing some mills to be closed and their weirs opened up to allow free passage for barges.

Thacker, in writing here of the lower river, presents us with a fascinating insight into the problems that weirs presented, of a similar nature or worse in those early days, because a lesser volume of water would have existed in the places above Lechlade, which I will presently describe. He writes:

> ... I present an excerpt from *The Acts of the Privy Council.* 'September 4, 1580. The Lord Mayor was required to send an account to the Lords of the Council how many weirs there were between London and Staines; and how many had been erected within the last seven years: her Majesty being given to understand that by the multitude of weirs the river is likely to be choked and made un-navigable; and is disposed to have some present redress taken therein'; her hostile interest having been aroused, I fear elsewhere, by certain stops insolently erected within direct view of her palace of Richmond; and also, perhaps, by such documents as those of 1572 and 1574 just quoted. Four days later the report was presented to the Council; no doubt the Lord Mayor was glad to obtain royal countenance for his prerogative, and quite conceivably delighted to get in a sly reference to Majesty's own delinquancies. For amongst other obstructions he mentions fifteen 'hatches' and six 'stoppes' commanded by letters from Mr Comptroller to be erected for the supply of 'lampreyes and roches' in her Majesty's household. The Queen gravely commanded that so many of the said 'weares, stoppes and hatches' as were illegal should be defaced...

Not only the weirs themselves were obstructions, but the dangers they caused are exemplified in these curious old verses:

Mylls weares and locks men do them call
that doe annoy that worthy streame
Against the lawe they doe stand all
but still the drownde thos simple men

One farmer hath a lock in store
That hath made many a Child to weepe
Their mothers begg from dore to dore
Their ffathers drowned in the deepe.

At ffarmers lock foure men be loste
of late I putt you in no doubt
Three were drowned the streams then toste
the fourth he had his brains knocked out.

Besides those early dangers, we can visualize the problems and difficulties once encountered by weirs obstructing commercial river traffic, by the following account by Thacker:

When a vessel desires to pass a sufficient number of paddles or rymers are hauled out and stood handy on the bridge or just ashore. This allows the water to rush through the opening in great volume, which continues until the water level above the weir is reduced nearly to the level of the water below, and the rush is considerably quietened. Then the vessel is dragged up through the opening; the old classical method being by means of a rope and winch stationed above the weir . . . . Other means were to pole her through, or for the crew or horses themselves to haul upon the line. The craft while passing up presents the appearance of ascending an incline. Going down the same rush is relied on to carry the craft through. It will be quite evident that this operation is attended with an enormous waste of water; the level of the whole upper reaches for perhaps a couple of miles being lowered a considerable number of inches, needing perhaps several days to recover its depth.

The immemorial mills were great offenders in the matter of erecting these weirs, whether convenient to navigation or not . . . . Flashes were required, not only at the weirs, but very frequently also to float barges over distant shallows. The miller would then, for a fee and at his own grudging choice of time, let down a flash for this purpose. Even so all trouble was not necessarily at an end for the much enduring navigator. For it often happened that a second mill intervened, whose owner would cheerfully divert the welcome abundance to his own wheel and rob the bargemaster of the accommodation for which he had not only paid, but walked many miles to arrange. These and other amenities naturally caused much friction between the millers and the barge traffic.

It was not until 1350 that Parliament passed its first Act against obstructions of the navigable part of the river, but for centuries after that one Commission followed another in creating, re-creating or dismantling that which had gone before, generally in localized areas rather than in the river as a whole.

I have no way of knowing if one or any of the weirs from Cricklade to Lechlade caused navigational problems, but imagine they would have done. Of the weir at Watereaton we learn that in October 1535 Sir Walter Stoner, who, although a Catholic, was Sheriff of Oxfordshire and Berkshire and remained in public office throughout the reign of Henry VIII, wrote to Thomas Cromwell, Earl of Essex and competent adviser to the King: 'I have pulled up the weir of Water Eyton according to the king's commandment.' The weir was probably connected with the stepping stones, said on the 12 February 1306–7 to have been in existence 'of olde time'. These stepping stones and the weir were probably situated where the Horse Bridge now stands; the former were the subject of a dispute in 1307 between the Vicar of Latton and Godstow Priory. (Not for the first time it seems had there been a dispute regarding the tithe land of Eisey.) I believe there could have been no reason for the removal of the weir other than navigational difficulties involved by its presence.

Virtually nothing is known about the weir (mill?) at Castle Eaton. Thacker makes mention of Samuel Ireland seeing it in about 1790 and says (*c.*1908): 'I do not know that there is now one stone left upon another. It was on the right bank, about a quarter of a mile above the bridge. I believe a new poundlock, already planned in the Conservancy pigeonholes, is intended some day to stand on the site.'

Blackford Weir at Kempsford was about three meadows below the village. The Conservancy had it removed in 1869 with the sill left as a foundation for stepping stones. Thacker could not find them when he was there in 1910. He mentions Krausse referring to the remains of an old mill there in 1889.

Of Hannington Bridge, Baskerville in 1692 writes:

> So here wee'l stop a while and cool,
> ffor Boats do oft come hither to lade
> Malt, Barley, other goods to trade,
> Down to Oxford and Abingdon,

And thence in barges to London
ffor wharfingers, a house provides,
To keep goods dry, on Wiltshire side.

Redpool was believed to have been situated at Map Ref: SU202971 where it is seen that the river turns sharply from an easterly to a northerly direction.

The last weir before Lechlade was a short distance above the Inglesham canal Round House. Thacker considers that none of the eighteenth century surveyors noticed it, and the earliest mention of it that he could find was in the 1850 copy of Wood's *Oarsman's Guide* which says that it was immovable, 'consequently the river is no longer navigable to Cricklade'. Ravenstein confirmed this eleven years later as 'the head of navigation on the Thames'. It was removed in 1868. Thacker says:

> Squire Campbell of Buscot complained the same month of its removal, and threatened to rebuild it. If this were objected to he would claim on the Conservancy for loss of water. There is a distinct pool and neck; but I could find no stones or stakes. A man told me at Godstow in the summer of 1912 that he could remember seeing craft hauled over the weir by a winch.

I paid a further visit to the site of the Cricklade West Mill in July 1993, and it is almost unrecognizable, so much has it been altered by farming activities. The original bridge over the river at the lower end of the mill site has itself been rebuilt of concrete. The site of the mill pond now appears impossible to place exactly. Above the site is a double weir built of concrete and its purpose I was unable to appreciate, and I could only think that had it not been built the river bed above as far as the aqueduct would be drained. The weir's presence does at least prove to future generations that a mill must have been there, the site of which I found entirely occupied by a large farm building of concrete and timber.

6 The Upper Reaches

Clear and gentle stream!
Known and loved so long.
Robert Bridges (1844–1930)

Although 'The Brook' may not have been one of Alfred, Lord Tennyson's greatest achievements, it is probably loved today more than any other of his works; born and bred in Lincolnshire, it is unlikely that he knew this part of England when he wrote it, yet the setting could so easily have been the Churn.

The River Churn has its beginnings out of several headstreams high in the Cotswolds at Seven Springs, a few miles south of Cheltenham. It falls for about 400 feet in a tortuous fourteen miles until reaching its confluence with the Thames at Cricklade. On the journey it touches villages and hamlets like Coberley, Cockleford, Colesbourne and Marsden, waters the deer in beautiful Rendcomb Park and then flows on to North Cerney, Baunton and Cirencester. Now running more gently it begins its last stages. Meandering across the valley, passing Siddington and through the willow-lined water meadows to South Cerney, the struggling Churn becomes almost strangled and lost on either hand by the Cotswold Water Park, with hundreds of acres of old gravel workings, before breaking free to join the brimming river in a corner of Priory Close at Cricklade, known in my younger days as the Priory Field.

With arguments still raging as to where the Thames's true source is, the Thames Conservancy hoped to settle the matter once and for all, and although water no longer poured out at that well known place, Thames Head, it was decided to mark the place permanently with a stone. The inscription reads: 'The Conservators of the River Thames, 1857–1974. This stone was placed here to mark the source of the River Thames.'

The source at Thames Head was referred to by W.G. Fernside thus: 'The numerous little fountains rise in infantine playfulness, four or five inches in height, at the foot of some rising ground planted with trees and shrubs.'

The *Encyclopaedia Britannica* summarizes the Thames's source as follows:

> Its traditional source is Thames Head, at about 356 ft (109 m) O.D. (Ordnance Datum, or mean sea level as defined by Ordnance Survey) in the parish of Coates, 3 mi (4.8 km) SW of Cirencester; but claims have been advanced for Seven Springs, the source of the River Churn, situated at nearly 700 ft, (213 m) O.D. 4 mi S of Cheltenham.

Walking down from Thames Head you may have to go some way before the first signs of water appear. Someone once wrote, I believe it was Gibbings,[1] that a little below the source itself a cow could drink the Thames dry. This lack of water at Thames Head was undoubtedly due to the pumping station erected in 1878. I received a letter from my namesake and kinsman from Cheltenham recently, who knew a great deal about this pumping station from his father Cecil Taylor Cuss (manager of the GWR works at Swindon) and he writes:

> I expect you know what happened to the spring at the start of the Thames at Trewsbury Mead near Kemble. The GWR at Swindon needed a secure supply of water for the works at Swindon and for the locos, and so they sunk a well at Kemble and introduced a steam pumping plant to take the water from Kemble to Swindon in a 9" (?) pipe, so that they did not have to rely on Swindon water. At the source the Thames nearly dried up.

Julius Caesar named the river Thameses; by King Alfred's time it had become Tames and in Queen Elizabeth I's day Themmes.[2] The name has also been varyingly written as Tems, Tames, Temmes and one or two others during man's long association with the river.

From its source to its mouth the Thames must hold more history than all the rivers of the world. It was the Parliamentarian John Burns who informed an American visitor that '... every drop of water is liquid history'.[3]

Let us see what others have had to say about this curious drying out of the Thames source and its upper reaches. Leland in the sixteenth century writes: 'I*f*is riseth 3 myles from Cirencester, not far from the village of Kemble, within a mile of the Fosse Way, wer very bed of I*f*is is In a great Somer Drought there aperith very little or no Water yet is the stream fervid with many offsprings re*f*orting to one Botom.'

The historian William Smith in his *History of England*: 'Cirencester . . . standith upon the river Churn, which is the principle head that Thames hath and springeth in Cotswold poole, six miles est of Closter.'

Fred S. Thacker writes:[4]

> You may now climb up to the canal towpath and, leaving Gloucestershire as you pass beneath the arch that carries Akeman Street over the canal, walk northwards for nearly half a mile until you pass the stone which records the seventeenth mile from Inglesham, and arrive within fifty yards of two cottages that lie across the water, go over the wall and down the embankment, and after a little search you will find the ivy-covered ash, with TH carved upon its trunk about a yard from the ground, leaning over the slightly hollowed earth where once rose Thames and all its history.

After a further visit he writes:

> I dropped down to the canal path and went to see if there was any water at Thames Head in April; taking with me a bottle to collect some if I found any, as men will preserve the water of Jordan. But all was as dry as in summer; only the waterless hollow, with white violets and early cowslips growing by it and overhead the cawing of rooks.

Ramsey the eminent geologist stated: 'The Thames rises not far from the crest of the Oolithic escarpment of the Cotswold Hills that overlooks the Severn.'

J.E. Vincent appears to be a little undecided but seems, on the whole, to agree with Ramsey, and after a lengthy argument as to whether the river's true name is Thames or Isis, writes: 'If we may not derive the name Thames, we may at least attempt to derive, trace as from the source, the river Thames. What, it is imperative to ask, is the spot where we may look for the true source of the Thames? That, again is not by any means a simple question.'

After quoting Leland, he goes on:

> He [Leland] meant the Thames Head of today, situated, as he describes, but for many years less water-bearing even than in his time, because the springs have been impoverished, or diverted from

their function, for the purposes of the Thames and Severn Canal . . .
the stream from Seven Springs is always visible, and that from
Thames is not; and the Seven Springs brook is a much more important stream in appearance. But it is a rather large 'but', the stream
rising from Seven Springs has been called the Churn until its junction with the Thames, and the stream which joins it has been called
the Thames for many centuries.[5]

This Royal river and principle river of England winds its devious
course eastwards to form part of the boundaries of no fewer than
eight counties, bisecting Greater London before entering the Nore
– the North Sea – 210 miles from its source. However, it is only
Gloucestershire and Wiltshire that are of concern to us here and
may rightly be termed 'The Upper Thames', being the river from
Lechlade to the source that can no longer be navigated commercially; I say no longer, because it was used at one time for this, as
far as Cricklade and, far less so, as high as Ashton Keynes. It is
extremely likely that it was of considerable importance to the
Romans for the conveyance of timber, principally oak from that
part of the river where Cricklade now stands, to *Londinium*, when
the Braydon Forest flourished on the clay soils south of the river,
right down to the Thames itself. According to the *Roman Chronicle*
the story of the Danes sailing their longships up the river as far as
Cricklade, might appear to show proof enough that the flow was far
greater then than it is today.

When the country's highways were little more than dirt tracks,
fit only for saddleback, before their gradual improvement and the
introduction of the stage coach, which was to be followed by the
canal builders, the river was Cricklade's vital lifeline. Today, as we
near the twenty-first century, only the occasional punt or kayak is
delivered there by road, ready for its leisurely journey downstream
to the boatyards at Lechlade, Abingdon or Oxford. Of Cricklade,
Hilaire Belloc mentions little of the place itself, his interest was of
course the river: 'How and when the old bridge at Cricklade fell, we
have no record, but one of the most important records of the
Thames we have in Anglo-Saxon history is connected with the
passage of the river.'

In 1877 a petition, headed by the Revd John Flood (Vicar of St
Sampson's) was made and signed by thirty-four prominent people
of Cricklade and presented to 'The Right Worspl, Sir John Ernle
Knight and Sir George Hungerford Knt., Burgesses in Parliament
for ye Burrough of Cricklade in ye county of Wilts':

   . . . these are humbly to shew yt whereas heretofore there was always a free and undisturbed passage for smaller boats and barges from ye town of Cricklade to Oxford and Abingdon and divers other places for commoditys of the said town and country, furthering the trade thereof and also beneficial to the country adjacent. Now of late the said boats have been stopped and interrupted at a certain place (St John's Bridge) by Captain Cutler and not permitted to pass upon the said river without payment of a considerable sum of money for severall [i.e. each] boat, so desire you to take the promises into your consideration, and we shall pray.

Farms along this fertile valley, from Ashton Keynes down to Cricklade and Lechlade were particularly famous for their cheeses and their disposition was at one time by the only means – the river. The canals were beginning to take the trade over when William Cobbett, lamenting the condition of Cricklade's poor, tells us of a few other products of this rich agricultural countryside. At Buscot, where the road is closest to the river, stood the storehouses for the produce, which was carried downstream from the upper reaches in small craft, for loading into larger barges, mostly destined for London. Thacker, writing in the opening years of the twentieth century about this commerce, says:

There was a great trade in cheeses in old times from Lechlade to Cricklade, which were collected, and loaded into the London barges down at the old storehouses at Buscot. One Ralph Mould, of Newgate Street, Cheesemonger, says in an old report that he receives great quantities of cheese from Lechlade by barges. Two thousand five hundred tons of cheese came down annually thence to London in peacetime; much more in war.

He goes on to complain of the rise in freights owing to new locks and increased wages.

A 1737 Act stated that the Thames was navigable to Cricklade. From 1770 the Commission was empowered to construct locks along the river in their Sixth District, from Cricklade to Oxford. Before the Thames and Severn Canal was constructed, boats of from seven to ten tons navigated to Cricklade. From 1790, the year after the first barge travelled successfully on the Thames and Severn canal from the Severn to the Thames with a load of coal, the Thames from Cricklade to Inglesham suffered severe neglect. Before 1611 the Commissioners District, from Cricklade to Oxford, spent no money at all on the river between Cricklade and Lechlade.

Westhall, writing in 1828, records that barges of only six to seven tons could travel as far as West Mill. A draught, with as little as twelve inches in these upper reaches between Lechlade and Cricklade, was sufficient for commercial navigation. Shallow, wide boats (barges) of up to ten tons burden were able to navigate in water of this depth. The modern punt is of similar shape and form and can float on water of only half that depth. It is easy therefore to understand why the Thames's higher reaches were utilized and, in these earlier days, how important the river was to life in Cricklade and the nearby villages and hamlets.

The Thames Conservancy was created in 1866 and given jurisdiction over the river from Cricklade to Yantlett Creek. In the previous year it had been stated that 'the part between Lechlade and Cricklade, is now almost grown up'. In 1893, Nevil John Cuss prepared a petition to the Board, signed by the landowners and inhabitants of Cricklade, in which it was requested that the minimum of twelve inches of water be maintained to the Town Bridge. The Board admitted liability, but were constrained through lack of funds to carry out the work. Seven years later the Landowners Committee persuaded the Conservancy to abandon any scheme for a proposed improvement between Abingdon and Cricklade. The committee reasoned, no doubt, that an increase in public intrusion of these quiet and peaceful upper reaches – for whose maintenance they could see no commercial advantages to their riparian ownership – could only be to their disadvantage and that wildlife in general and their game in particular would be disturbed. The poaching fraternity probably disagreed.

In 1889, L.L. Krausse mentions that the Thames Conservancy had recently dredged the river between Lechlade and Cricklade, but in a few years it was choked again. Shelley with his wife Mary, rowed up from Windsor with the objective of reaching Thames Head by way of the Thames and Severn Canal and so to the Severn, but when the Canal Company demanded a fee of £10 for their journey, the poet refused to pay such a large sum. They attempted to row on upstream but the choked conditions eventually defeated them.

Thacker writing of Hannington Bridge: 'The river was terribly choked with weeds; and I think most upward craft got stopped here in the summer of 1908. I heard rumours that a thorough dredging and cleaning is intended soon between Lechlade and Cricklade, and hope it will come about.'

The following year J.E. Vincent writes of the difficulties encountered to boating upstream from Lechlade, describing them as 'mere labour and sorrow'. He writes that:

One or two allusions, however, must be made to the part above Lechlade. Everybody is tempted when there to push up as far as Inglesham Round House, marking the junction with the Severn Canal – much talked of before it was constructed, little used since; but if I may judge the inclinations of others from those of myself and my friends in the past, the temptation to penetrate farther upstream will vanish at this point. Mr Hutton, enthusiast as he is, is not encouraging. He has made the effort many times, but once and once only, has he succeeded in penetrating the reeds past Castle Eaton and Kempsford to Cricklade.

The Revd Hutton writes that:

... above Lechlade the river has been left almost to itself. The weeds are cut; they ought to be everywhere, but they are not. That is all that has been done, and thus it is not often that a boat can make its way over shallows and through sedge and rushes in summer from Lechlade to Cricklade. The water runs swiftly, and even a canoe can not be forced upstream. Often you may tug and carry and pull, and yet you will not succeed. I have got as far as Hannington and Kempsford and Castle Eaton, but never till the year 1903 to Cricklade itself; and then – in a canoe, with very hard work, and not more than half an hour's rest – it took from 10.30 a.m. to 5 p.m. But what compensations! The glorious summer day, never too hot, though hot enough to tan the cheeks and burn the arms; the fresh strong wind, playing among the rushes by the bank and the elms and poplars by the shore; the clear swiftness of the stream, swollen by the rains, but pure and bright like a mountain spring; the birds, the cattle, the haymakers at work. There can be no other happier sights than these ...

The Revd Hutton mentions 'the palmy days' of traffic by water, and considers the Upper Thames 'must have been' much used in those days. If he paddled his canoe, as is most likely, I can appreciate his trials and tribulations, for I knew the river in the 1920s, as far as Castle Eaton, very well, but very little of it beyond that village by water.

In boyhood and early youth I had a canoe and a punt at my disposal for several years. Although coming near to a spill from the canoe on one or two occasions, I never got a wetting. However, the first time I fell from the punt, it was a winter's day, and snow began to fall as I hit the ice-cold water. On one or two later occasions, but in summertime, the same thing happened again. On one such my old schoolboy friend, the late-twentieth century North Wiltshire poet, was with me. He portrayed the accident in verse, one of which is below.

Punting in his canoe, under the conditions the Revd Hutton had to contend with, could have caused him less distress and shortened his time considerably, but it is an art needing long and careful practice. A canoe, by its very design, tends to roll alarmingly when one stands upright in it for the first time. One has to find and hold the centre of gravity precisely, for at the first attempt a wetting could be imminent:

> On infant Isis we would float
> In an old unwieldy boat,
> Intent upon far voyaging
> To Cowneck or the distant ring
> And at times 'twas not unknown
> That I should be left on my own
> There in the boat, for you, no doubt
> With some dismay, had fallen out.[6]

The story is taken up once more by Fred Thacker of the navigational difficulties encountered, he writes:

Do not attempt to force the Thames above Inglesham in dry seasons, with a heavily laden double sculler! I tried it once, . . . it is often as I have just said, impracticable for anything heavier than a canoe to travelling very light and easy to float over the shallows, which are frequent and show in places but an inch or two of water rippling over the white chalky pebbles. And there are stretches of clotted reed that sullenly clog the whole width of the course for a quarter of a mile at a time. These scours recall what must often have been the state of the river even as far back as the olden days. Dr Plot wrote: 'In dry times barges do sometimes lie aground three weeks or a month or more, as we have had sad experience in past summers.'

Flashing was often resorted to in dry seasons. Stanches were placed above the shallows to dam the river and, when suddenly released, the craft floated off by the sudden rush of the torrent.

J.E. Vincent tells us that:

Tiny craft are occasionally met upon it here to batter their way through the undergrowth to Lechlade, the accepted starting point for navigation. Cricklade never had the commercial justification to set itself firmly on the river. Navigators may disagree but I estimate the end, or start of shipping on the upper Thames to be near Inglesham Church, at a line marked by an ash, its bark rubbed smooth by generations of itchy cows.

As early as July 1607, commissioners surveyed the river from Cricklade to Radcot, and in the preamble to the subsequent Act, it is stated that the Thames is navigable for boats of good burthen west of Oxford. How far west, was apparently left unspecified.

J.R.L. Anderson[7] mentions Thames Conservancy plans to make the river navigable for small cruisers as far as Cricklade.

In the early 1980s a scheme was submitted by the Inland Waterways Association to make the river navigable to Cricklade once more. My letter of enquiry, made to Mr T.T. Ramsden-Binks, a Cricklade historian and its museum curator, about certain hoped-for intentions of the Association brought the reply:

> ... that boating enthusiasts of the IWA (Inland Waterways Association) attempted to drum up support for making the river navigable again as far as Cricklade, but this later developed into a scheme for reinstating the Thames and Severn Canal. This was opposed by the Cricklade inhabitants and by riparian landowners for reasons of cost, the harm to wildlife and the effect it might have on riverside scenery.

To gain publicity for this scheme the IWA used a purpose-built boat of shallow draught, having the appearance of a punt. The barge, named the *Token Ton*, left Coventry on the 7 May 1984 and reached Cricklade on the 9 June. Her cargo consisted of bricks, aluminium ingots, paint, wine bottles and building equipment. The occasion received a good deal of publicity and attempts to further these ambitions were still being made nine years later but I understand that public opinion remains against the scheme.

The present course of the Upper Thames is all that is left, and only a trickle of its former self, as it meanders along the southern rim of a once great gravel-bearing river of a mile and more in width, its origin unknown and its geological history defying analysis. So ancient is it indeed that we are tempted and excused in thinking the river as we know it is indeed immutable, and in post prehistoric terms, it would certainly appear to be so. Man, however, with a little aid from nature, has wrought many changes in the stream as we know it today. Before leaving this chapter it is interesting to see that Mr R.T.C. Rolt, in his excellent treatise on the Thames, in a year unspecified during the first half of the century, found the scene about the Thames and Severn Canal at Inglesham Round House disturbing, grieving at the dereliction about the old canal lock. He did not apparently make any attempt to row on upstream past the old canal entrance.

The *Token Ton* on its arrival at Cricklade

He tells us that much of the timbers of the old gates were rotted away but that one gate was still hanging, and the derelict lock chamber was nearly 'lost in a tangle of climbing roses'.

Notes

1. Gibbings, Robert, *Sweet Thames Run Softly* (J.M. Dent)
2. 'Sweete Themmes runne softly, till I end my Song,' 'Prothalamion', Edmund Spenser
3. 'I have seen the Mississippi, that is muddy water, I have seen the St Lawrence that is crystal water, But the Thames is liquid history.'
4. *The Stripling Thames* (1908)
5. *Story of the Thames* (Smith, Elder & Co., 1909)
6. Shipway, George, *Things Dear to the Country Heart* (R.J.C. Publishing, Blunsdon, Swindon, Wilts, 1992)
7. *The Upper Thames* (Eyre & Spottiswood, 1970)

7 Life Beneath Thames Waters

A fisher sat where all was green . . .

The Atlantic salmon (*Salmo salar*), king of all the river fish, was once so common in the Thames that it was said medieval London apprentices turned up their noses at salmon 'sandwiches'. As long ago as 1338 there is a record of salmon together with other fish being destroyed illegally in the Thames, and forty years later, during Edward III's reign, salmon were still so plentiful in the river that the fry were taken in great quantities and fed to pigs.

By 1536 all this had changed and the people of Staines, so it has been said, obtained 20s for a fresh salmon sent to the King, Henry VIII.

In 1746 in an essay written by Roger Griffiths (the water bailiff of his day), he writes: ' . . . though some of our northern countries have as fat and as large [Salmon] as the River Thames, yet none are of so exquisite taste'. In 1781 there were complaints made at Kingston on Thames about fishing for salmon out of season, and this was possibly the beginning of the end of what had by then been deemed a delight for the taking. In 1843, one Purvis importuned the City to grant him a lease of the Victoria Embankment there to establish a salmon fishery, which delicacy he imagined might still be taken in abundance from the Thames. However, by then the fish were no more, according to other records, for the last salmon had already been taken and it was to be more than a hundred years before the next fish was caught in the river and that at West Thurrock Power Station.

Since 1979 salmon parr (young salmon in their first year) have been introduced in secluded parts of the river with their adipose fins

67

removed – quite harmless to the fish or its movements – for future identification. Smolts (young salmon in their second year, the second phase in a fish's development before it is ready to leave for the sea) were introduced further downstream. It is thought that at this stage in their lives the scent of the river is implanted. More than 60,000 parr are now introduced annually and some 40,000 smolt of which about 10 per cent may survive. Following their return they are caught in salmon traps at Moseley Weir. Between 1982 and 1985 an average of about 100 fish returned each year, increasing to 175 in 1986. I do not know where the parr are introduced, but it is possible that the clear, cool waters of one or two of those Cotswold tributaries are chosen as well as parts of the upper river itself.

The Thames Salmon Trust was launched in 1985, with commercial sponsorship encouraged to provide 'ladders' at certain weirs, which the fish would otherwise find impossible to negotiate; several having already been completed. The Inland Rivers Authority, launched four years later, keeps close watch over our rivers and streams, for all of us who love the river will be hoping that its pollution will soon be a thing of the past. By the dawn of the twenty-first century the Thames may be designated a salmon river once more and perhaps fine specimens will be taken in those wide open stretches of water.

In July 1993 one of the biggest salmon caught in the Thames for a hundred years was taken on rod and line more than eighty miles upstream between Henley and Marlow. It was described as a two-year-old female measuring three feet and weighing twelve pounds. Major John Hyslop, Appeals Director for the Thames Salmon Trust, believed it may be the same fish he caught and returned to the water the previous month. The psalmist's 'things creeping numerable and innumerable . . .' are as plentiful everywhere along the Upper Thames and its tributaries, as are to be found in any like rivers in Britain. From the most lofty and prized of all the creatures nurtured and sustained by Thames's waters, I turn now to the most lowly and insignificant, which can provide food for man yet was once the dish of epicures, that little creeping crustacean, the freshwater crayfish, *Orconnectes virilis*. Few people today would have any idea how to catch him and I suspect fewer still ever bother to do so, with the consequence that he is more numerous now in the Thames's upper waters than he ever was.

Like most of the arthropods the crayfish is a nocturnal creature, a skulker, and seldom seen in the daytime but for his probing claws extending from his hole, ready to grab any passing morsel that may chance to be floating by. He makes his home in holes in the bankside, in crevices in the stone and brickwork of bridges and culverts or under large stones and boulders on the stream bed. From these he can easily be lured by his acute sense of smell to a bait of meat or offal. A grown specimen can measure anything from about six to sixteen inches (15 to 40 cm). In England's rivers they are seldom much longer than five to seven inches (12 to 17 cm) and eight inches (20 cm) would be a large specimen. The flesh of this 'river lobster' makes excellent eating. C.J. Cornish writes:

> ... ten years ago the banks of the river from Staines to the upper waters at Cricklade were honeycombed with crayfish holes, like sand-martins' nests in a railway cutting. These holes were generally not more than eighteen inches below the normal water line. In winter when the stream was full fresh holes were dug higher up the bank. In summer when the water fell these were deserted. The result was that there were many more holes than there were crayfish, and for hundreds of miles along the Thames and its tributaries these burrows made a perforated border of about three feet deep.[1]

Cornish tells us that disease, which first appeared near Staines and spread upstream, led to virtually the complete destruction of crayfish in the river. Their bodies turned almost red and they crept from their holes and died. Before the pestilence crayfish were so numerous that making crayfish pots was a local industry. I have never heard of pots being used in the Upper Thames and have no experience of them, but they would undoubtedly have been made on the same principle as the lobster and crab pots with which all who have visited seaside fishing ports will be familiar. To make the pots, smaller osiers were used, so Cornish says, of about the size of a straw, baited and lowered to the stream bed near the crayfish holes. So insignificant had this lowly creature become in the countryman's economy, twenty-five years after Cornish wrote about it in 1902, that I was unable to buy the equipment for its capture. The shopkeeper today in hardware stores or fishing tackle shops will probably wisely shake his head to hide his embarrassment if you ask for such things. He will probably not have the faintest idea what you are talking about. If you want to taste the flesh of this little freshwater lobster you will have to be prepared to make your own equipment.

Cornish says:

> In the canalised stream which runs into Oxford itself there were great numbers which not only burrowed in the bank, but made

homes in all the chinks of stone and brick river walls, and sides of
locks, and in the wopod and weiring, where they sat ensconced as
snugly as crickets round a brick farmhouse kitchen fireplace . . . and
were regularly caught by the riverine population of boatmen,
bargees, and waterside labourers and sold in the Oxford market . . .
at six pence a dozen.

Cornish describes a dish of crayfish 'as scarlet as coral' and such
was not infrequently seen at an Oxford College luncheon.

The mature freshwater eel appears today to be more a nuisance
to fishermen than it is worth, but the flesh is delicious and the
elvers are a great delicacy and always in demand. On reaching
maturity eels leave the ponds, lakes, rivers, canals and estuaries
where they have lived since their early life as elvers and travel
great distances. Our own European species (*Anguilla anguilla*)
migrates to waters off Bermuda to spawn, and back there, it is
believed, to die. The larval life is spent in the ocean where they drift
slowly easterly with the warm Gulf Stream. It takes three years to
become an elver of about as many inches in length, when it enters
the rivers, sometimes in enormous numbers. Like crayfish they are
practically omnivorous.

When I was a boy, after the First World War, the more enterprising countryman would resort to all kinds of methods to feed a
hungry family and the capture of eels with night lines was
commonly practised. Such illegal methods were used later during
the great depression of the 1930s, although by that time few went
without sufficient food to sustain themselves and their families and
food rationing had long since ceased. The poor man however,
caught them to sell to the nearest MacFisheries or to eat at home
as a change from his meagre diet. At that time farm butter was 7d
(3p) a pound, eggs were less than a penny each and the
Unemployment Benefit for a married couple was under £2, and for
a single man only 17s 3d (87p).

It was under the slope of Eisey Hill that Cromwell's troopers
had rested before their hastily dug fortifications – visible today
only as soft contours made by grazing cattle and time itself. From
there they would have seen the distant ancient church of St
Sampson's in Cricklade, towering above the houses of this little
community, as they waited in vain for Prince Rupert's advancing
army to stream across the meadows from the west. Here there is a
deep pool at the bend beyond the trestle bridge already
mentioned, and as a boy, I watched two local men and saw for the
first time how fish were 'tickled', as one fine trout after another was

being taken by hand from the river. It was something that one day I would have to try for myself: it looked so easy. In my younger days the law on river poaching was not as strict, neither were riparian owners as mobile. The modern poacher, although considerably more sophisticated, was matched in cunning by his predecessors. A press report dated April 1991 states: 'A huge operation to catch poachers on the River Wye in Gloucestershire was launched yesterday by police and the National Rivers Authority. Poachers are estimated to take £250,000 worth of salmon a year from the river.'

Jack, or pike as they are known after they reach a larger size, are our largest predatory native coarse fish, and on rare occasions a catch has been recorded of well over thirty pounds (13–14 kg); however, such catches are generally taken in lakes and gravel pits, although specimens of twenty pounds have been taken at Eisey from a hole on the bend. This fish makes very good eating and has for long been a valuable addition to the countryman's diet.

Notes

1. *A Naturalist on the Thames* (1908)

8   Kemble, Gloucestershire

> There was a rocky valley between Buxton and Bakewell, . . .
> you enterprised a railroad, . . . And now, every fool in Buxton
> can be at Bakewell in half-an-hour, and every fool in
> Bakewell at Buxton.
>
> *Praeterita*, John Ruskin (1819–1900)

During this exciting period in the history of transport, John
Ruskin's wit might have applied to Kemble or elsewhere, but
before the line broke through from Swindon to Cheltenham and
gave a branch track to Cirencester, the place was almost unheard
of, and then, opened as Kemble Junction in 1845, it was soon to
become a household word to rail travellers, and the village, preg-
nant with history, was at last 'put on the map'.

In the book edited by Mr Christian Brann[1] we are told that
Kemble is a modern derivation of Camele. The name appeared in
Charters of 682 and 688, for certain land grants made to
Malmesbury Abbey by Cedwalla, the King of Wessex (AD 685–88),
which may have been when the Saxon settlement was founded on
the original, ideally situated Roman site. For as we know,
Christianity by this time was already becoming established in some
parts of Britain, introduced by Augustine in AD 568.

Camele, meaning 'boundary', was likely to have been the northern edge of the Braydon Forest. It is not surprising perhaps that
with Cirencester, Roman *Corinium* so near (four miles) which was
the most important town of Roman-Britain after *Londinium*, that
irrefutable evidence of their occupation has been found in the
village.

I understand the first intimation of a Roman site at Kemble –
although apparently this was not realized at the time – was in 1983,
when a retired engineer from the Kemble estate, Mr J. Gillett, was

building his house on the site of an old barn and unearthed a Roman fourth-century sarcophagus. It might have remained undisturbed for another 2,000 years had he not decided to lower the floor and in doing so struck the overhanging limestone lid two feet down. The coffin, which was also hewn out of limestone, contained the remains of a Roman lady. She would have been of about five feet in height and, according to a paleo-pathologist she was about forty-five years old when she died. Death may have been hastened by the chronic arthritis from which she had suffered. Since that time further burials have been discovered and the Cotswold Archaeological Trust has confirmed the existence of a Roman cemetery of this period.

It would not have been very long after the Battle of Dyrham, about twenty miles to the north-west in AD 577, when the Saxons routed the local tribes before they established themselves in Kemble. This great battle was with the rightful occupiers of the territory the Dobuni, who had long since been tolerated through necessity, and absorbed to a great extent by their Roman conquerors and had, until the Saxon onslaught, been fiercely independent. History does not tell us what then may have happened to these people, but many were taken into slavery.

This subsequent Saxon occupation has also been established by burials, and in common with many such sites all along the valley, including the large cemetery at Lechlade, burials were generally in very shallow graves. Graves were first discovered at Clayfurlong Farm in 1856. There were twenty-six interments found up to that time, all about six inches beneath the surface, and like many Anglo-Saxon burials, it was not unusual to find some artefacts buried with their owners, among which were articles of everyday use; of war and of peace. Among these were spearheads, umbones, brooches, a brass coin, a bronze spoon, a bronze earring and a bronze hairpin.

It was apparently 130 years before further Saxon inhumations were discovered at Kemble. This was in 1986 when a man was digging his garden at Clayfurlong Grove. The bodies found were females, aged between twenty-five and thirty, one of whom had been buried with a silver pin, with a garnet set in a circular head, which may have been one of a pair linked by a chain. Also found was a decorated silver hoop about three inches (6 cm) in circumference together with hollow beads of coloured glass, possibly belonging to a necklace; these artefacts helped to date the graves.

The oldest living thing in Kemble must be the churchyard yew tree. The wood of the English yew is hard, heavy and fine grained because its growth is slow. Its toughness and great strength made it almost indispensable for such bows as those used by the yeomen of England and the longbows used by the English archers at Crecy. Few village churchyards have been without their yew tree, where it was safe from stray cattle and horses. Its heavy green foliage is alkaloid and can be injurious or even fatal to animals; for this reason the truth of the local legend of Cromwell's troopers tying their horses to this tree in Kemble must be cast in doubt. The yew tree can live to a great age. Mr Brann[1] tells us the Kemble tree measures twenty feet in circumference, and its age, by the rule of thumb method, makes this fine specimen about 500 years old. Within its hollow trunk its roots have thrown up another bole in healthy growth. The tree is described as the 'Anglo-Saxon Yew tree by the church' because it is 'generally considered to date from Anglo-Saxon times'. However, as I have said, some yew trees are of great size; the gigantic specimen that grew in the churchyard of Selborne in Hampshire, and came to an ignominious end in the great storm of 1989, revealed nine skeletons among its roots and was certainly more than 1,000 years old.

For ever the most revered building in any of England's ancient villages is its church – many date back to the Normans. The Early English Church of All Saints, Kemble has seen many changes. It is not exactly known when the derelict chapel of ease at Ewen (see chapter nine) was demolished and removed to Kemble and rebuilt there exactly as it had been found, to form the entire south transept. To do this each stone must have been carefully marked before its removal. The whole operation by today's standards, was not anything very out of the ordinary but an extraordinary achievement nearly three centuries ago. The holy water vessel was also transferred to its new home, having been used for many years for the lowly purpose of feeding poultry. The chapel door key survived.

The church has a beautiful eighteenth-century tower, and the graceful steeple, added in the sixteenth century, rises to a height of 120 feet. The music and song of the Christmas of 1823 must still have been echoing in the ears of the villagers when, in a great storm a few days later, the steeple was struck by lightning and so badly damaged it had to be rebuilt. Since that time considerable changes have taken place in the fabric. Much rebuilding was carried out in the nineteenth century, which included the porch, the chancel and the nave. Unhappily this made it lose something of its ancient beauty – perfectly illustrated by a watercolour reproduction made before the restoration, a black and white photograph of which may be seen in Mr Brann's book.

The church at Kemble

To help carry the enormous weight of the spire, arches were constructed across the tower's four right angles and the tower arch sealed in. We are told that twelfth century stone coffin lids were used in the process. The spire was subsequently found to be in a dangerous state of repair, and was strengthened with iron bands and tie rods, with the inevitable result that damage was caused by the expansion and contraction of the metal, and rust allowed water to creep into the crevices. Two engraved sundials were built into the stonework near the base of the tower. Again in 1952 further repairs were made to the spire, the weathercock refurbished and the iron bands repainted. Eleven years later the bells were again silenced, when the steeple needed further attention and £8,000 was estimated for the work. However, further more minor repairs and painting has preserved the grace and beauty we see today.

On the west wall of the nave is a tablet, taken from the chapel, commemorating a London lord mayor who was buried in the old churchyard. Removed from the Ewen aisle and hidden away in the vestry behind the organ is the recumbent effigy of a thirteenth-century knight in a flowing surcoat and holding a shield. Much of it is worn away and his coat of arms can no longer be recognized. It must once have been exposed to the elements and possibly used as a step, until it was brought inside: nothing else can account for its present appearance. The stone lid of a coffin, upon which he once rested, is in a recess in the aisle; gracefully canopied cusps flanked by carved heads are surmounted by a seven- or eight-membered hood mould with a delicately carved capping. Fragments of medieval glass, found near Salisbury Cathedral in the 1920s or 30s, are in one of the windows; in it there may be seen a small figure of a woman in a white robe. There is an Early English piscina and a sedilia in the south chapel. The north chapel has a rather unusual triple lancet east window. The rather plain font is fourteenth century with a modern base.

A memorial plaque to a member who was not destined for succession in the local Poole dynasty, may be seen high on the west wall of the church which reads:

> 'Edmund Poole second son of Edward Poole Esq
> being but two years of age was here bvryed the 4th
> day of March 1661.'

Some events in the history of this important family in the area are in chapter ten on Poole Keynes, to which, in the first part, the family gave its name.

Burials in the churchyard ceased in 1882, the exception being stone vaults, or graves of not less than five feet deep without exposing other remains. The desecration of graveyards was once commonplace in late centuries in England and Ireland. Churchyards were commonly filled to over-capacity; that of Cricklade St Sampson has been estimated to hold the remains of more than 30,000 people.

Well known names in the parish that have influenced its history are the Phillips, the Biddulphs and the Gordons. Mr Brann's book gives no fewer than fourteen Biddulph entries in his index, seven of the Phillips and there are numerous entries relating to Anna Gordon and Robert Gordon.

In 1969, after cracks appeared in the old vicarage walls at Kemble, the floors began to give way and a staircase started to move, temporary accommodation was found at Blackbird Cottage until a new vicarage was built. Unfortunately we learn it was constructed cheek by jowl with farm buildings.

Kemble has a seventeenth-century manor house. The nineteenth-century owner was able to make alterations to it as a result of the sudden wealth the coming of the railway had engendered. Its size was reduced in the early 1950s.

The Coming of the Railroad

The coming of the railway to Kemble, undoubtedly the most momentous event in its long history, could only have been commensurate, in the lives of Kemble people, to the airfield named after the village that came into being nearly a hundred years later with the Second World War. Both railway and airfield are still there to remind the village of its recent history.

It is not necessary for me to give more than a broad picture of the railway line, whose coming was such a momentous event in the lives of the inhabitants when it passed through their village, for its story has already been so admirably told in Mr Brann's book, under the title *The Dear Old Great Western* by Mr J. Thomas, secretary of the Cirencester Railway Society.

Support for a rail link by a western route to the north from London, joining the existing link from Paddington to Bristol at Swindon, came from many quarters and finally a Bill was given Royal Assent in 1836. A line would be built from Swindon with stations at Purton, Minety and Kemble and so to Gloucester and Cheltenham by way of the Stroud valley, tunnelling the Cotswold ridge. This would be in a similar manner to, and almost in parallel with, the famous Sapperton Tunnel built for the Thames link by canal with the Severn. The line was estimated by Brunel to need a capital outlay of £150,000, and it was surveyed by him on horseback for a broad gauge twin track. During much of the time he stayed with his staff at Oaksey, two miles south of Kemble. The Cheltenham and Gloucester Railway Company was formed for its construction.

Although there were numerous obstacles, both human and physical, to be overcome before the railway was completed, one of the greatest obstacles appears to have been a recalcitrant landowner at Kemble by the name of Gordon. Squire Robert Gordon of Kemble House, Secretary to the Treasury 1835–41, was determined to have his 'pound of flesh' if he allowed the railway to pass through his estate and he made a very thorough job of doing so. The demands made on the company were daunting. In the first instance, where the track was to pass close to the manor it had to pass underground by the cut and close method, for a distance of 400 yards, so that there could be no disturbance from the noise of the trains or by smoke from the locomotives, the deep cutting was to be planted with trees and shrubs. Further, the junction for Cirencester was not for access by the public, except for the transfer of passengers; the only exception to this was Mr Gordon's exclusive right of its use by his family and friends. A certain route was laid down for access by the company's employees to the junction so that they might not be seen from his house or grounds. The cost of the seventy-five acres bought by the company from the Squire was £13,500 and he obtained compensation for disturbance and damage of £7,500. A similar sum was paid to the Thames and Severn Canal Company whose canal was crossed and recrossed two miles to the north of the village. These were very large sums of money.[2] A station, which the company called Tetbury Road Station, had to be built for the use of Kemble residents half a mile north of the village by the Roman Fosse Way and a stone's throw from the source of the Thames. At that time the two tracks on the main line were still of the old broad gauge of seven feet and a quarter inch; this was not changed until 1872, when the thirty-five miles of the up line from Swindon to Gloucester was relaid in only four days. It was followed by a similar change in the single line to Cirencester. The seven miles line to Tetbury from Kemble Junction was completed and opened in 1889.

Eventually, in 1882, Squire Gordon's heir, Anna Gordon, relented and permitted Kemble Junction to be used as a station, referring – as well she might – to the company as 'the poor dear Great Western'. The new station was of a new design by Brunel and built within the inverted apex formed by the main line route and the branch line to Cirencester and reached, for passengers, by a footbridge.

In a period that I would term as the unstoppable heyday of railway construction, when all else became subservient to the needs of the railway companies, another branch line of seven miles was opened in 1889 from Kemble Junction westerly to Tetbury. The branch closed down in 1965 and the branch line to Cirencester later that year.

The construction of Kemble airfield, like that of Down Ampney a few miles down the Thames valley was already under way at the outbreak of the Second World War, but unlike that of Down Ampney it did not share a part in Operation Market Garden when airborne and parachute divisions left for Arnhem in September 1944, rather was it used as a maintenance and storage unit for the RAF during those troubled years. Down Ampney with many others is gone, but Kemble aerodrome lives on.

Notes

1. Brann, Christian, ed., *Kemble, Ewen and Poole Keynes: Three Villages by the Infant Thames* (Collectors Books Ltd., 1992)
2. Costs and relative values have been a study of considerable interest to historians. Henry Phelps-Brown and Sheila Hopkins have met this challenge in a rather unusual way and have come close to answering this virtually imponderable question in their book: *A Perspective of Wages and Prices* (Methuen, 1981).

9 Ewen, Gloucestershire

> Sweet is thy course, and clear, and still
> By Ewen's old neglected mill.
> Green shores thy narrow streams confine.
> Where blooms the modest eglantine,
> And hawthorn boughs o'ershadowing spread,
> To canopy thy infant bed.
> > Thomas Love Peacock, (1785–1866)

This 'unique and delightful' man, T.L. Peacock, as the Revd W.H. Hutton described him, also wrote of the river he loved so much in more general terms in *The Genius of the Thames*, a lyrical poem in ten parts:

> The woods are roaring in the gale,
> That whirls their falling leaves afar;
> The crescent moon is cold and pale,
> And swiftly sinks the evening star,
> High on the mossy bank reclined
> I listen to the eddying wind,
> While Thames impels, with sinuous flow,
> His silent rolling stream below;
> And darkly waves the giant oak,
> That broad above his stature rears
> On whose young strength innocuous broke
> The storms of unrecorded years.

Half a dozen roads converge upon this tiny cluster of cottages and farms. Thacker described it in his all too brief dissertation: '... a charming little cluster of cots and farm houses,' he wrote, 'with a level bridge across the stream that whispers through, cradled in forget-me-nots'. Little can have changed since Thacker saw it in the dawn of the century. Some new dwellings have been added since the Second World War but, as the 1989 published Ordnance Survey *Landranger* series shows, the place is not overwhelmed by their presence. Should you have a special love of the Cotswolds, on whose extreme southernmost edge it lies, you might well wish to stay awhile and explore, talk to its friendly people and breathe in this peaceful gift from heaven in a still unsettled world.

The land limits of Ewen, which is in the parish of Kemble, were set out with stones until quite recently and are given in a charter of King Athelstan (AD 931) as 'five mansas in Aewilme', donated to the Abbey of Malmesbury. There is a certain confusion about the source of the *Tamyse* in this charter and numerous springs are referred to as rising in the parish of Aewilme.

If we look at the water in Ewen today after normal rainfall, it is hard to imagine that there could ever have been a sufficient flow to operate a watermill. Standing on Parker's Bridge, Father Thames's second road crossing – a place that used to be known as the Blue Arms, because it was believed by older inhabitants that an inn or hostelry of that name once stood there – the terrain appears too level to sustain a watermill. There is, however, a fall of more than twelve feet from the source at Trewsbury Mead, hidden by trees a mile away beyond Clayfurlong Farm until the river leaves Ewen behind under its third bridge on the Poole Keynes road. From there it continues through the meadows to Somerford Keynes and the first of the flooded gravel workings referred to earlier.

The Thames's source has already been described quite fully (see chapter six) but the following, as seen and told by Walter Armstrong[1] in the opening paragraph of his charming old book, merits inclusion here:

The head waters of the Thames bubble up in a brick-bound spring, a kind of Artesian well, in a meadow about three miles from Cirencester. The meadow is known as Trewsbury Mead, from the site of an old encampment called Trewsbury Castle, which lies close by. It is enclosed on one side by Acman Street, one of the four great Roman roads which meet at Cirencester, and on another by the Cheltenham branch of the Great Western Railway, while it is bisected by the embankment of the Thames and Severn Canal. The Thames Head is close to the bank, and the water it sends along the ancient channel is greatly lessened by the demands of the artificial river which is kept up to the required level by water pumped from the spring. This however, is so abundant that until lately it scarcely failed even in the driest seasons, while in winter its waters flowed over the wall and bubbled up through the earth for many yards around, to wind away through the meadows on their long course to the sea.

To make the mill operational in days gone by, the volume of water must have been considerably greater than it is today, but Thames Head was producing then an adequate supply of water for the purpose, its volume increased by numerous runnels, at Bicknam Spring, which is now known as Bittenham Springs. The ancient name of Aewilme (meaning the place of the springs) bequeathed its name to the modern Ewen. These springs are believed to have been places of pagan worship, long before the Anglo-Saxons or the Roman invasion. Being a part of Kemble in ancient times, Ewen village is not entered in Domesday.

There is an interesting story in Mr Brann's book of the vagaries of the water supply from these springs in the extreme Thames upper reaches. Mr Colin McHugh, whose family lived at Bittenham Springs, the house by the waters of that name, was greatly concerned in 1980 when his small lake, anciently known as Old Monks Pond began to dry up as a result of the Thames Water Authority taking further quantities of water from their subterranean supply. The Authority excavated the pond and in doing so discovered it was lined with cobble stones believed to be of Roman origin. The pond was lined with a rubber compound such as may be obtained for garden pools to hold the water, but after the autumn and winter rains the pressure of the water puddled with clay, the underground pressure burst open the fissures and when it subsided, left a sieve through which the water could drain away almost as quickly as supplies from elsewhere were found to keep the barges afloat. This was one of the factors that hastened the canal's demise, perhaps sooner than it might otherwise have done.

There have been several Roman finds in Ewen but little to indicate that it was seriously occupied. There appears to have been some mild speculation that a Roman villa existed, brought about by no more than the find of a Roman hypocaust pipe which, as Mr Brann writes, could well have fallen from a cart intended for delivery to some new Roman villa at Cirencester. He tells us that Mr McHugh has found Roman coins on his land and also a Thames and Severn Canal token, probably similar to the one shown in chapter three.

Samuel Thacker, William Cobbett's walking counterpart of a later era, whose devotion to the Thames makes him stand apart, wrote of what he found at Ewen in the first decade of the twentieth century in the bitterest terms:

... But very little beyond this, except in wet summers as 1907, the desolating and depressing spectacle ensues of a river bed six feet deep in places, with no connected streams running through it. All you get in arid seasons is an infrequent pool of still and not always sweet water. One's first emotion is almost of tears; the second of absurd anger at the inhuman engine sucking away the streams of the springs that should send a pleasant rivulet herealong! So I felt in the exceptional drought of 1906; but they say the bed had not been quite so waterless for eighteen summers previously.

Ewen Mill, *c.* 1850

The south chapel in Kemble Parish Church is known as the Ewen Aisle. There was a chapel of ease standing at Ewen for many generations, which eventually became derelict; in the seventeenth century it was removed stone by stone to Kemble and now forms the south transept in the church there. Surviving this chapel is its door key, which for some time was treasured by the Cumberland-Jones family then living at Elm Green. Another Ewen resident, the retired Revd Spence Woolward suggested that it might be handed over for safe keeping to Kemble Church where it was on display in a glass cabinet.

Ewen was the home of the founder of the Pathological Society, Professor Boycott, who died there in 1948, and his son William Boycott who lived there until his death in 1989. Both showed considerable interest in Ewen's historical associations, and Mr Brann says they undertook excavations in the search for the foundations of Ewen Chapel. They worked in a disused quarry, finding Roman sherds and coins and a good deal of information about the occupants of the village in the Middle Ages.

Every village, almost by tradition, has its manor, and where one does not exist, as at Ewen, then sooner or later, one will be created. Here it was a fine old square Georgian house of three stories with a hipped stone-clad roof and the nostalgic name of Elm Green. This was to be renamed Ewen Manor before the late, locally much lamented, Col. St J. Valentine Gibbs took over the property. There is also the seventeenth-century Ewen House, which has mullioned and transomed windows.

The line of the disused Thames and Severn Canal can be seen on the modern maps as a tortuous winding course, following, as faithfully as it can, the contour that brings it in a southerly direction to within half a mile of Ewen at Ewen Wharf, which must, in its heyday, have meant so much to the hamlet. Here remains the only bridge carrying the disused railway line from Kemble to Cirencester where it spans both the road and the canal.

Places of refreshment are traditional, and in Ewen, in earlier days, a beer house was closed down by the owner because the tenant had cast his vote elsewhere in a General Election![2] We read of a local man named Cornelius Uzzel eating with his beer no less than six pounds of bacon, half raw and half par-boiled. Time, and a little exaggeration has no doubt made the scales weigh heavier through the years.

Here at Bittenham Springs is the Wild Duck Inn and it was the site of Ewen Mill. The Wild Duck Inn was converted from a cottage and an old barn into the property we see today and where its hospitality can be enjoyed. It consists now of inn, hotel and restaurant, and was relicensed in 1937. There had been many owners until, in 1990, it was taken over by the current owners.

There had been a timber yard in the village for many years but its last owners closed it down in the early 1950s. Few people now can appreciate the labour intensive days when planks were cut by hand labour. Two men, one above and one below, would operate the long hand saw.

Four men of Ewen fell in the First World War. Their names share the memorial in Kemble Parish Church with those of eleven others of Kemble and tiny Smerrill, a place with only two houses a short distance away. Mr Brann does not tell us if any men from the village itself were lost in the Second World War, but only of the seven who gave their lives from Kemble.

Between the two great wars Ewen children had to walk to Kemble to school. No doubt this is a delightful walk in summertime but hazardous in winter for we learn of a child on one such journey being drowned in the Thames at Parkers Bridge.

The first footbridge over the Thames

Notes

1. Armstrong, W., *The Thames: From its rise to the Nore*, 2 vols (c. 1890)
2. Brann, C., ed., op.cit.

10 Poole Keynes, Gloucestershire

We must, however, acknowledge, as it seems to me, That man
with all his noble qualities, . . . still bears in his bodily frame
the indelible stamp of his lowly origins.

Descent of Man, Charles Darwin (1809–82)

The earliest evidence of habitation by man who lived 1,750,000
years ago in the Paleolithic period, has been recorded here in the
gravel beds as well as in Lechlade, in the form of flint implements
and actual human remains. The same have also been recorded in
nearby Meysey Hampton and at Bourton-on-the-Water.

Great families, many with known origins in the remote past, still
bear their stamp on the place-names of England. We are aware that
a few had their beginnings with the Conqueror, fought with him
and in the grant of lands received their just rewards. Male heirs
may have died out, inheritance by marriage to female heirs may
have changed the titles, but still, however tenuous the hold, ancestry can still be claimed by some to the Norman French who landed
on the shores of Kent to do battle on that fateful day in 1066. Wars
have not extinguished them, unsympathetic governments have not
blighted them nor have taxes completely impoverished them. In
the stately homes of England it is rare today to find any of these
great family names who are either decadent or despised; that they
do exist we all know, but most have long since become the back-
bone of our learning and culture, and are respected and honoured
by us.

Poole is one such name; it litters a page of *Who's Who*, and its
roots have been put down from Kent to Dublin to Tanzania. No
members of this family live at Poole Keynes today, nor can it be

found that they have ever done so, but that there was some age-old affinity with the village can be of little doubt. One member at least has been buried there, and their homes have been in the vicinity for centuries, their mark indelibly etched in the surrounding country-side. So where did the name – village or family – come from? Did the family give the name to the village or, as appears more likely, did it adopt it from the village? It cannot be coincidental?

Poole as a place-name appears in Cheshire, Dorset and the West Riding of Yorkshire, its origin in every case being obscure. The Sapperton estate and the manor, about six miles from Poole Keynes, was purchased from the Nottingham family and the house rebuilt by Sir Henry Poole, High Sheriff of the county in 1487. No Poole exists on the bronze plaque in Normandy's Castle of Falaise,[1] nor, as far as I am aware, is it contained in the so-called Battle Abbey Roll, which, however, is also thought to have been unreli-able, so the origin of the name has to remain a mystery that will probably never be solved. However, as mentioned earlier, we are aware that Keynes had undoubtedly been taken from the family of that name and joined as well to Summerforde (now Somerford) as well as to Ashton.

Poole Keynes village cross

By a deed of Elizabeth I, Richard Purcell, gent, and Thomas Dennis, yeoman, both of Cricklade (and to their heirs and assigns for ever), transferred certain land and town properties as a charitable trust for the benefit of the inhabitants of Cricklade (5½m). In order to perpetuate this charity, it was enfeoffed by a deed to eighteen persons of whom Edward Poole, described as a substantial landowner, headed the list of names for this purpose. This is an early enfeoffment and is worthy of note. It reads: 'Ther is non other or meanynge of this feoffament, but that the rents, yssues, proffitts and comodities of the said premisses from tyme to tyme, shall be bestowed and employed uppon the said highe waies about the Town and Burrough of Cricklade in manner and fourme and to non other use or uses intents and purposes.'

Sir Henry Poole of Cirencester (4m), was son and heir to Edward Poole and his wife Margaret Walton. Sir Henry held the seat for Cricklade with Sir John Hungerford from 1604–11. He married Anne, daughter of Sir William Wroughton of Broad Hinton, Wilts. – and here we begin to see a little more of how the names of these great families were endowed upon the places where possibly they had first settled, or whose names they had adopted: the village of Wroughton itself is close to Broad Hinton. In 1620, when Sir Henry was MP for Malmesbury (12m), Wilts., he entered into a debate on the scarcity of coin, blaming the shortage on much finding its way to Scotland and from thence abroad. Very early we learn that the family had strong Protestant leanings, which one day would cost it dear. He advocated that papists should pay double subsidies, thus classing them with aliens. It was on 14 December 1620 when he raised the hope that certain bills would be passed, 'that we may not go home again with empty hands'. In his will he counselled 'Sir Neville Poole, my son, to be careful, loving and kind to his brother and sisters and to be good unto my tenants, suffering them quietly to enjoy their several estates'. This was proved by Neville Poole on 14 November 1632.

Sir Neville Poole (1592–1653), eldest son of Sir Henry, raised a regiment for Parliament in 1642. He had been knighted by James I at Newmarket in 1613 and the following year became MP for Malmesbury. Later, in 1626 he represented Cirencester and then again Malmesbury in 1640. He was married to Frances, daughter of Sir Henry Poole, of Sapperton.

The third generation (of the Poole line) to sit for Parliament was Edward Poole (1618–73), described as of Kemble (1m) and Oaksey (1½m), and son of Sir Neville Poole above. He metriculated from Oxford in 1635 and entered Lincoln's Inn a year later.

He sat as a member for Wootton Bassett in the Long Parliament of 1640, then for Cricklade with John Hawkins, and finally for Chippenham in the Rump Parliament 1659–60. His name appears in a Wiltshire county list of 1667 as 'a Justice of the Peace with £1,000 a year'. The changes after the Civil War may explain why, unlike his father and grandfather, a knighthood was not eventually bestowed upon him. He represented Malmesbury for five years until his death in 1673.

In the heart of Normandy, near midway between Vire and Bayeux and five kilometres south-west of Gaumont, is the village of Cahaignes. This was the birthplace of Guillaume de Cahaignes, who fought with William at Hastings alongside Robert, Count of Mortain, the half brother of the Conqueror. Their names appear on the bronze plaque with more than 300 others (who are reputed to have fought at Hastings) in the Conqueror's birthplace, the Castle of Falaise in Normandy. Of these only a list of sixteen names can, with certainty, be said to be authentic and of whom their descendants are living today; it is thought that the Cahaignes (Keynes) are among them.[2]

The Conqueror bestowed the Earldom of Cornwall, together with vast estates and manorial holdings in Sussex and Northamptonshire, on his half-brother the Count as a reward for his services in the battle. From these the Count gave twenty-five manors to William de Cahaignes. In Henry I's reign, these were divided up between William's two elder sons, while his third son, Ralph, was given most of the Northamptonshire estates. Five lines of inheritance were eventually created from these three sons, of which only one was to survive. As a result Keynes came to be added by William's son Ralph de Keynes, to the Anglo-Saxon villages of Poole, Somerford and Ashton. All of which were but a small part of the de Keynes original holdings, still well known today. Nearly a page in *Who's Who* is occupied with this illustrious family, that of Sir Geoffrey Keynes (Langdon), taking up the best part of a half page, proof of a status that is undeniable.

Domesday reading states:

Azelin holds Poole Keynes of Edward. Wulfwynn held it TRE,[3] and it paid geld for 5 hides. There is land for 5 ploughs. Of this 5 hides are in demesne, and there are 3 ploughs and 6 slaves, and 6 villans and 2 bordars with 2 ploughs. There is a mill rendering 10s, and 60 acres of meadow, pasture 3 furlongs long and 2 furlongs broad. [and] woodland 1 league in length and breadth. Worth 100s, now £6.

One of the greatest claims to fame throughout the de Keynes inheritance is undoubtedly that of John Maynard Keynes, first and last Baron Keynes CB FBA (1883–1946). He was a Fellow and Bursar of King's College Cambridge, and a man who could be described as standing high 'in the company of the great'; that his obituary takes up sixty-eight pages in the March 1947 issue of the *Economic Journal*, which he himself had edited for many years, needs no more eloquent testimony to his greatness. As a school-boy and in his later years he had an absorbing interest in the family name. He married Lydia Lopokova of St Petersburg, whose mother carried the name of Douglas. His father Neville Keynes had a Cambridge scholarship in mathematics and became University Lecturer in Moral Science. His grandfather, John Keynes, established a business in flower horticulture and was Mayor of Salisbury shortly before his death in 1878. Maynard Keynes joined the Treasury in 1915, received a CB in 1917 and at the Peace Conference 'was a natural choice as financial represen-tative for the Treasury'. He became a friend of Lloyd George and Winston Churchill. The family had suffered vicissitudes, going right back to William de Keynes of Somerford and Ashton etc. who married Margery, a daughter of Adam de Periton, who died about 1266.

Adam's estates were shared by his two daughters Catherine and Margery, whose share was vested in William de Keynes. Their grandson Robert de Keynes conveyed the property to Hugh le Despenser, most of which passed to the Crown on the execution of Hugh le Despenser the younger in 1326. However, the nephew of Robert, Sir John de Keynes, became possessed of some of his uncle's property, but the part forfeited was given to Queen Isabella, widow of Edward II for help in suppressing the Despenser rebel-lion. Keynes Court, Keynes Rag and Keynes Place remind us of their origin. Tilton, Sussex, had an historic association with the de Keynes, having once been a de Keynes family seat. It was purchased by Lord Keynes (John Maynard Keynes) as his country retreat where his wife Lydia continued to live after his death. There was no issue.

Remarkably enough, other than a stone tablet in the church of St Michael and All Angels in memory of Francis Poole, dated 1644, I have found no other evidence of the family in the village.

The church was consecrated in 1399 but most of the fabric, with the exception of the square embattlemented tower was rebuilt in the 1770s. Extensive repairs were undertaken in 1845 when the church was restored. The Gothic west window of the tower is dated

The church at Poole Keynes

1775 while the font is earlier, being 1700. There are good examples in the Gothic windows. The oak pulpit richly carved with roses and tracery is possibly Elizabethan. The wide, elaborate candelabrum was a nineteenth-century memorial to the vicar, Joseph Myles, and has an angel blowing 'the last trumpet' together with two cherubs. Built into the wall of the nave is an arrangement of figures, consisting of two women in Elizabethan dress and five girls, and is probably the remains of some elaborately sculptured tombstone. We see there the memorial to the fallen in the First World War, when seven of the men of this tiny village were lost.

The manors of Poole Keynes and Kemble were inherited by Sir Robert Gordon through his marriage in 1806 to Elizabeth Anne Coxe. Their daughter Anna inherited the estates and was well known and respected in the area. Her grave is enclosed by ornamental wrought iron railings under the yew tree in Kemble churchyard. She was the last to be buried there.

Besides the Gordons, there are many names that have held importance in the recent history in Poole Keynes and its immediate environs: the Bathursts, the Biddulphs, and the Phillips to name but a few. Many are frequently mentioned, with some interesting anecdotes, in Christian Brann's book (op.cit.). Cromwell's soldiers are said to have burned down the Manor House because of the Lord's sympathies for the Royalist cause. With its mullioned windows and gables this is now Church Farm. Built, like all the older dwellings, of Cotswold stone, the Old Rectory too has many gables, stone mullioned windows and label moulds, with a stone-tiled roof and handsome chimneys it is altogether a dwelling of considerable character. Leading to the church is a pleasant avenue of yew trees of about 200 years old. We see there the memorial to the fallen in the First World War.

West End Farm is sixteenth century. Lower Farm appears to be of similar age and both are such as may be found anywhere in this area of the Upper Thames.

Thacker (op.cit.) brings the sad, protracted ending of the water-mills in the area hereabouts into sharp focus. The mills were once an integral part of every English village. Wherever a stream had a sufficient head of water to turn a wheel, there surely, a mill would be built. Thacker writes:

> ... at the stone bridge that carries the lane between Somerford Keynes and Oaksey ... I found myself stopped again at the end of a meadow ... Getting in to the lane I struck Thames again across a large field, and went along to Kemble mill; and the Somerford upper mill, silent and ruinous, though the adjoining farm looks prosperous. Many other mills appear in the maps: Skilling's, Washbourne, Poole Keynes and the rest; but they are only names now, and the three or four I have mentioned are all that still remain.

Notes

1. The Castle of Falaise, Normandy, is the birthplace of William the Conqueror.
2. Camp, A.J., *My Ancestors Came with the Conqueror: Some Who Did and Some Who Probably Did Not* (Society of Genealogists, 1988)
3. TRE is a Domesday reference to pre-conquest times.

11   Somerford Keynes, Gloucestershire

Mine be a cot beside the hill;
A bee-hive's hum shall soothe my ear;
A willowy brook, that turns a mill,
With many a fall shall linger near.
                    Samuel Rogers (1763–1855)

The village in Saxon times was known as Summerforde; a rough interpretation being 'a place that could be crossed by a ford in summer'. It has also been suggested that it derives from 'sump' or marshy land crossed by a ford: *English Place-Names* gives a more detailed analysis.

The infant Thames wanders peacefully past the village over its gravelly bed where a ford was eventually replaced by a bridge, but sometimes after heavy rainfall this baby shows it can have a violent temper. The terrain is level and low so flooding of its meadowland is not infrequent. It was no surprise therefore that in early January 1994 after rainfall overtook previous records almost everywhere in England, the village made headline news as one of the places worst affected by floods.

It appears that, unlike Kemble a few miles away, nothing has been found to indicate that any settlement existed before the arrival of the pagan Saxons, who formed the settlement after the Battle of Dyrham in AD 577 (see chapter eight).

Very early records tell us that Somerford Keynes was associated with St Aldhelm (639–709), a cousin of the King of Wessex and pupil of Maildulf from Ireland, who had created a Christian school in Malmesbury (Caer Bladen). Aldhelm continued his studies at Canterbury and was later made the first Abbot of Malmesbury in 675. Ten years later, a charter by Berhtwald a nephew of King

Aethelred of Mercia granted land consisting of forty hides, (considered by some to have been an exaggeration) 'at Sumerford on the east bank of the river called Thames'. This was made for the support of the monks of his abbey at Malmesbury, which was a great mission centre. Domesday states:

> The same bishop (the Bishop of Lisieux) held a TRE, and it paid geld for 10 hides. There is land for 7 ploughs. Of this 5 hides are in demesne, and there are 3 ploughs and 5 slaves and 14 villans and 8 bordars with 4 ploughs. There is a mill rendering 10s, and 100 acres of meadow, [and] woodland 3 furlongs long and 2 furlongs broad. It is worth £7.

The earliest church of All Saints was Saxon and was probably built by Aldhelm (*c*.690), in his later years. It is stated by Professor F.M. Stenton[1] that: 'The modern church of the place incorporates a megalithic doorway surmounted by an arch cut out of a single stone and ornamented by narrow parallel mouldings. As Aldhelm is known to have been a builder of churches there is at least a presumption that a church was built for the peasantry on his new estate.' Until this church was built the first Saxon converts to Christianity were probably baptized in the Thames, in Somerford, and later in Ewen, Poole and Kemble.

The Saxon doorway at the church at Somerford Keynes

The oldest and most treasured relics of the past apart from the unique Saxon doorway, are portions of Saxon sculptured stone, carved with two distorted animal heads facing one another, to give the appearance of biting a spherical ball, all presently resting on a window ledge just inside the church. There is a resemblance here to a pair of stones, which can be seen built into the south wall in St Sampson's church at Cricklade, above the main arcade. To return to All Saints, while these fragments, placed as they are on the high window ledge are not in the best position for observation, the Revd Gilbert Martin who came into the church when we were there, told my daughters and me, that having them placed in a wall recess was being seriously considered.

All Saints' Church at Somerford Keynes

The unusually narrow doorway, 'one of the quaintest doorways of our land' could have been built to suit its high arch, cut as it was from a single stone. Quoins of roughly cut stone are set in horizontal and vertical courses, as was the Saxon fashion in building and are in a part of the original north wall of the nave. This opening had long since been blocked up and plastered over on the inside until, in 1968, happily it was reopened.

Somerford Keynes, together with Poole Keynes, Shorncote and Kemble were originally in Mercia until its king approved the grant of the land. Since King Alfred's time when one of his great defensive fortifications was built at Cricklade to defend Wessex against the Danes, Somerford became one of her many daughter churches and remained within the Cricklade Deanery until 1897. Then, after being in the Salisbury diocese for 900 years, it reverted to within its old boundary of Mercia, the Gloucestershire county boundary as we know it today. Nearby Kemble, Poole Keynes and Shorncote are also now in the Worcester diocese. When I was a boy I believe these places came within the Cricklade postal district, but are now within the district of Cirencester. No further boundary changes were made in this area in 1974 and indeed the whole of Wiltshire was left alone.

Somerford had been granted to the Bishop of Lisieux, Gilbert Maminot, after the Norman conquest and was still held by him when Domesday was written. Baron Guillaume de Cahaignes fought with William at Hastings, and, like so many others, was rewarded with land for his services (see chapter ten).

As to the church, it is thought that only this remarkable doorway, the section of the south wall of the nave in which it is built, and the pieces of decorated stone remain of its Saxon origins. There are of course few stone-built Saxon churches surviving today, and among these rarities are Aldhelm's St Lawrence at Bradford on Avon and Escomb Church near Bishop Auckland, although numerous churches have remnants of Saxon work remaining. Cotswold inferior oolite taken from a local quarry, was used in the building of All Saints and it has been suggested that the squared quoins may have been taken from some ruined Roman building in Cirencester. It was plastered both without and within and probably originally roofed with thatch for at that time the use of Cotswold stone for roofing had not been thought of. The great stones of the door openings were the thickness of whole wall, and so it stood for 500 years.

By 1200, when the church was rebuilt, the manor came into the possession of Ralph de Keynes through his marriage. William, his grandson, gave the advowson and the great tithes to Merton Priory as a thanks-offering for the recovery of his lands from King John to whom they had been forfeited after he had taken part in a rebellion. This was a time of church building in England, and such a concentrated spell of church activity was not to come about again until the nineteenth century period of rebuilding and restoration, when, in 1875, this church was also restored.

In the early rebuilding, some of the Saxon work was incorporated, which it is thought was carried out by the second William de Keynes, who by then had acquired through marriage other properties near Cricklade in north Wiltshire, including Ashton Keynes. He was also Warden of Braydon Forest. He probably first noticed the bare, uncomfortable and damp interior of the church with its earthen floor strewn with rush and straw and the complete lack of seating. Had there been higher ground in the village no doubt a new church would have been built there, for burials beneath normal water tables, particularly in a gravel subsoil, were always a problem.

The early lancet window in the north wall, the chancel arch and the nave arcade help to date the work. The existing nave was probably built on the original foundations, the Saxon nave being the same size. The font is early Norman; the south wall of the nave was built of squared stone; the porch may have been built later, and four two-light windows were in this wall. Medieval paintings on the plaster walls have all disappeared, the last, of St Christopher, had been on the wall of the narrow doorway but was lost when this was reopened.

The north wall of the much restored chancel has a deep window, which is probably late Norman. The two bays of the arcade are thirteenth century. The oak screen in the chancel was already erected by the fifteenth century and the large west Perpendicular window was installed to give light under the tower and at the dark end of the nave. Small as it was, the church originally had three altars. A faculty dated 1713 mentions a 'wooden tower and belfry' wherein were hung two bells.

With the Reformation came changes. During Henry VIII's reign, all the silver (except the chalice), the vestments and nearly everything else of value were removed. The chalice itself 'was melted down and made into the Communion cup', although what the difference in its conversion might have been we can only speculate; this is still in use today. With Puritan fervour the stone altar was removed, and in its place an oak table was provided. The other altars were taken away and the wall-paintings whitewashed over. It is thought that at the time a lectern for Bible readings may have been provided and possibly a pulpit.

There appear to be contradictory accounts of the ownership of Somerford Keynes Manor. In the brief, most readable history of the church (copies of which can be obtained in the church) it is stated that Sir Anthony Hungerford of Down Ampney (see chapter twenty) purchased the manor in 1547, the year of Henry VIII's death, and installed there Bartholomew Ferrys, a poor relation, whom he knew would do all to conform to the changes that had been brought about during Henry's reign, but we are told by

Geoffrey Gibbon, MA, a vicar of Somerford Keynes, that it was surrendered by Merton Priory seven years earlier to the Crown who sold it to Richard Andrewes and Nicholas Temple in 1543, who in turn sold it two weeks later to Roger Pateshale of Minety.[2] It later came into the hands of the Strange family, wealthy wool merchants of Cirencester.

Robert Strange, with strong Roman Catholic leanings, appointed by the last abbot as a life mayor and high bailiff of Cirencester, in 1543 took a lease of Somerford Keynes Manor for twenty-one years. The following year he purchased it outright for £586 16s, which included the large Pillesmore meadow and two mills. Although he himself never lived there, to establish the family hierarchy his son Michael lived in the new Manor House which he had built for him. On an old door frame are carved the initials of the owner 'R.S.'.

In 1547 when the vicar died, his successor was appointed by Sir Anthony Hungerford, mentioned above. Gibson (op.cit.) tells us that little is known of the vicar presumed to have been appointed by Robert Strange, but that a terrier agreed to have the manor lands exempted from tithe by payment to him of £10 annually. Robert Strange died at the age of ninety, when his son Michael was twenty-four, and came to live at the manor with his wife and young son Robert. Seven more of his children were baptized in the church and are recorded in the original register between 1588 and 1597. Nominated by the Crown, John Snead became vicar in 1587 and was married in the church in 1600. The marriage was childless. There is a terrier telling us of his tenure of office, that he had 'one dwelling house – the Vicarage – with one barn, stable, edifice and courts' and 'the Parsonage Barn', very probably the Tithe Barn.

Michael Strange who died in 1613 is buried in the church together with his wife and his son Robert. His daughter Bridget married Thomas Nicholas of Stratton near Cirencester. Their daughter Mary married the third son of John Coxwell of Cirencester, after which Coxwell Street was named, and there was John, who acquired more wealth even than his grandfather Robert. Mary, with a dowry of £700, quite a small fortune in those days, lived with her husband in Bibury. Robert, the eldest son, graduated from Brazenose College, Oxford. He married Jane, the daughter of Sir Anthony Hungerford; they had six daughters and one son Robert.

Robert, Michael's son, was fined at the time of Charles the First's coronation, under some ancient and almost forgotten statute for not taking up the knighthood permitted to him by his great wealth. He gave £20 each year during his lifetime to his brothers Anthony and Michael, and in his will he left £2 to the Vicar John one time Bishop of Salisbury. His tomb is near the church porch. By 1700 the church building was said to be in a ruinous state, and very probably by that time the growth of 'flowers, roses and honey-suckle, intertwined with green ivy from ground to roof' was already doing damage to the structure. During the restoration services perforce were held in the village school. It was said that 'the church is lovingly cared for by its present incumbent and is a model of cheerful aspect and beauty'.

Two vicars, Christopher Fawcett and his son William, between them served this church from 1829 for nearly ninety years, and are commemorated by some windows; the first a scene from the Nativity and the other showing Christ with children in a field of flowers. Another window depicting St Christopher, is dedicated to a boy of the family and there is a fourth, also to the Fawcetts, of St Dorothea and St Elizabeth, garlanded with roses. There is also a stone memorial 'to ten men who died for peace' with a coloured medallion of St George and the Dragon.

The old manor near the church is part fifteenth and part sixteenth century, the east wing being later. The hall, once probably extending to the roof, has a beautiful Elizabethan fireplace and a second fireplace has a carved overmantle with the arms of the great Hungerford family. According to other sources the old tithe barn with its twelve bays and stone-tiled roof dates from 1753.

In the church is a most noticeable memorial to the last Robert Strange, who died unmarried at the age of twenty-four. His figure, of white marble, with long hair and pointed shoes, is in elegant Jacobean dress and is beautifully sculpted. Legend has it that whenever a death is imminent in a family at the manor, he is seen to appear there.

It was during the reign of Queen Anne (1702–14) that Edward Foyle carried out both new and repair work to the church fabric. The ancient bell tower was in a ruinous state and a half-crown rate was imposed for a new stone tower to replace the former timber structure and, as can be seen, it blends perfectly with the rest of the building. The squire at that time altered the seating, probably by high pews graded in position according to the status of their users, which we learn caused complaints to the bishop, who, however, then obtained a retrospective faculty to authorize it. It is thought that at about this time the roof timbers may have been renewed.

Early in the nineteenth century the church was repaved and paid for by George Foyle's son George. It is then we read of the creepers covering the external walls.

The church's three bells were joined by a fourth in 1747 on which is inscribed 'When you ring I'll sweetly sing'.

A report rendered by the Gloucester Cathedral architect Frederick Waller, dated June 1874, stated that the walls of the church be restored and the south wall of the nave rebuilt, the church reroofed and a new vestry built, and we are told that further drastic measures were found to be necessary when the creepers had been removed. Only the tower itself and the nave arches were left *in situ* before the restoration work began.

Of the church itself little further need be said. Although its restoration may have meant some archaeological impoverishment, particularly when all but three memorials were removed from the walls and floor and went unrecorded, the rebuilding gave it more light and the new arches made the interior more attractive. When the plaster was removed it was said 'the gains far outweigh the losses'. Later, the heating stoves were replaced by radiators and in 1947 electricity was installed, replacing oil for lighting and coke for heating.

In the early nineteenth century Somerford Keynes shared with many others the considerable impoverishment caused by the enclosing of common land. In 1806, the poor were soon to become poorer, when they lost their right to grazing on no less than 500 acres in and around the village and, although they got some recompense it soon went. Most of this land was taken by two of the biggest landowners, the Crofts and the Foyles. Three fields went to the vicar, by which he had to forfeit his annual £10 tithe. Some idea of the condition to which many of the labouring classes were brought in these parts has been described by William Cobbett, after he had been riding near Latton on a cold November day in 1821, some part of which may be seen in the chapter on Latton. Within the next two decades there was considerable turmoil in England, when a revolt of farm workers in Gloucestershire and Wiltshire in 1830, known as the 'Swing Riots', was a direct result of these dreadful conditions Cobbett had so dramatically portrayed. Near starvation had brought desperation. The Chartist Riots that rose to their peak in 1839 when these two counties were particularly affected, was the result.

Nathaniel Woodruffe (see chapter twenty-one), one of forty clergymen to attend the consecration of the new Eisey Church, was vicar here at the time of the riots. He built the new vicarage costing £90 in 1804, which is now a private house near Neigh Bridge, and we may well wonder how his conscience smote him, if it did at all, by accepting enclosed land in lieu of his tithe. In some notes he made of his sermon dated in 1822 one reads: 'Address the poor – you have little – give of that little – 1d. or 2d. or 6d. as you can: for the Lord loveth a cheerful giver.'

The Revd Gibbon (op.cit.) tells us that in 1830 the village had three shopkeepers, a smith, a wheelwright and a baker, and by the time (1968) when he was writing his delightful little book, there was only one shopkeeper 'and no butcher, baker or shoemaker' and he tells us the last cottage industry was that of glovemaking by 'old Mrs Bennett in the 1930s'. By 1994 there were no shops.

Vicar Woodruffe, possibly needing to augment his stipend by any means he could, apparently acting as overseer, made notes in 1821 that today throw further light on the conditions of his time in rural areas. Such an office was usually carried out by the church-wardens who, in those days carried heavy responsibilities and were overseers of the poor, supervising relief by raising local taxes (rates) from parishioners to pay for it. They oft times acted also as waywardens or surveyors too, and this the vicar had chosen to take upon himself, when he had taken over from Maurice Washbourne who, in the previous year, had repaired the road to Ewen, 'then called the Farm Road' and had put up gates at either end. The repair of the street in the village was carried out by three women who were paid 9d a day and broke up stones for the purpose. Men were paid 8s a week and 1s 6d beer money. When Vicar Woodruffe was eighty he employed a curate at £90 a year and retired from public duties four years later. After his death another chapter in the history of Somerford Keynes opened with the induction of Christopher Fawcett, who came of a wealthy, well-known Dyrham family, as vicar and squire. An interesting account of his tenure and his family may be read in Geoffrey Gibbon's book, to which I am considerably indebted for much of the foregoing information.

At one time there were five water mills; the one mentioned in Domesday is thought to have been Old Mill, known in 1653 as Bond's Mill and nearly 200 years later as Pool Mill. In 1327 this mill was worked by 'Geoffrey of the Mill'. It was situated near the manor by Old Mill Farm. Only a stone bank now shows where once was Skillings Mill below Lower Mill where, according to the church register, a child was drowned in 1827. Lower Mill was still being worked as late as 1954. There was also Upper Mill, pulled down in 1924, and Kemble Mill, once in a part of Kemble parish.

The oldest dwelling house in the parish is undoubtedly the Manor House where the ghostly figure of the young Robert Strange has sometimes been seen. Somerford Keynes House, the old vicarage, is now privately owned. There in 1969 was also Somerford Cottage, Croft House, The Close, Number Two Water Lane, Kemble Mill and, if we want to include Shorncote, there is the Manor Farm.

Gravel extraction has now practically surrounded the village with water on three sides.

Notes

1. *Oxford History of England*, vol. 1
2. Cuss, H.W. John, *Through the Saxon Door: The Story of Somerford Keynes and Shorncote* (published by the author at Somerford Keynes, 1969)

12   Ashton Keynes, Wiltshire

This is a little paradise with flowing waters everywhere, and
fine trees and flowers, and charming cottages and old houses,
a place of quietness immersed in a long peace.
          Highways and Byways in Wiltshire, Revd W. Hutton

The name derives from Old English (Anglo West Saxon) 'esc', an
ash tree or trees and ton, tone, 'land', or it might thus be translated
as 'the settlement near the ash trees', for here on the fringes of the
Braydon Forest the ash was probably the most common tree.
'Keynes' was added as early as the eleventh century, and represented land within the confines of that awarded to Baron de
Cahaignes by the half brother of William I for his services following the Norman Conquest. He had fought with them at the Battle
of Hastings and his name appears with 315 others on a bronze
plaque in Normandy (see chapter ten).
     The village, perfectly sited with an abundant supply of water was
like so many other settlements of neolithic age (3000–1800 BC);
axe heads of that period having been discovered to the north-east
of Clayhill Copse and near Packers Lane cottages. East of Kent
End aerial photography has revealed crop marks and a site dating
from 2000 to 750 BC with sherds of this period found near Ash
Cover. The Dobuni would certainly have settled here, although
some have considered that the Celts may have been the pre-
Roman inhabitants.
     The Romans in their turn found the area much to their taste and
close enough to their capital Corinium to be perfect for settlements. The site, known since between the two World Wars as the
Cotswold Settlement is now preserved as an Ancient Monument
where once a large Roman settlement existed, and Roman coins
have been found in places in or near the village. A Roman temple

Keynes (see chapter eleven) and, neither Latton nor Kempsford churches escaped the hand of the modern architect. So forthright indeed was Hutton that he goes on to say:

> It is when we come to the chancel arch that we remember the trees. It is a hopeless fraud. It masquerades as twelfth century work, and yet it is dated all over by incompetence – 1876. It is, nevertheless, what the clergy and the architects call a restoration. It is a lie and a vandalism, and as such we say no more about it.

The Church of The Holy Cross is some way from the village. This is not all that surprising with churches of this early period, when based on Saxon foundations, or early Norman. Sycamores line one side of the long, gentle, pleasant sweep of a macadamed pathway from the village, with seats here and there. Entering the churchyard from that direction, there is a pleasant avenue of yews planted *c.* 1780. The opposite entrance to the churchyard is from the Minety to Siddington road, where one has the feeling of being in open country, as indeed is the case, and the village dwellings are left far behind. I do not remember the elms spoken of by Hutton, but no English landscape was once complete without them, alas they are gone now.

The church has seen many changes, with additions, alterations and the inevitable nineteenth-century restoration in its 800 years. William Butterfield, an architect who specialized in church restoration, was responsible for the 1870s' changes so derided by Hutton. The font, which Butterfield considered with the altar to be the most important features in a church, is almost facing as you enter. A sketch of the Norman chancel arch before Butterfield enlarged it can be seen on the wall to the left as one faces the altar and, still facing east, the arch, also on the left, is infilled with a wooden screen sealing in the 'beautiful late 13th century chapel' now used as a junior church. The triptych in the chapel with the four evangelists above is much praised by W.H. Hutton:

> At the end of the aisle, above the arch into the chapel, is a very lovely triptych. In the midst is a solid mandorla, and above it the symbols of the Four Evangelists; on either side is a canopied niche. The south aisle, in which there is a good perpendicular window, was rebuilt soon after the north aisle [thirty years, *c.*1380], and both keep their 14th century roofs as does the nave, which seems to have been reroofed at the same time these aisles were built. The north porch and the tower of three stories are also of the fourteenth century. It

thus appears that we have here a church containing much decorated work, and yet it makes far less impression upon us than we might expect. In the Perpendicular window in the south aisle are some fragments of fifteenth century glass. There we see a Blessed Trinity, God the Father, holding the crucifix upon His knees, His right hand in benediction; but the brooding dove is missing. Another fragment shows us a figure with a model of the church in his hand. I suppose this is the founder.

Thacker also thought the interior of the church was very beautiful and mentions the following inscription:

> Here lieth the body of Henry Hawkins Esq. the grandfather, and
> Henry Hawkins ye Grandchild both dyed the 27th Day of April 1658
> and lyes interred both together vnder this Gravestone
> Read here ye mortals all your owne lifes date
> How quickly Age and youth does terminate
> The Grandsire & Grandsone hence both of them
> Past in one day to their Hierusalem

The cost of the restorations amounted to a total sum of £2,018 17s 10d with the largest donation being made by the Duke of Cornwall with £1,700. It was reopened on 12 July 1877. S.M. Knocker[1] gives the date of the aisle to about 1380 and the wall within from the porch reveals an originally arched opening, its apex 'rising a foot or so' above the present door opening. Behind the plaster was found a niche for holding a statue above the hood moulding with jambs, sill and lintel, the last decorated with fan-vaulting. Mr Knocker says that this was a time at the end of the fifteenth century when fan-vaulting reached its peak of excellence with examples at Christchurch, Oxford and in the Chapel of Henry VII in Westminster Abbey, and contemporary with this south door-way it can thus be dated at about 1480. The niche had been filled with three stones, one of which had been a scratch dial, with the hole for the gnomon and a portion of the circle still bearing the inscriptions.

The little booklet we found on sale in the church describes the chapel:

> Now go behind the organ and cross over to the other side of the church. Here is the Lady Chapel with an altar in use today. An Altar that stood here in olden days and you can see the outline of the Piscina on the window ledge. At the topmost part of the beautiful 15th century window you can see the only remaining pieces of Pre-

Reformation glass. One picture of a man holding a model of the Church (Which Church? Ours has no spire). This is known as the Milling window. The Revd M.J.T. Milling was Vicar for over 50 years from 1884. You can see on the pillar to the left as you enter, the list of incumbents from 1304 onwards.

The vertical-sided font has been broken and repaired. The church guide asks if this had been the work of Cromwell's troopers, but much depended, in those years of great upheaval, on the officer or the sergeant in charge.

The church registers date from 1582, in which there are several entries worthy of further description:

'[1740] ... on the 22nd October in the evening fell a great snow which did continue until Simon (?) and not all the snow melted until 28th day of October.'

'[1775] ... upon the 8 day of September it was sopozed with sum people in Wiltshire to be an earthquack in some parts of the same county by severill people as found the earth to shake and tremble as they lay in bed with great surprise to them that felt it and many counties in England and Wales as reported by the newspapers.'

'[1781] ... highest winds that any man did ever know took down trees, hedges, hayricks, cornricks, killed many cows, some people and some sort of all cattoll of all kinds to the surprise of all people in England and Wales. Pray God we may never see the like again.'

At this time the manor house in the centre of the village (now known as Cove House) was owned by the Richmond family, three of whose table tombs can be seen in the churchyard near the ancient village cross. This family too found itself divided between the Royalists and the Parliamentary forces.

The Parliamentary force marched from Cirencester to Latton, Cricklade and Swindon *en route*, to take part in the Battle of Newbury. We read: 'The army marched through Swindowne, Chizelton, Abern Chase (where the army in a deep valley came under attack from Cavaliers), Hungerford, Skelton and to a village called Embry on September 19th about a mile and a halfe from Newbury.'

It was here that the famous Battle of Newbury took place. The story goes that it was at this time that John and Henry Richmond, officers of distinction, who were on opposing sides, were encamped on the dark night preceding the battle and one, deciding to try and find his brother in the camp of the enemy to make an affectionate farewell in case they might not see each other again, skilfully eluded the sentinels and found his brother's tent. His brother, alarmed at the sudden appearance of a stranger 'rose upon his bed and shot him on the spot'. In the cold light of morning the terrible truth was revealed. In his remorse he fled to America; today his descendants return from time to time to visit the village of their ancestors and their graves in the churchyard.

The cross in the centre of the churchyard is one of four in the village. It was restored for the purpose of converting it into a War Memorial, 'the missing stones being discovered in the village in a quite remarkable way'. John Milling tells us in his *Great Days with Rod and Gun* that it is 'A fine old cross indeed', with its ancient well-worn steps, the result of countless people sitting upon them. Milling mentions his father, who first came to Ashton Keynes as vicar in 1884, and who himself discovered the base of the cross – the steps – in a very unusual way, for only the pedestal and base then existed. It happened over a period of thirty years. The large stones from the second step were found near the old Tithe Barn that once belonged to the monastery a short distance away from the church. He later noticed two stones, built into the wall of the Old School House which proved to have been the head of the cross. However, the owner would only part with them if the whole wall was pulled down and rebuilt. So the matter remained *sine die*, until the property changed hands, and the new owner a Mrs Cove gave her permission to remove them. Meanwhile the good man had found two pieces of the shaft cross, one apparently in the yard of the White Hart and the other used as a flower pot stand in a cottage garden. It was not until the end of the First World War before the cross was restored to its former glory and was then dedicated as a War Memorial.

The crosses are thought to all have dated from the fourteenth century. In 1812 the following is noted in the parish register: 'The Gumstool Bridge was taken down, rebuilt and lengthened. The cross was taken down, removed a few paces and rebuilt, and a bridge was built over the Thames opposite Vicarage House and a new carriage road was made from Gumstool bridge to the Mill.'

We learn that the cross by the White Hart was moved for a short distance in 1958–9 to avoid the risk of damage by passing vehicles. It is thought by some that the village crosses, remarked upon by the Revd Hutton, were placed strategically as preaching crosses. I could find only three in the village, each approximately equidistant and about a furlong apart, with the exception of the last, which was about twice that distance from the church, placed, it has been said,

The village crosses at Ashton Keynes

at convenient intervals for funerals, with a pause at each, for prayer and rest by the bearers and the mourners. We wonder how often they were used for such purpose and by John Wesley during that great eighteenth-century religious revival, and will they ever be preached from again by some other such charismatic figure? There is little doubt that John might first have taken his stand on the steps of this cross by the White Hart in the village centre in a scene that was to become familiar everywhere he went. However, many churches were closed to him, and thus the sky became his roof. He taught up and down the land and we are told that he travelled 250,000 miles by coach or on horseback, and preached more than 40,000 sermons:

> At Church with unaffected grace,
> His looks adorne'd the venerable place;
> Truth from his lips prevaile'd with double sway
> And fools who came to scoff, remained to pray.

The story of John and Charles Wesley, and of John in particular is extraordinary. John was ordained priest in 1728 at the age of twenty-five. Thereafter for the next ten years he travelled widely and in London met the Moravian, Peter Bohler. It was Bohler who first made him realize that faith alone was an almost forgotten Anglican teaching. John described in his journal the events at a Moravian meeting in Aldersgate Street, London, and his thoughts as Martin Luther's *Preface to the Epistle to the Romans* was being read:

> 'About a quarter to nine while he was describing the change which God works in the heart through faith in Christ, Christ alone, for salvation: and an assurance was given *me* that he had taken away my sins, even *mine* and saved *me* from the law of sin and death.'

Thereafter the story is well known. It was his elder brother Charles who wrote most of the well-loved hymns, many of which John thought were too sentimental. 'Love Divine all Loves Excelling', 'Soldiers of Christ Arise' and 'Jesu Lover of my Soul' were perhaps three of the most famous. At Bampton (a few miles outside the confines of this book), John Wesley preached his first sermon on the 16 October 1725. Later, when he was there again, he wrote: 'Here it was I preached my first sermon six and forty years ago. One man was in my present audience who heard it. Most had gone to their long home.'

Writing of Ashton Keynes in 1826 William Cobbett, with his practical and singularly secular outlook, showed no interest in its place of worship, and I do not recall reading of his ever having done so, other than to mention one in passing. He thought it had once been a large market town: 'and such numerous lanes crossing and cutting the land into such little bits that it must have been a large town. A very curious place.'

Fred S. Thacker, on the other hand, writes of the village with his usual enthusiasm and in glowing terms:

> The village has several parallel streets, joined at the ends only. Do I exaggerate? But it always seems so far round from any one of these ways to the next. There are four more or less mutilated crosses; the books mostly say three; perhaps they miss the one in the churchyard whose base and plinth alone remain. The dedication of the church to the Holy Cross may be the cause of this unusual number. But its host of little bridges is the peculiar, the perennial delight of Ashton Keynes. One is tempted to herald abroad that it possesses as many in its tiny area as span the whole of the rest of the Thames. The wide and generous road leads you up one side of the village, at its left runs the stream, over which lean these little crossings to the quiet grey houses and flowery gardens beyond.

These little bridges, and the Thames itself flowing past the cottages, remain much as they might have done nearly a century after Thacker so lovingly portrayed them. Baskerville, on writing of the bridges along the Upper Thames, mentions Ashton Keynes:

> The Bridges and Casway to go into Gloster shire from Cricklade are 580 paces or yards long, to the farther side of ye Bridge over that stream which comes from Cyrencester [the Churn]. The other stream which runs by Ashton Canes comes in by Cricklad town. The 2d Bridges *viz* That Bridge over Ashton Canes stream, and the bridge over Tems or Cyrencester stream and ye Casway wch leads from Tems Bridge to Latton in Glocester shire (a mile fro' Cricklad Town) has no arches.

Thacker writes that: ' . . . it is very noticeable that the writer [above] deprives the Ashton Keynes stream of the name of Thames, and bestows it upon "Cyrencester stream".'

Johanna, heiress to the Lord of the Manor, in the late seventeenth century, became the second wife of Edward Foyle of Somerford Keynes. Her mother was Alice Chapman who bought fields in Somerford for the benefit of the Ashton Keynes poor.

Edward Foyle, in the right of his wife, was appointed to Ashton Keynes Church shortly before his death in 1719, and the manor then passed to Hawkins Chapman, the eldest son of Johanna's first husband.

For some further interesting and knowledgeable details of Ashton Keynes it is recommended that you read *Ashton Keynes: A Village with no History* by Madge Patterson and Ernie Ward. Published by Keith Cowley, Oaklands Road, Chirkbank, Shropshire and first printed in 1986. Though why such an unworthy title has been used for such a well produced book must remain something of a mystery.

Notes

1. *Wiltshire Archaeological Magazine*, vol. 60, pp. 122–3

13   South Cerney, Gloucestershire

I knew a little garden close
Set thick with lily and red rose.
William Morris (1834–1896)

In common with other ancient country places, South Cerney has its complement of modern council houses and small groups of modern private dwellings. There still survive, however, many old cottages, with their attractive 'old world' gardens (hence my misquotation) with roses around their doors and flower-beds of night-scented stock and sweet-williams beloved by generations of country-dwellers.

The cottage homes of England,
By thousands on her plains;
They are smiling oer the silvery brooks
And round the hamlet fanes.
By glowing orchards forth they peep,
Each from its nook of leaves,
And fearless there the lowly sleep,
As the bird beneath the eaves.

The pen of William Morris and others more able than mine have praised the scent of old-fashioned garden flowers. Dobson wrote:

Here in this sequestered close,
Bloom the hyacinth and the rose;
Here beside the modest stock
Flaunts the flaming hollyhock;
Here, without a pang one sees
Ranks, conditions and degrees.

South Cerney is a large straggling village, built over gravel, which in places is eighteen feet thick; deposits of melt waters of fifty million years ago lie beneath a thin topsoil.

Someone in 1840 wrote of the soil being of oolitic limestone and guessed at the commercial potential of the gravel lying just beneath the surface, by saying that if its value were realized it 'might form one of the best materials for repairing the highways'. More than half a century was to pass before commercial excavation in the area of the Upper Thames was to begin in any quantity, mainly for the manufacture of concrete and concrete products. The excavation of these immense deposits of gravel (from every available piece of land that could be used for the purpose) have left many expanses of water. This amenity is itself being used for recreation of many kinds. Known as the Cotswold Water Park, it is shared pretty equally by both the counties of Wiltshire and Gloucestershire, through whose common, curiously shaped boundary, it passes. See the OS *Landranger* Map No. 163, revealing how the exploitation of these immense gravel deposits has used every available area, up to the very edges of the roads themselves and the banks of the River Churn, which in places almost appear to merge with it.

This pleasant stream leaves its water meadows above the village to flow through its very heart, having given the place its name Churney, South Churney or Cerney, as well as North Cerney higher in the hills and elsewhere. The stream emerges half a mile to the east and continues its winding course through the waters of the gravel pits on either side.

The Revd William Grey, a village curate, writing in the early nineteenth century tells us: 'the pasture being water meadow is extremely good but the arable, lying on the ground or gravel, is shallow and poor and worth on average less than 25s an acre, and will not bear a crop of wheat oftener than once in four years.'

Although I have failed to find it mentioned elsewhere, Thacker (op.cit.) tells us that the spire, which once graced the lovely old church of All Hallows, was struck by lightning and insufficient funds could be raised to rebuild it. It has, however, little pinnacles remaining on each corner of its battlemented tower, which sets off its proportions to perfection. Thacker says, after mentioning 'a huge new copper band', that 'they are touchy here on the subject of lightning' and he goes on to say: 'Against the south west corner of the church is a sepulchral slab, upon which a male and female figure are cut in high relief as far as the waist, where they die into the stone; it covers the Manor House vault, which the last burial in 1900 filled up.'

When I saw this box grave (which dates to *c.*1370) in early 1994, time and the elements had long since told their story, the features, which no doubt were once clear cut by a craftsman's hand, were rounded and shapeless and a dark green moss was growing in happy abundance in the water-filled fissures.

Thacker described the whole southern side of the churchyard as 'dark and romantic with the shadows of ancient yews'. Nearly a century on there can be very little difference today. The church was restored in 1862 when the south aisle was added by J.P. St Aubyn. Although it was originally a Saxon edifice, it has many Norman features including the tower whose top is probably thirteenth century.

The fourteenth-century north porch has a Norman doorway, with zigzag carving. Much of the south porch has late Norman work. The stone plaque over the arch is thought to be Saxon and was probably once housed in another part of the original building; on it Christ is represented bringing the message of the Gospel to departed spirits, with figures in kneeling positions to welcome him. Our Lord carries a cross whilst treading on some snake-like figure of evil. Above this Christ is seen as King with angels holding a canopy on either side of him. The elaborate shafts of this remarkable doorway are held together by stone hands and have unusual capitals, and around the doorway are some twenty vigorously carved heads of strange creatures. This altogether beautiful doorway has an oak door, opened and closed through five centuries by tens of thousands of hands, long gone.

Through a double arch from the tower can be seen the beautiful chancel with its sedilia. There is a delicately sculptured piscina with the basin formed like a shell, and above it a tiny face garlanded with tracery and leaves on either side. The east window has bell-flower ornament together with other interesting features; it was rebuilt in the fourteenth century.

The church's heavily carved oak chest is dated 1634. The importance of keeping records under lock and key had by then been long since realized. This may have been why parliamentary forces during the Civil War generally felt the need to protect them for by that time a decree by Thomas Cromwell, Earl of Essex, that records of baptisms, marriages and burials were to be maintained in every parish in the land, had already been in operation for more than a hundred years.

Parish registers can be of immense value to the historian and family historians alike. The researches into several branches of my family tree have disclosed some strange facts. Other than that of a

All Hallows' Church at South Cerney

romance of long ago, the writings in that old oak chest also revealed some unusual relationships within my Stephens's ancestry in the village of South Cerney. Curiosity was first aroused when

'Stephens' as a given name was noticed in a Peters family name to the elder brother of my great-grandmother Elizabeth, the more so because Stephens was to become her married name. It was the wish of their father to perpetuate his mother's maiden name (Stephens). If only he had known that his daughter, yet unborn, was destined to marry his uncle's son.

Many consider the most interesting features of South Cerney church are two facsimile fragments of an exquisitely carved wooden crucifix of the twelfth century that W.R. Latherby described as 'a work of great intensity'. These two fragments, one of the head of Christ and the other of a foot, are indeed thought, very probably, to be the earliest pieces of wood carving in England; the work may be seen in a recess of the chancel wall, sealed behind glass in a wooden frame. This can be conveniently studied with the aid of a small strip light operated by a switch on the outside. It is understood the original fragments are in the British Museum, where their purchase for a substantial five-figure sum is being considered. The complete crucifix might have been of about nineteen inches to about forty inches in height: seeing what remains of it makes this difficult to judge.

There are a few fragments of medieval glass and there is glass of a far greater age in another window in the north aisle, with its clustered pillars and five arches, which is considered to be one of the finest thirteenth century aisles in the county of Gloucestershire.

In this church the memory of two people who reached their centenary is perpetuated. The earliest is a stone to Walter Porlock who died at the age of 100 in 1701 and there is a wooden cross to the memory of Anna Billiald who died in 1930, aged 102.

In the village there is a particularly fine building, containing twelve dwellings, that is greatly admired by visitors. It is a benefaction by Mrs Anne Edwards, widow of a curate, Isaac Edwards, who at some time after her husband's death was left a considerable sum of money with which she did good works for the remainder of her life. The College, as it is known, would probably cost upwards of £3,000,000 to build today and was exclusively for the benefit of clergymen's widows and orphans in the county. We read the following from a letter written by an admirer after Mrs Edwards's death:

> Upon every case of sickness, accident or loss her purse was never closed. But it was her regular pensioners, fourteen in number, that most constantly experienced her bounty. Two aged, crippled or poor pensioners came to her house every day for food, so that the couple, once a week, were largely provided with meat, beer and bread. When any of her pensioners died, another was sought out and provided for.[1]

South Cerney College at the turn of the century

In the central light of the church's west window she is seen kneeling, offering up the model of the college to Christ for his blessing.

The foregoing reminds us once more of the dreadful conditions of the poor during this first part of the nineteenth century, the vivid description given by Cobbett (see chapter nineteen) of the young female agricultural labourers when he saw them on a cold November day looking 'as ragged as colts and as pale as ashes' their shoes tied with pieces of rag to hold them on their feet. Such distress is hard to imagine, but matters were to get even worse before they got better. We might say that in part Chartism was born out of a series of bad harvests during a serious economic depression and, as Thomas Carlyle put it when deaths among the poor were brought on by semi-starvation, it became a 'knife and fork question' culminating in what history recalls as 'The Chartist Riots' of 1839. We read in this informative little book[1] about the village and of how it was entirely dependent on agriculture, and its ancillary occupations, for survival. In letters to a local newspaper, the *Wilts & Gloucestershire Standard* in 1839, the Revd William Gray of South Cerney 'stated that the labourers of Cerney were paid between 9s and 12s a week.' In his opinion this was a good wage and any higher rates would bankrupt the farmers. 'What would then become of the labourers?' Gray agreed that some people in

Cerney were badly off but he suggested that this was inevitable. 'I do not attempt to deny,' he wrote, 'that there is much and severe suffering among the poor – such always has been the case and always will be.'

In another letter, replying to Gray, the anonymous writer painted a grimmer picture of the state of the poor in Cerney, and insisted that 9s a week was the highest wage paid to any labourer and a long list was given of particular labourers and their earnings. 'John Townsend and Charles Parker have been at task [piece] work for John Pollard and did not earn more than 8s a week, sometimes less; they are now at breast ploughing for the same farmer and cannot earn more.' 'William Dunn, now out of work, has not earned at any time more than 9s generally only 8s, and cannot get any work in the parish at the present time.'

The book goes on to tell us that 'Cornelious Simpson, aged 19, a hale and hearty young man, works for Mr Large as a fodderer at only 6s a week with his breakfast on Sunday mornings' and a particularly enlightening statement goes on to tell us about James Simpson who 'works for Mr Howell at thrashing etc. for 9s a week, has ten children two only of whom are capable of regular work, one earning 6s [perhaps this was Cornelious above] the other 4s. a week: his wife has a child at the breast'. The letter states that the labourers' families had a monotonous diet of 'barley bread and potatoes only'. This anonymous letter ends by urging the poor of Cerney to take political action in order to win a fairer deal. This was probably a reference to Chartism, a left-wing movement of the time. It is surely no coincidence that in the same year, 1839, William Gray wrote a letter to the Home Secretary complaining of Chartist meetings in South Cerney.

Nearly every old English village has its cross and South Cerney is no exception. In the physical sense village crosses are rarely crosses at all; any symbol of the Crucifixion was generally removed during the Civil War by Parliamentary forces in whatever village they happened to enter. Most are left as a plain shaft of stone set on a stepped base, as seen in many of the photographs in this book. Some may be surmounted by a ball as in this case or a tabernacle as for that of the two crosses in Cricklade. The exact origin of village crosses remains something of a mystery. That they were of considerable importance to the life of a village there can be no doubt, for hardly a village exists without a cross within its precincts and, as in the case of Ashton Keynes, even an exceptional three or four. South Cerney has its modern cross to the memory of its fallen with the words:

Sons of this place, let this of you be said:
That you who live are worthy of your dead.
These gave their lives that you who live may reap
A richer harvest ere you fall asleep.

South Cerney village cross

In *Glimpses of Victorian South Cerney* there is mention of the Pollards, a nineteenth-century farming family. I once came across a cutting from an old local paper listing items to be auctioned after the death of one Elizabeth Pollard. The list gives us some idea of the status and wealth of a farming family of Victorian England, which is in stark contrast to the conditions of farm workers of the period. The account reads:

When Elizabeth Pollard died in 1881 all the contents of her farm-house were put up for auction. The auctioneers published a cata-logue of the goods which provide a very full picture of Mrs Pollard's world. The farm-house had five fully furnished bedrooms, a large kitchen, a drawing-room, a sitting-room, a dairy fully equipped for cheese-making and a well-stocked cellar. The kitchen was obviously the centre for the work of the farm; it contained an office desk, a variety of farm tools including billhooks and hatchets and an iron door scraper and three iron spittoons for the use of visiting labourers. The dairy had a 'double-screw cheese press' and a 'box cheese press'. The drawing-room appears to have been packed with a variety of furniture, including eighteen chairs and several tables. A typical Victorian touch was provided by the presence of 'two cases of stuffed birds and sundry stuffed animals'. The sitting room had 'five old-fashioned Windsor chairs and cushions' around a 'capital oak leaf table'. Four out of the five bedrooms had four poster beds, as well as a mixture of commodes, dressing tables and chests of drawers. Further evidence of Mrs Pollard's cider making is shown by 'fifty gallons of good cider' in the cellar. The overall impression that one draws from the inventory is that Mrs Pollard led a busy life and enjoyed a good standard of living.

The interesting village guide, mentioned above, tells us of the state of illiteracy in South Cerney in the 1840s when 50 per cent of the men and 44 per cent of the women were unable to sign their names in the marriage register. The results after the 1870 Education Act changed all that, when, fifty years later, in the 1890s, illiteracy, in as far as the signing of registers was concerned, shows us that 96 per cent of men and all of the women were able to sign their names.

'Using age at death in the registers as a crude guide to life expectancy', Tony McLeavey[1] says, and adds, 'We see a similarly dramatic change during Queen Victoria's reign. In 1852 the average age at death was 36.3 years, by 1899 this had risen to 56.9 years. These figures reflect the national trend in life expectancy'. The guide book continues:

> The highest mortality rate [in South Cerney] was among the elderly and the very young. In 1854, for example, 27 deaths are recorded of which 10 are of children under two years old. There are occasional accidental deaths and some curious entries such as that of John Wheeler, who died in 1848 'by visitation of God'.
>
> The register of baptisms gives some information about the level of illegitimacy in South Cerney. In the 1840's as many as 10% of all births recorded were of unmarried mothers. By the 1890's the rate had fallen to 6%. In the 1840's the curate sometimes wrote the name of the father and lightly crossed it out so that it remained perfectly legible. We can find out more about these unmarried mothers by looking for their names in the census.

Even by 1851 conditions, though probably not nearly as bad as in the 1820s and 30s, were yet by any standards still very low indeed. One Mary Sly, aged forty-eight, unmarried, living with two of her four children, obtained a living by running errands for people. Elizabeth Haines and Rachel Bayliss, aged fifty-seven and forty-two respectively, are quoted. Elizabeth shared her house with her three single daughters and a grandson, whilst Rachel lodged, together with her son Thomas, with a farm labourer named Charles Jones. The guide book goes on to say:

> The Poor Law Amendment Act of 1834 tried to reduce the number of people receiving benefits from the rates by insisting that anyone in need should go to a nearby workhouse where conditions were, to say the least, unpleasant. For the poor of South Cerney the local workhouse was at Cirencester. In a large parish, Cerney supplied the workhouse with many of its inmates, but it is clear from the records that there were too many poor for the workhouse to take and many continued to receive payments while living at home. In 1835, for example, no fewer than 38 people in the village were receiving money and bread from the poor law authorities. These 'paupers' were either very old people or widows with dependent children. On average the old people were given 2s. 6d. a week and a loaf of bread. In the same year there were eleven inhabitants of Cerney in the Cirencester workhouse.

I cannot allow this chapter to pass without a brief mention of the Thames and Severn Canal that passed close to the northern edge of the village; its coming, like in the other villages mentioned, brought South Cerney an increased prosperity. I am reminded of the canal there soon after it was brought into disuse, by the great abundance of the beautiful little winter aconites that grew along its south bank under the tender willow saplings which, by 1932, were already beginning to colonize the ground on either side.

Notes

1. McLeavey, Tony, *Glimpses of Victorian South Cerney* (The South Cerney Trust, 1987)

14 Cricklade, Wiltshire

Greeklade, whose great name yet vaunts that learned tongue
Where to Great Britain first the sacred muses songe
Which first were here at Isis bounteous head
As telling that her fame should through the world be spread
And tempted by this flood to Oxford after came
There likewise to delight her bridegroom, lovely Tame
Whose beauty when they saw so much did they adore
That Greeklade they forsook and would go back no more.

> Michael Drayton (1563–1631)[1]

It has been asserted that it was Panda of Mercia who established
the university at Cricklade in AD 650 of which Michael Drayton
thus gives us some confirmation that the world's oldest university
was founded here before being transferred to Oxford. So much
that has been said or written about this ancient borough would be
of little interest to the serious student of history, other than that it
glorifies what has been, and still is to the eyes of many, a beautiful
old town. The earliest description (c.1140) we have is by William of
Dover, when he 'arrived at Cricklade situated in lovely surround-
ings (*in loco delicioso*) abounding in all kinds of riches':[2]

Tower and turret crown your height,
Thames lay babbling at your feet.
Ghosts of Druids glide by night
Up and down your busy street

Light men laugh and hurry past
Sentry of the Roman Way;
Shall you live to laugh the last
Wise old Cricklade? You or they.

John Leland, antiquarian to Henry VIII in his tour of England and Wales *c.*1540, wrote: 'Crekelade is in the farther Ripe of I*f*is, and standeth in Wile*f*hire,' and of neighbouring Braydon in its parish he wrote: 'Loke here wher Braydon Water cumming out of Wile*f*hire doeth go into I*f*is.'

Ireland thought the town remarkable only 'for a very large parish church, and for which they convey their dead for interment, which is by fastening the coffin in the front of a postchaise; and for which while they have the power, they were accustomed to make a living; by a more high priced, than constitutional estimate of their borough franchises?' and he adds a further version of the founding of Oxford University at Cricklade thus: 'A Greek school was anciently founded here, or rather restored, by the learned archbishop of Canterbury, Theodorus, and afterwards translated to Oxford.'

Not all were inclined to sing Cricklade's praises and it was made very obvious that William Cobbett (most famous for his *Rural Rides* written in clear uncompromising prose) found little there to his liking when he gave the town a visit on 7 November 1821 and must have taken a meal there, probably at the White Hart or another of the dozen or so inns of which the town then boasted: 'I passed through that villainous hole Cricklade about two hours ago, and certainly a more rascally looking place I never set eyes on. The labourers look very poor; dwellings little better than pigbeds and their food nearly equal to that of a pig. This Wiltshire is a horrible county.' However, he took the poor of the town much more to his heart on his next visit five years later. He rode through the river at Hatchetts 'it not being above four or five yards wide, and not deeper than the knees of the horse'.

As time has passed no others appear to have written of Cricklade as disparagingly as Cobbett or Ireland. Charles Dickens, jun., in his detailed *Dictionary of the Thames* (1893) says it was a 'pleasant town, clean and well paved, but it has not been the scene of any particularly remarkable events, since it shared the fate of so many Thames towns and was plundered by the Danes in 1015.'

Fred Thacker[3] writes:

> . . . Now a farm blocks the way, but if you persevere round you will arrive at a rustic bridge called Hatchetts on the outskirts of Cricklade, where baptisms have been performed within memory. Rose Cottage[4] adjoins it, well known to men who navigate through to Cricklade; above which Taunt marks an old weir site; perhaps the

is also believed to have existed on a site near Cleveland Farm. Domesday states:

> The Church of St Mary of Cranborne holds Ashton Keynes, and held it TRE, and it pays geld for 20 hides. There is land for 16 ploughs. Of this land 10 hides are in demesne, and there are 2 ploughs, and 5 slaves. There are 20 villans and 12 bordars and 4 cotsets with 13 ploughs. There is a mill rendering 5s, and 100 acres of meadow, [and] pasture 1 league long and half a league broad. The woodland is of like extent and is worth £15.

In the late 1960s some excavation work was carried out by members of the Cricklade Historical Society to the earthworks in a part of the village named Halls Close, some five furlongs east of the church and sometimes known as 'The Battlefield'. A test trench revealed wall foundations and a rubble trench. Here a considerable quantity of unglazed pottery was found. The site was thought to have been a fortified manor at the time of Stephen (1097–1154) and the pottery, which is thought to date to about the first half of the twelfth century, confirms this opinion.

Then came the Saxons, speedily crushing any resistance they may have met with, culminating in the Battle of Dyrham. Ashton Keynes belonged to King Alfred who left it to his daughter Aethelgeofu, Abbess of Shaftesbury, at which time a community of nuns or monks established themselves where the farmhouse near the church now stands. A part of the moat, long since dry, with its sides eroded but still of good depth, may still be seen, and must have been very deep. It runs parallel with the south side of the churchyard and once encompassed both the church and the monastery.

The Revd Hutton says:

> I left Cricklade regretfully very early one morning, and came on my way to the beautiful village of Ashton Keynes ... and the whole village, I know not why, is scattered with crosses. There are no fewer than four of them beside another in the churchyard, yet why they are here, close to the frontier of the county let it be said, I cannot say nor could anyone explain it to me.

Elm trees led to the Church of The Holy Cross, 'lovlier', he says, than is the church itself which 'has suffered too much at the hands of the accursed restorers'.

A similar fate befell the church in neighbouring Somerford

St Sampson's, Cricklade, as it was in 1814

ruinous old house on the right bank was the weir-keeper's, it stands at the head of the pool, and then the walk is barred by 'nimble footed Churn'; and I went to my night's rest back across Hatchett's bridge and into Cricklade.

St Mary's, Cricklade

'Now when I had seen all this,' writes Edward Hutton,[5] 'I went on through the lingering summer afternoon beside the childish Thames to the noble town of Cricklade in the meads.'

Thacker who, like Cobbett, appeared wont to return to Cricklade because the town appealed to him very much, wrote:

Cricklade has two beautiful churches; St Sampson's crowning the hill with its splendid tower of about 1550, St Mary's bejewelling the valley down by the Thames bridge. St Sampson's was built in the time of the first pointed builders, and displays fine later perpendicular work. There are two curious and interesting carvings both inside and outside the tower; the four aces, shears and sickle, the Paveril's pepper garb and the Warwick bear and ragged staff; the latter over the south arch of the tower. The remains of a cross stand in the churchyard, and built into the porch is some tenth century sculpture; perhaps in evidence of a church here from that date. At the restoration of the church in 1864 many old things were got rid of as at Minster Lovell. One, they say, was a fine screen, and another was the original sanctus bell, long left lying about, and ultimately given by a workman to a stranger and deposited by him in the Devizes museum as they relate. The beautiful flying buttress outside the Hungerford Chapel was added by one of that family in 1569; perhaps Sir John, who died fourteen years later. I have not been able to resist a thought that St Sampson's looks out over the wide adjacent parishes a suspicion like fine old Sir Roger de Coverley, who would stand up in the middle of the sermon to count the congregation, and learn if any of his tenants were absent.

Thacker continues:

St Mary's in the valley complements the grandeur of St Sampson's with delicacy and charm, and adds a prestige of Norman work .... The barbaresque Norman mouldings are rich on the chancel arch, surviving from about 1150 ... the porch is green with ivy and the cross in the churchyard is in much better preservation than that of St Sampson's[6] ... Robert Jenner (q.v.) member of Parliament for Cricklade was one of those inclined towards the middle course with Charles I, when it was debated to bring him to justice as the 'chief delinquent' towards the close of the Civil War; and with Ashe, member for Westbury, got a reprimand from Cromwell for his tenderness.

I left the same Cricklade one August morning by the left bank to walk upstream. I noticed again what always seems so striking: the inconsiderable brook it is that runs under the town bridge. 'Is that the Thames?' has been the amused question from many lips.[7] It manifests just there no likelihood of greatness; although in the meadows above you may often discern the unmistakable promise of a River that by the Thanet shall merge into the infinite sea.

I passed West Mill (q.v.) an ancient building bought up by the Conservancy for disuse. In the meadow in which it stands, is still called the 'Rustling Ground', an old nurse yet alive, (*c.*1907) the granddaughter of a former miller at this very mill, remembers hearing as a child the shouts of the wrestlers and the noise of the backsword play.[8,9] She recollects too being taken to the Vale Hotel[10] in Cricklade three quarters of a century ago, and held to one of the windows to see the morris dancers, and in her wise old ears there still echoes the jingling of the little bells they wore upon their leggings'

A brief account of Cricklade by Gareth Hugh Davies in his most enjoyable book,[11] brings us suddenly into the present: 'In the dimming evening I trudge into Cricklade. I shall carry the image of this miraculously surviving tapestry (The North Meadow) (q.v.) as far as the sea.'

West Mill, Cricklade

The first land enclosures began in the reign of Queen Elizabeth, but it was not until The Enclosure Act (1783) that the medieval system finally ended and most, though not all, of the remaining parts of common land were enclosed within the Cricklade parish. One example of this is The Dance Forty, more locally known as simply The Dance of some ten or more acres, it runs in a narrow ribbon alongside the Purton road (B4041) beginning half a mile from the town centre. This was never enclosed – common land if ever there was. The name probably has medieval origins. Situated at the town's southern end, it was convenient for local jousting, archery and other open-air pastimes, with dancing on May Day and other anniversaries. Five hundred years later, their descendants danced there again in celebration of the ending of the First World War. I can remember the dancing and the huge bonfire, with another at the crossroads by the Vale Hotel, on the very spot where once had stood the Town Cross; its base, column and head, but not its series of steps, now stand in St Sampson's Churchyard.

I have a vague recollection of the remains of one of the two town pounds near Tom Peare's house, 'The Dance House', at the north end of the Dance Forty. Here Tom Peare[12] aided by his son Jack, broke in their horses.

The other pieces of common land in Cricklade were also enclosed, the papers for the enclosure of Chelworth Common dated 1789 are in the Devizes museum. The Acts for the enclosure of Common Hill are dated 1814 and 1815. There was also a small triangular-shaped parcel of land known as Calcutt Forty; much of this is now engulfed by the road junction leading to the Cricklade By-pass, opened in 1976. On this site Cricklade's second pound was sited and it is thought that the name Forty denoted that here again archery was also carried out. From this same piece of land, wild and uncultivated, I heard my last Wiltshire corncrake in 1927, a bird that sadly has now become virtually extinct in Britain, except for a few scattered places in the Outer Hebrides and in the far north.

Cricklade had many inns, as I have mentioned, among them the White Swan, now a greengrocer's shop on the south-west corner of the cross roads; the Vale Hotel is on the other side. It became notorious for the political meetings that took place there at the time of the infamous bribery and corruption trials, which came to be known as Petrie's Cricklade Case.[13] The occupier in 1797 was William Barnes. Thomas Mann Gunn became landlord *c*.1813 and John Packer in 1840. Subsequent to its demise as an inn, the property was owned by William Clark, a coachbuilder. He displayed in his shop a life-size dummy of a horse drawing a coach or wagon. After this the property was owned by William J. New and subsequently by members of his family until 1981, when it continued as a greengrocers and general store until the present day.

The White Hart in the centre of the north end of the High Street has always been Cricklade's principle inn and was the chief posting house. Opposite the site was the old Market House or Town Hall that once stood in the middle of the wide street. Those owning this inn from *c*.1700 have been Francis Bristow, John Smith; *c*.1780, Nevil Cuss (the writer's very distant cousin); *c*.1840, Joseph Craddock; *c*.1870, Hollister Forrester and Joseph Townsend (who lived in the Dance House during his retirement), followed by Roy Scott *c*.1930 and others. It is now a Trust House.

The Three Horse Shoes, about a dozen houses north of the White Hart, has had an interesting history and has been known by several names. After about 1691 it was called the George Inn and subsequently the White Horse and the Star, possibly not in that order. It has been occupied by John Harper *c*.1715, Richard Clarke *c*.1721 and Thomas Skilton. Daniel Peare *c*.1840 and others until shortly before it closed down in 1975. At that time the landlord was

Harold Brooks, always known locally as Doctor Brooks, his grandfather having been Charles Brooks a qualified LSA (1830)) practising in Cricklade until his retirement to 17 High Street.

The Red Lion is still extant. Little of the history of this house is known. Its ancient sign is the badge of John of Gaunt, and Dr Thomson has stated this 'may be associated with the Duchy lands now forming the parish of Braydon'. The building is sited directly upon the line of the old defensive wall running through the garden. The limestone blocks of coral rag incorporated in its construction are obviously some of those once taken from the wall. In 1840/41 the property was owned and occupied by William Sadler, and George H. Webb was occupier in 1869. I particularly remember the Red Lion when, as a lad, *c*.1920, in a building attached to the property, I saw the only privy (earth closet) seat of its kind, then reputed to be still in the town. It had accommodation for two large and two small posteriors all on the same long elm seat.

The King's Head is also still in use. It was established by Lord Porchester as a political headquarters in 1841, when William Blake was occupier, and then Sampson C. Russell in 1869, and in 1875 by Edward Barnes. I became aware that it was occupied at least for a brief period *c*.1869–*c*.1872 by W.H. Stephens sen. I refer to a letter written by his eldest son, my maternal grandfather of precious memory, William Henry Stephens in 1870 from the USA, wherein he requests his parents to look after certain of his special belongings at the King's Head before they vacated it to move to their permanent address where their bakery and corn business was situated at 29 High Street next door.

The White Horse, now the Vale Hotel, was kept by the Godbys in the late eighteenth century. John Wood succeeded them in about 1797 and it was occupied by the Landsdown family until *c*.1825 to *c*.1870. Frank Laing was the licensee in 1875 and in 1892 it was George R. Griffin.

The Sun was 'John Harvey's house' now 21 Calcutt Street. Chelworth Courts were held here in 1792 and 1793. A (later) Chelworth Court House is marked on Byrt's map as on the site of 1 Spittals Lane.

The Crown, long since disused, occupied the site of Gunning's Sadler and Harness Maker's shop, which was closed *c*.1928 and was directly opposite the White Hart Hotel. The first mention of it as an inn was in 1551 and so it remained until possibly the late 1770s or early 1800s. It was no longer an inn by 1826.

The New Inn was a Waylands Estates property and stood next to The Bell opposite the White Hart, it has long since been a grocer's shop. It is mentioned in the 1670 St Sampson's vestry book. Some subsequent occupiers were William Hill and William Cuss.[14]

Among the numerous inns that once existed in Cricklade, I have mentioned just a few, but there is one still extant, its street face scarcely altered since its medieval beginnings; this was originally known as The Saracen's Head, seemingly derived from the times of the Crusaders, until when, in *c.*1786, it became known as The Bear, and remains so to this day. Thacker states that: ' . . . about twenty years ago (probably the 1880s) it displayed the sign of The Bear and Ragged Staff. No confirmation of this has been found, although there are local reasons why it might not be so called.'

It would be of interest to know what these reasons could have been. Between 1690 and 1940 the names of a few of the occupiers are known. There have been John Clerdew 1697, George Pike approximately 1795 to 1841. Joseph Brooks about 1869 and Thomas Smith in 1875. William Turk was landlord early in the twentieth century, followed by his daughter and her husband, Edgar Newman, after which their son in law George Osman, became landlord *c.*1940.

Old Bear Inn, Cricklade

Today the number of public houses in Cricklade stands at only six: The King's Head, The Vale Hotel, The White Lion, The Red Lion, The White Hart Hotel and The Bear.

At one time or another the owner or licensee of an inn has been described as alehousekeeper, innkeeper, innholder, tippler, taverner, victualler and now in modern terms, publican.

A survey[13] was carried out for the War Office for the billeting of troops, and probably used also by the Board of Excise. From this survey and some other sources Mr John Chandler[14] has compiled a most useful account with illustrations, tables and charts, covering the accommodation and stabling in the county of Wiltshire in this area.

Before the age of turnpike roads, with the exception of Salisbury, Cricklade was still one of the most important towns in Wiltshire. It will be useful to compare its population and other factors with that of neighbouring Swindon now Wiltshire's largest town. The adult population there in 1676 was 580. At the same time at Cricklade it was 640, being 500 in the parish of St Sampson and 140 in that of St Mary's. Twenty years later, stabling for horses was 75 in Swindon and 91 in Cricklade, while the number of beds available for travellers is listed in Swindon as 14 and in Cricklade as 68. In 1620 Cricklade innkeepers numbered 12 and Swindon's 2, the Goddard Arms in the High Street and the King's Arms in Wood Street.

Notes

1. Hebel, J.W., ed., *Complete Works*, 5 vols (1931–41)
2. *In loco delicioso* has been adopted for the town's motto and means 'in a most delightful place'.
3. *The Stripling Thames* (1908)
4. Owned at that time by my great grandfather, Joseph Cuss.
5. *Highways and Byways in Wiltshire* (Macmillan & Co Ltd., 1917)
6. It has to be remembered that the St Sampson's cross had once stood in the centre of the crossroads until its removal in about 1818.
7. This makes one wonder what these people would have said if they had seen the same stream flowing under the bridge at Ewen.
8. This has not been spoken of within my memory.
9. The cavalry backsword, a simple and handy weapon on which the knuckles were protected by a single or basketlike guard, sometimes double-edged and sometimes single. The sport came to be practised with such wooden weapons as the quarter staff, singlestick and cane, hence the noise of the play. It gradually became the forerunner of modern fencing.
10. Formerly the White Horse Inn
11. *A Walk Along the Thames Path* (1989)
12. One William Peare was a notorious robber. He was born in 1756 and hanged in

1783. He was one of a family of blacksmiths, some of whom lived at the Three Horse Shoes in the High Street. The Cricklade Museum has notes of his crimes and associates. See *The Highwaymen of Wiltshire*.

13. This case resulted in 'An Act receiving the royal assent on 17 May 1782 (Geo. III, xxii, c.311)' for prevention of bribery and corruption in the election of members of Parliament for the Borough of Cricklade in the County of Wilts.

14. Abstract of a 'particular account of all Inns, Alehouses etc. in England with their stable-room and bedding in the year 1685', PRO–Kew WO 30/48.

15. *Wiltshire Archaeological Magazine*, vol. 84 (1991).

15   Cricklade – Religious Foundations

At church, with meek unaffected grace,
His looks adorn'd the venerable place;
Truth from his lips prevail'd with double sway,
And fools, who came to scoff, remain'd to pray.
'The Deserted Village', Oliver Goldsmith (1728–74)

The reasons for believing that it was here that St Augustine met the English and Welsh bishops have been well founded and set out by the learned ex-Bishop of Bristol, Dr Forrest Browne, in his lectures on 'Augustine and his Companions'.

Ancient local legend (in whose folds the truth is oft times wrapped) has claimed two places for these historic meetings, both in the Cricklade area, which took place a few years before St Augustine died in AD 604 and, as will be seen, there is a high possibility that each was a rendezvous.

The Venerable Bede states that they met 'at a place which is to this day called Augustine's Oak ... on the borders of the Hwicce and the West Saxons'. The Hwicce occupied the southern part of Warwickshire, Worcestershire and Gloucestershire, and the West Saxon boundary was along their southern border, so the conferences would have taken place somewhere on that boundary. Bishop Forrest Browne points out that the Roman Ermin Street would cut the county boundary 'as near as may be to St Augustine's Oak' and 'cuts it at Cricklade', which would be equidistant between Canterbury and St Asaph. At that time the Welsh were in bitter feud with the West Saxons but there existed a close alliance with the Hwicce, so they would have been free to pass through this territory, and the first meeting may well have been with the Welsh bish-

135

ops – a mere mile and a half from Cricklade – near Down Ampney and in Hwicce territory (see chapter twenty). Cricklade being a seat of learning at that time, the town would have been an eminently appropriate place for St Augustine and the British bishops to stay after their meeting.

The only evidence that remained for one of these meetings until the 1920s, was the bole of an ancient oak, three miles from Cricklade in the Forest of Braydon. The last resting place for this tree, known as the 'Gospel Oak', was in the church of St Sampson in Cricklade.

The historic meeting is purported to have taken place beneath this oak at SU 05258875. There the Norman kings hunted the wild boar and King John hunted there more than once in 1200 and four times in 1204. From what is known, Charles I was the last king to have used the forest for hunting. This time-worn and weather-beaten oak was wantonly cut down in 1865 and its remains were carried to Cricklade.

The ancient pollarded bole, in height more than six feet and in girth, as I recall, more than three feet, stood by a pillar behind – and south of – the chancel choir stalls in the church since my earliest recollection. With the bark long gone, it presented a sere grey—brown, bald, appearance and was in an advanced state of decay. J. Lee Osborne wrote:

> Though absolute certainty in such a matter is, of course, impossible, the belief that this is part of the oak mentioned by Bede (who died in 735), and that beneath it St Augustine held at least one of his memorable interviews with the bishops, may claim at least a high degree of probability. If this is indeed so, there are few more sacred relics in Britain than this fragment of scarred timber.[1]

At the time I was too young, but as far as I can recollect, no hand was lifted, nor voice raised in protest at its desecration when the incumbent vicar (*c.* 1924) caused its removal into the churchyard, where it stood leaning against the corner of a pier and the outer wall, to the east of the south door until it finally disintegrated and its remains were removed. There is no doubt that this oak was of considerable antiquity, and was the oldest religious relic in the church's possession.

W.H. Hutton writes:[2]

> Near Cricklade it was, as the Bishop of Bristol has clearly shown, that St Augustine met the bishops and doctors of the nearest

province of the Britons. 'The northern end of the bridge or ford of the Thames at Cricklade' comes thus into almost our earliest history. Two miles further on, by Down Ampney, on the road as you drive from Fairford to Cricklade is Oak Farm, now only a cottage or two. It was at 'The Oak' that the meeting took place. Very likely it was by this very farm.

The 'Gospel Oak' in the garden of St Sampson's Vicarage

William III's accession to the English throne would have had little effect at first upon the inhabitants of the Upper Thames, but it brought consequences of far reaching import to its history when Britain was declared a Protestant State. The Act of Toleration, 1689, restored the rights of most of the religious denominations outside the Anglican Church, which had earlier been taken from them. Catholics only were excluded. The Baptists, for example, who had strong roots in every village, were no longer compelled to baptize in infancy and many found their 'River Jordan' in the

Thames at Hatchetts, Cricklade, where adult members of the faith were baptized in its waters. However, toleration was only superficial and complete freedom of worship was yet a long way away. Lord Hardwicke's Act of 1754 made it compulsory for all marriages, Catholic marriages included, to take place under the rites of the Anglican Church. This of course caused considerable unrest in Catholic communities. Only Jews and The Society of Friends (Quakers) were excluded from this Act, and continued to worship undisturbed and maintain their own records.

The liberation of Roman Catholicism from the yoke under which they had suffered for their faith for so long, did not come about until the repeals of the Test Acts of 1673 and 1678, the last (of three) of which was not made law until 1889. Broadly speaking these Acts were to ensure that Catholics were debarred from holding any form of public office; any person who did so had first to swear an oath of allegiance, declare against transubstantiation and additionally receive the Sacrament within three months of holding office.

To return to earlier history for a moment, it was to be nearly a hundred years after St Augustine's arrival in England in AD 597 before the conversion of all the heathen Anglo-Saxon tribes had been completed. We know that a church of some kind must have existed in Cricklade in AD 973, and without any doubt it stood where the great church of St Sampson now stands on the highest piece of ground within the town. The first recorded reference to its existence was in the year when Aethaelmar, Ealdorman of Hampshire (who died *c*.983) left one pound in his will to 'the church of Cricklade', which was by that time stone built. Before that date enough stone had been brought, on royal (Saxon) authority, to Cricklade to revet a mile and a quarter of the town's defensive wall of five feet in thickness, which had been preceded by a wooden structure.

The numerous tribal kingdoms were brought together into a single church teaching by Theodore, Archbishop of Canterbury from 668 to 690, and helped, more than anything else could have done, to bring about a united England. Pagan practices were hard to eliminate, but Christianity was welcomed; people at that time were impoverished and pleasures were few. The introduction of this new faith brought with it a reason for social intercourse and it gave hope where before none had existed and created a sense of purpose. With Christian Biblical teachings came unity. Adult baptisms were normal but the baptism of infants was practised from an early date. The Eucharist, or Holy Communion, was the principal Sabbath day service and sermons, although long, were eagerly listened to.

The church became the centre of English village life, in part because it was the only substantial building a village possessed. Later on, even cock-fighting (which was prohibited in 1849) was commonly carried out in village churchyards. Sometimes it appears that this took place even in the church itself. Churches had no pews in the earlier days, so standing throughout the service was a general rule and, in the case of sport, if the weather was bad, the open floor was an ideal setting from which to view the fight. We know that during the Civil War horses were stabled in St Sampson's Church, but this practice was not uncommon and we read later on of Parliamentary elections taking place within its consecrated walls. The practice of the use of the church for other than normal Christian worship and observances, is now reverting, if only a little, to the tendencies of an earlier epoch.

The Puritan form of worship within the Church of England is far less common as we approach the end of the twentieth century. There would appear to be in many of us, a certain love of ritual, no doubt inherited from our pagan ancestors, and we hear less and less of matins and evensong being taken in the Anglican parish churches.

I shall quote from the work of Dr T.R. Thomson,[3] particularly from his history of Cricklade's two churches. These churches have influenced so many generations of those who have lived within their shadow and the sound of their bells; and whose lives have been centred around these beautiful and revered churches through the centuries.

The earliest work that is visible in St Sampson's is that of the lower courses of the west wall of the nave, before the restoration half a century later. The possibility that this stone, which is inferior oolite, may have come from the town's defensive walls cannot be ruled out. During the restoration of 1864 the south wall was rebuilt.

The construction of the two newer eastern windows is evidenced by the lowering of the outside string course, and the rebuilding of the wall between. The eastern of these two windows displays tracery of a most unusual pattern. The modern glass commemorates a family by the name of Nott, long connected with Braydon Forest.

It was a member of this once well known family, Lieut.-Col. Nott, a Royalist, who was thought to have been the cause of Cromwell's army under Essex losing many horses at Cricklade.

The Widhill 'chapel' (the north aisle) was once used for children's services and various meetings and after 1814 for the parliamentary elections. Until 1864 it was shut off by an oak screen.

This picture of the interior of St Sampson's Church looking east clearly
shows the misalignment of the chancel. This is understood to represent
Christ on the cross at Calvary with his head leaning to one side.

The following is copied from the vicar's notebook:

> Patsy Giles tells me (Jan 1813) that she remembers when the church was on fire. Her father got up early one morning to go and make some candles; looking over the church gate, he saw a light in the church. At that moment something burning fell from the ceiling – her father summoned assistance, and after a long time the fire was subdued, many of the surrounding walls being emptied for the purpose.

On the 25th a fire broke out in the Widhill Aisle in the church, and had it not been for very prompt assistance, the whole church would have been destroyed; the keys of the church being at the time in the church through the vestry room window.

The Hungerford Chapel was built probably by Sir Edmund Hungerford, first of Down Ampney, who died in 1484. The work is rich but the appearance from the outside is shoddy. It looks 'stuck on'. The thrust of the new tower necessitated a flying buttress in 1569.[4] There are ornamnetal niches with the initials R and H to commemorate the parents of Richard Hill, Bishop of London, who are buried here. In the Bishop's will of 1495 . . . he gives 'to the fabric of the chaple of St Sampson's . . . one hundred marks'. Prior to 1864 the chapel was shut off from the chancel by a plaster screen and was in use as a vestry . . . Phillippa (1821) says, 'In the vestry is the iron frame of the hour glass which formerly the minister preached by.' The tower was rebuilt in the sixteenth century, and shows affinities with those of Fairford and Kempsford; it has been called the Glory of North Wiltshire.[5] The rebuilding must have begun or was under discussion early in the century. It is mentioned in the will of Thomas Rusley, (1512–13), '. . . towards the construction of the tower 20/- (£1)'. The will of John Jane, vicar of St Sampson's, 1526, gives to the building of St Sampson's 'three quarters of all my goods'. About 1540 it was completed as far as the lantern vault.[6]

'A strong case was made out that John Dudley, Duke of Northumberland, was the chief mover of the rebuilding. In 1547 he acquired from the Crown the manors of Calcutt and Chelworth Parva for his son John, who was created Duke of Northumberland. His ambition was now at its height. In 1552 he married his son Guilford to Lady Jane Grey, and had planned to alter the succession. He was very near the throne indeed.'

The restoration was carried out in 1863 and 64. The oak pews, a jumble of all shapes and sizes, extending up to and under the western tower arch ... were removed and replaced with crude pine seats. The floor formerly of stone flags was laid with encaustic tiles and channelled for heating pipes, and the galleries at the west end were taken down. The organ (1820) was in the centre gallery of three at the west end and here sat a choir of men and women, formerly an orchestra of flute, violin and bassoon took their place here. The galleries on each side contained appropriated pews. The present pulpit, said to be of Barnsley stone, was erected at the same time. The very dilapidated oak screen (already mentioned) 'surrounding' the Widhill Chapel was wilfully destroyed.

The entries in the vestry book, under dates 1 April 1700 and 7 April 1704, throw some light on the construction of the 'detestable pews of all shapes and sizes and galleries ... in some of the arches'. They run as follows:

'A vestry then held it was allowed that Edward Nott Esq, have liberty to erect a gallery in the north east corner of the middle aisle. During the restoration services were held in the town hall.'[7]

A memorial to my father Joseph John Cuss with a picture the *Light of the World* presently hangs in the Widhill Aisle (1993).

Of the Vestry Minute Books two, 1670–1730 and 1731–63, are in the (Cricklade) museum, and four, covering 1818–60 are in the custody of the Clerk to the Parish Council.

Payments to the poor in money and clothing (indicating the particular garments granted) are set out. For many years the Cricklade poor had to bear the letters C.P. (Cricklade Parish) on their arm .... Under the same heading are found entries concerning expenses, persons in transit, distressed soldiers and sailors and apprenticeships. Miscellaneous payments constantly recurring, are for the dog-keeper, bellropes, pulpit cushions, cleaning linen, scouring the branch or sconce (candle holder), mending the surplice, oil for the clock and bells, repairs to both, repairs to the mounds and churchyard gate, gaol and marshalsea money, ejection of strangers, road repairs, ringing bells on the 5th November (after 1605) and money paid to the constable of the hundred for the repairs of county bridges. In 1677 is a reference to Hearth Money, in 1685 to a 'Board for the King's Arms above the arch'. In 1683 there is a payment of one shilling to Robert Harper 'for making a frame for the paper concerning His Majesty's touching of the evil'. In 1726 it is agreed that a gallery be built, for the use of the singers provided same be done at their own proper cost and charge.

It was the duty of church wardens as overseers of the poor, to see that the rate was correctly levied and distribution made to the poor and the destitute of the parish. Begging was illegal and some kind of order was attempted in the granting of assistance for those who – just as we find them today, 200 years later – for one reason or another were unable to help themselves. Vagrants were actively discouraged from remaining in the parish for their presence would mean a drain on the rates and less help for those who were 'settled' within its confines, unless their condition was so bad that a benevolent disposition and common humanity forbade their immediate removal. 'Settlement' meant that a person would be established by owning his own property, or the parent would have done so, or he may have served an apprenticeship there and perhaps his father before him had been born there; in short he or she was virtually a native. Many interesting things come to light from time to time in these old records. For example in the churchwardens' accounts of a village in Staffordshire is an entry of 1s 6d (7½p) given to a travelling woman with smallpox and three others paid by the overseer; 16s (80p) 'Pay'd to Widow Dickens towards the keeping of her cow'; 1s 6d 'pd to Thomas Stokes in hard weather' and 1s 6d 'pd to Samuel Fowkes for fetching Thomas Lightwood to church, he being dead in the snow'.

Undoubtedly the office of churchwarden was of particular importance. Churchwardens' accounts ante-date the parish registers but are rare and not of a great deal of interest in research itself; as parochial officials they carried a heavy responsibility. There were waywardens or surveyors whose duties were to see to the maintenance of roads and bridges within the parish, elected at one time by the villagers themselves. This task was sometimes also taken on by the churchwardens.

The Parish Hall borders the churchyard on the north side. In the early days of its existence it was the Poor House with an upper floor and a lock-up, together with living quarters for the Poor Master and his family. The building would house as many as twenty-five paupers. There are references to the employment of male paupers in stone breaking, to the appointment and clothing of the town beadle and in inoculation against cow-pox, a mild disease which, once contracted, made the 'fortunate' victim at once immune from the dreaded killer, smallpox. Dr Thomson writes:

In the church chest are scores of bundles of receipted accounts and apart from modern service books and registers there is only one further item under this head, 'The Vicar's Note Book', also in the museum. This is a modern exercise book containing extracts from newspapers and articles in the *Wiltshire Archaeological Magazine*

(WAM). The few other items contain valuable scraps of information.

St Mary's Church

Beloved by more than thirty generations, this beautiful little church of St Mary's had been shared equally by firstly Catholics and then Protestant worshippers until, in 1977, it reverted once more to Roman Catholic worship.

The church is close to the north end of the High Street, just within the east-west line of where once stood the ramparts of the Saxon Town Wall. The structure blends well with the architecture of the town.

The early history of the church is unknown. Whether or not the church was originally the parish church cannot be said for certain, but the probabilities are against it, and the smallness of the parish would seem to confirm this view. The building is planned on the traditional pattern for small churches, with a western tower, a nave with north and south aisles, south porch, and chancel with a north chapel. There is a fine and well preserved chancel arch, which is a richly carved specimen of the purist Norman period, 1120–50.

The church has a chained Bible in good condition. The parish of St Mary's is the smallest in the Bristol diocese, of only about fifty hectares, its bounds can be seen on the 1885 edition of the six-inch OS Map. The parishes of St Sampson's and St Mary's were united in 1952 and the benefice of Cricklade and Latton was created.

I have mentioned parish registers before but it will do no harm to elaborate here on the context of losses. The value of church or parish registers (once maintained for both religious as well as secular purposes) was generally considered of sufficient importance to keep them under lock and key. Registers were kept in this way in iron-bound oak chests of great strength, but even so, they were sometimes tampered with. In time it may come to light that many an inheritance was obtained by the dishonest removal of proof of a baptism (and thereby of a birth) from the register. An example of this can be seen in the earliest register of the church of St Sampson's, where neatly cut from the edge of a baptism page is a space that filled a single entry; an idea romanticized in *Oliver Twist*.

The Parochial Records Measures Act 1969 brought together the older parish registers from out of their church safes and ancient chests for assembly and permanent storage by each County Record Office (CRO). They were to be put into good repair, classified and microfilmed for public use. The order was carried out with few exceptions. To many people I am sure, including myself, the wisdom of the act is questionable. The risk of damage by fire or other means to a large assembly of priceless documents cannot be over-estimated. Experience gained from similar happenings should never be forgotten. Probably outstanding among these was the loss of documents (of which there were no copies) in the 1922 Dublin riots, in the destruction by German bombing raids during the Second World War and in the damage by flood to the State archives in Florence in 1966. When these original registers have been repaired and microfilmed and their storage facilities have been found by the county archivists to be satisfactory, they should be returned to their original homes. By such means, if an odd one should be lost or damaged, there will be a record of its contents. In fact all could be lost for a whole county, if they were under the same roof as the copies – catastrophe indeed.

The registers of St Mary's Church date from 1663, and the earliest one has that magic word 'Abracadabra'[8] written on the inside front cover, presumably as a charm against plague. In addition to their storage now in the Wiltshire Record Office, there is also a copy transcribed and indexed in the Cricklade Museum. There is also in the museum, diocesan transcripts of earlier date,[9] from 1605, and the names of many of the earlier churchwardens can be traced.

There is in the Devizes Museum a very beautiful water-colour drawing of St Mary's Church executed in 1810 by John Buckler, and a pencil drawing, made before 1862, which was owned by Mrs A.M. Nash in Cricklade (1950). A photograph of the church (with the Revd Hugh Allen, rector for 48 years, standing at the gate), showing the 1862 east window and the roof without dormers, is in the (Cricklade) museum. The plain glass in the windows is very noticeable.

The Non-Conformists

What exactly we may ask, is Non-Conformity? The question can be answered by simply stating that in the true sense Non-Conformists represent most of those Christian separatists who have broken away from the Anglican Church or Church of England – the established church. At once we may think of the Wesleyan Methodists, the Baptists, the Congregationalists and so on. Yet, in a sense, the Anglican Church itself falls into this category, breaking as it did from the Church of Rome at the Reformation. However, there has always remained a certain continuity with the pre-Reformation English church by the Church of England, as the Anglican Church with the Church of Rome. A handful of what we might term the new Non-Conformists's denominations set themselves up in Cricklade and their influence has been of considerable importance in the day-to-day religious life of the community. The number of adherents, however, has steadily declined since the end of the Second World War, until today only the Congregational Church remains as a place of worship, joined by a few scattered groups of the other denominations remaining to form the Cricklade United Churches.

The Wesleyan Methodists were the best known of all the dissenters and had their chapel by the river and Town Bridge, which is now a Youth Centre. The Primitive Methodists worshipped in Calcutt Street, where is now a doctor's surgery, the Baptists also held their services in Calcutt Street (those premises are now used as the Cricklade Museum) and the Congregationalists, remaining the strongest, and situated in Calcutt Street as well, now share their church (built in 1772), as The United Reformed Church.

Thacker (op.cit.) writing in the opening years of the twentieth century says:

> The non-conformists of the little town of Cricklade perpetuate the ancient feast about the 12th August with a great camp meeting and tea; though not now, as formerly, in the large north meadow or 'Nor' Mead' as the old generation called it. At the old proper religious observations of this festival there were wrestling and racing and backsword encounters, and fights in earnest for personal grudges were often adjourned, they say, so that they might be enjoyed without suspicion under cover of a holiday. No doubt there was a certain laudable character about it all, and the non-combatants, imitating the ancient Christians, seized upon the occasion and gradually turned it into their own sober uses. They should at least share the credit with the Rev. F. Dyson, long the vicar of St Sampson's, a fine specimen of the old hunting parson of bygone days, and much loved by all who knew him. He seems to have instituted donkey rides and other innocent amusements on the Monday as an inducement to his parishioners to abstain the Sunday feast.

When I was a child my maternal grandfather had a serious difference of opinion with the incumbent of St Sampson's and left the church to join the Congregationalists. From then on we grandchildren were treated to a fine tea and games each August which took place at Mr Freeth's farm at Calcutt. Children assembled at the

Congregational Chapel for conveyance in immaculately clean four-wheeled haycarts, to the feast. By 1923, more than ten years after Thacker wrote his book, festivities in this form were consigned to history; but ever since there has been an August Bank Holiday Show and sports (once held in Paul's Croft), preceded by a fancy-dress parade, starting at The Knoll near the Town Bridge, and led by one of the two town bands with the other in the rear, each taking the lead in alternate years. The procession ended at Paul's Croft where the judging took place for the best turn-out.

> Wherever God builds a house of prayer,
> The devil always builds a chapel there;
> And 'twill be found upon examination
> The latter has the largest congregation

Notes

1. *Cricklade: The Meeting with Augustine and the British Bishops* (1921)
2. Hutton, Revd W.H., *By Thames and Cotswolds* (1908)
3. Materials for a History of Cricklade
4. A flying buttress might also be described as 'a detached buttress with a flying arch'.
5. In all the literature I have read about this church, I have come across only one writer who disagrees with this description; 'although with its unduly massive turrets and pinnacles (spirelets)', he writes, 'and its blank tracery, it is a rather cumbersome piece of work with little of the grace of the other wool churches'.
6. Bond, Francis, *English Church Architecture*, pp. 374–6 and notes of pp. 332, 374 and 377 concerning patterned vaulting.
7. Contemporary accounts of the restoration may be seen in the *Wilts and Gloucestershire Standard* 30 May, 22 June and 31 July 1864, and the *Swindon Advertiser*, 26 December 1864. The architect in charge of the work was Mr E. Christian.
8. This is a cabbalistic word – one with a hidden meaning; cryptic, magic, mysterious. It was used supposedly to ward off evil, e.g. during outbreaks of plague.
9. The entries for christenings in the Bishops' Transcripts for St Mary's Church are for 1605–09, 1615–23, 1666–79, 1694–7, 1707–10, 1725, 1751–62, 1757–9, 1767–1837. Those for St Sampson's are for 1599–1609, 1619–23, 1632, 1666–80, 1694–8, 1709–11, 1720, 1724–9, 1751–2, 1763–1837. All may be seen at the WRO in Trowbridge.

16 Cricklade – Topography

Change is inevitable. In a progressive country change is constant.
Edinburgh 29 October 1867, Benjamin Disraeli (1804–81)

At the turn of the century entertainment was of the simplest kind.
My mother was impressed by 'some poor man' (*c*.1895) in the High
Street, singing a parody on a popular song of the time. The jolly lilt
of a barrel organ playing in the High Street was always very popular and a common sight in the first quarter of the century; my elder
sister recalls one with a performing bear. There were concerts in
the old Town Hall, now long since a glove factory, by travelling
troupes of players, and after the First World War came the Royal
Cinema, with silent films, which were shown with a piano accom-
paniment, in an old converted school in Gas Lane. There were
bucket seats at the rear costing 1s 3d (6¾p) and forms in the middle
and front priced at 6d and 9d (2½p and 3¾p).

There was little otherwise to entertain, but market days, on the
third Tuesday in every month, brought a few hours of bustling life
to the town. Temporary pens for livestock flanked the pavements
from the crossroads down the north end of the wide High Street.

Of four crosses once believed to have existed, two remain and
stand in the churchyards of St Sampson's and St Mary's. The original Town Cross was once in the centre of the crossroads from
where it is said to have been removed in about 1817. It now stands
in St Sampson's churchyard, north west of the east lychgate, near
Jenner's School – the Parish Hall. The gate is wide enough to allow
vehicles to enter, as they did when coal had to be delivered for the
church's heating system.

Robert Jenner was buried in the church in 1651. His epitaph
reads: 'Here lies the body of Robert Jenner Esq., Citizen and goldsmith of London who out of piety and charity built . . . a free school

148

in this parish and left twenty pounds a year for the maintenance for ever . . . . He deceased this life the 7th December 1651 aged 67 years'. His endowment was one of several lost charities and has produced nothing, certainly for over 200 years.

In the first decades of the twentieth century tradespeople were still relying on the horse for transport, and many had their own field named after them; 'Blackwell's Field' (Saddlers and Harness-Makers), which was behind the cemetery, now extended; and a part of it, 'Stephens's Field' (Bakers and Corn Dealers), was at Dudgemoor beyond the Dance Forty; 'Carter's Field' (Butchers) was north of the Vale of White Horse Kennels adjoining 'Blackwell's Field' and part of Culverhay, now a housing estate; 'Cowley's Field' (Local Carriers) was by the railway bridge on the south side of the high embankment, where visiting fairs used to set up their round-abouts and swings, and lastly I remember 'Little Double Days', that part of Double Days severed when the railway was built and mentioned elsewhere, that was always known as 'Clifford's Field'; the owners were farmers.

Until the Second World War, when they were removed to be melted down for the war effort, a pair of Russian cannon, trophies of the Crimean War, stood on either side of the War Memorial. It was a great occasion for a sleepy little market town, when these cannon were delivered by rail to Minety Railway Station and Nevil John Cuss hired forty white horses to haul them the five miles to their destination at the Knoll.

Transport by Road and Rail

In 1824 Cricklade still had no post-chaise, and neither was there yet any regular stagecoach service, but in summertime a coach, plying between Bath and Southampton would pass through the town two or three times a week.

Two enterprising Cricklade brothers named Clark still ran a horse-drawn carriage to Purton Railway Station as late as 1916. A similar service had probably been in use since the rail link by the Great Western Railway (GWR) was opened in 1841 between New Swindon and Cheltenham. This served Purton and Minety and does so still, as well as Kemble Junction where it passes through the valley of the Upper Thames within half a mile of Thames Head. Purton, four miles away, where passengers could embark for Swindon and Cheltenham and so connect to other places, was an important station for Cricklade.

The Clarks's carriage was enclosed and painted yellow below

and black above. It was drawn by a single horse, and entered by a high step at the rear; it held about eight passengers on hard seats along either side, the driver sitting outside at the front.

After the line through Purton was opened, it was to be nearly another forty years before the opening of the single track line by the Midland and South-Western Junction Railway Company (MSWJR) in 1883. This passed through Cricklade, linking Southampton to the south and Cheltenham to the north. The station was ceremoniously opened, with the newly formed Cricklade Town Band playing the first train across the bridge at The Forty and into the station to the tune 'The Flower that Bloometh'. The line was closed in 1963 under the so-called 'Beeching Axe'; nationalized long since, its dying decade would have had to see it closed far sooner under private ownership, but the taxpayer supported it with dwindling resources until its eventual demise.

In the railway's earlier years, this single track carried more than twenty trains each way every weekday. During the First World War, between August 1914 and December 1918, 6,452 troop trains and 1,485 ambulance trains passed through the town's station. Milk trains carrying tall, tapered milk churns, left the station every evening from a special sidings platform, for delivery to London. Four-wheel milk carts that took their daytime turn with farm chores, were a common sight every afternoon as they trundled through the town from all points of the compass and from as far away as Castle Eaton. In the days when motor cars were still an unusual sight on the roads, after dark on winter evenings George Keylock at Court Farm would go out and put his ear to the road to see if he could hear his milk cart coming. Now about 24,000 vehicles pass by this same farm every twenty-four hours.

Where the railway line once ran there is now the new Malmesbury or Bath road, the earlier road having been closed off near the north entrance to St Sampson's churchyard. South of this new road are now domestic dwellings, built on grass pastures to the Chelworth road from The Forty.

To the north of the new road, behind where the railway station and goods sidings used to be, there is now a council housing estate covering all of the following: the sidings with the long, narrow field alongside, the large, deep cattle pond, the Parsonage Farm home pasture, gardens, farmhouse, farm buildings and rickyard and the ancient tithe barn.

The pond held the largest concentration of the, now rare, crested newt that I have seen anywhere, and every summer I was certain to find a pair of spotted flycatchers returning to nest in the crown of one of the many old pollard willows around the banks. Now all is gone and uninspired council housing stands on the site.

I have belatedly suspected that the final depository of the bronze plaque from the 'stone yard' (mentioned later), was that old pond, close as it was to the scene of its damage in the upgraded stone yard. It was only a short walk from the north to the south end of the churchyard with the pond a few metres away.

The stone yard before its conversion to a 'place of beauty'

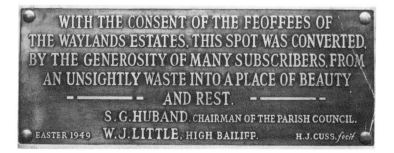

WITH THE CONSENT OF THE FEOFFEES OF THE WAYLANDS ESTATES, THIS SPOT WAS CONVERTED, BY THE GENEROSITY OF MANY SUBSCRIBERS, FROM AN UNSIGHTLY WASTE INTO A PLACE OF BEAUTY AND REST.

S.G.HUBAND. CHAIRMAN OF THE PARISH COUNCIL.
EASTER 1949 W.J.LITTLE, HIGH BAILIFF.   H.J.CUSS.*fecit*

The missing plaque commemorating the conversion of the stone yard

I watched the last passenger train, travelling north to Cirencester and Cheltenham, pass near the bottom of my garden. Every carriage was full to capacity with railway enthusiasts making their last nostalgic journey to turn another page in local history. Soon the last locomotive to use the line hauled away its own track, sleepers and chairs. In a year or two all that was left was a wilderness, to become a wildlife haven. Here was a new bird highway – just as were the derelict canals half a century or more before – partially replacing the hedgerows, which had been removed right across the floor of the valley, where now are hundreds of hectares of water, much of it known as The Cotswold Wildlife Park. Some parts of the trail have been broken; bought up by enterprising landowners, perhaps to rejoin what once had been a whole before the railway passed through. In an annual bulletin, published by the Cricklade Historical Society, David Hoad tells us of domestic dwellings near Siddington having caused a diversion to be made in his perambulation of the track from Cirencester to Cricklade. Embankments and cuttings, along these tracks, once rigidly control-burned to eliminate the risk of fire by sparks from passing locomotives, are now a brambly wilderness, where plant and animal life is thriving. An outstanding example of the contribution by the railways to the increase in our flora, is in the Oxford Ragwort (*Senecio squalidus*); this escaped from Oxford Botanic Gardens in about 1770 and has now spread to much of Britain, mainly found along railway verges.

Between the railway station at Cricklade and the bridge on the up line – demolished in the changes made to the road system – which carried the Malmesbury road across the track, were fields on either side, now covered in dwelling houses as already mentioned.

As well as the two sites in the town where fairs were held in recent times, it is possible that the north-west corner of Great Double Days may have been another. Immediately following the end of the Second World War, I built my house here on a half acre of bare field and many are the coins I have found there when turning over the virgin turf. It would be of interest to know if any of the hundreds of new owners of dwelling houses on these Cricklade fields, have themselves found anything of note.

With the great increase in twentieth-century vehicular traffic, the roads and bridges and their upkeep were always a problem. The Parish was once responsible for the repair and until the 1920s the District Council employed workmen, each of whom was in turn responsible for a stretch of road surface together with the verges and ditches over a distance of about four miles. Stone for repairs was delivered by horse and cart and stored by the roadside at convenient intervals to be broken down into suitable sizes, for patching up the potholes as a part of their duties.

After the Act of 1750 the Cricklade Feoffees contributed to the Turnpike Trusts – the Seven Bridges Turnpike, the Cricklade and Malmesbury Turnpike (1837) and the Swindon, Calne and Cricklade (third district) Turnpike. The repair of the road leading from Ermin Street, past Widhill Farm and Widhill Chapel to leave the parish by the west side of Tadpole Lane, was for long a matter of dispute. St Sampson's Parish, in the end, managed to escape further responsibility.

The modern road from Cricklade to Purton, passing through Purton Stoke, reminds me of the story of the robbery, by one Watkins, of monies that were destined for election purposes. Watkins escaped detection for a while, but was eventually apprehended in Wales and brought back for trial. He was publicly hanged near the scene of his crime, by the road bend at the foot of the hill beyond the village. This has since been known as 'Watkin's Corner' or 'Hangman's Corner'. The date and fuller details of the story may be found in the local newspaper archives.

Industries and Growth

The growth of Cricklade itself has been already touched on. It is hard to think of Bermondsey, Twickenham, Putney – name any of the areas of Greater London that spring to mind – as once having their willow-bordered streams, little fields and patches of bluebell woods, visited no doubt by nightingales in summer-time, but they did, of course. With the approach of the twenty-first century can it be possible that Cricklade itself is awaiting the inevitable and will be engulfed in tarmac and concrete that appears to be inexorably creeping towards it from the south west? The town of Swindon, halted in the opposite direction by geographical features that discourage growth (and, as a glance at the latest OS map will show, apparently by the new dual carriageway of its eastern boundary), continues its steady expansion. As the century draws towards its close, older people still have memories of some of the farms, fields, hedgerows, patches of woodland and narrow country roads and lanes that linked the villages of Pinehurst, Moredon, Rodbourne Cheney, Haydon Wick, Upper Stratton, Lower Stratton, Penhill, Kingsdown, Westlea and Shaw.

By 1960 Cricklade's population had increased from *c.*1,500 in 1930, to about 2,700 in 1990. The town's largest employer is the glove manufacturer Charles Ockwell & Company, whose history may be read in the *Victoria County History* (17.239). Nearly every dairy farm once made cheese and butter. Bricks were made on Common Hill and there were two iron foundries in the town, one at the Parsonage and the other near Knoll Cottage. Both ceased producing in the 1880s.

The area of land adjacent to St Sampson's churchyard, known as the Stone Yard, was so called because of its use by the banker masons, possibly as early as when the tower was rebuilt in the sixteenth century and certainly since the time of the restoration in 1863–4. However, Dr Thomson has concluded that:

> This was not so called until after the restoration . . . when it was used by the banker masons. It was manorial roadside waste enclosed before 1850 by the feoffees by permission of the lord of the manor of the borough . . . . In 1858 the fire engine house was built upon it, and later it was let to the District Council at a nominal rent.

The Stone Yard story was brought up to date in 1949, when history in Cricklade might have been said to have repeated itself. The bronze plaque, fitted to commemorate the occasion of the improvements made to the site, went missing. Three years later, another bronze plaque, missing for fifty-five years with, among others, my grandfather's name on it, was found one morning by the landlord of the adjacent Vale Hotel. It was propped up against the Queen Victoria Jubilee Clock from whence it had been removed; it contained the names of members of the Committee. The plaque from the Stone Yard held the names of the High Bailiff and the Parish Council's Chairman. Some person, or persons, unknown had objected to these names, and, after at first unsuccessfully attempting to remove the plaque itself, made a crude attempt to erase the offending names. My name – my firm had been contracted to carry out the work – was, however, not disturbed. A few nights later, probably the same person (or persons) unknown, tried once more to remove their eyesore, this time with more success, breaking the stone to which the metal had been secured with high tensile steel bolts, and it has never been found. See the following newspaper account which was of considerable local interest.

Missing plaque returned after fifty five years

Cricklade is becoming famous for its missing plaques. A few years ago a plaque erected on land adjoining the churchyard to commemorate improvements carried out there, vanished overnight and no trace of it has been found. Now a second plaque has come into the news, but this time it is a plaque which been returned after 55 years! The plaque is one that was fitted to Cricklade's Jubilee Clock erected in 1897 when Queen Victoria celebrated her diamond jubilee. On it were inscribed the names of the twelve members of the committee responsible for the arrangements.

A few months afterwards the plaque disappeared, torn from its position at the base of the clock, and nothing was heard of it again until one morning a few days ago when Mr A.G. Elbro, licensee of the Vale Hotel, who winds the clock gratuitously found it propped against the base of the clock and the clock had stopped! Numerous suggestions have been put forward as to the possible whereabouts of the plaque for the past half century, but Mr Elbro, who has been at the Vale Hotel for some 12 years, strongly refutes a suggestion that it had been lying in the cellar of the hotel, outside of which the clock stands.

COMMITTEE

W. HALLARD
W.J. CARTER
A.E. CLARK
M. GILES
H. HICKS
A.E. OCKWELL
J. ROOGES
W. SADLER
G. SELBY
W.H. SMITH
W.H. STEPHENS
W. WEBB

At a meeting of the Parish Council on Monday it was suggested that a place for the plaque might be found in Cricklade's museum.

The decision to erect the clock as a permanent memorial of the Queen Victoria Jubilee was made when it was found that funds collected in the town exceeded the cost of the celebrations. Further subscriptions were obtained and various functions organized to meet the cost, which amounted to £107.10.0. – £40.10.0 for the clock and £67 for the gas illuminated tower. Erected at the junction of Calcutt Street and High Street. It has three faces.

On Jan. 26 1898, the clock was officially started and a crowd gathered at the Town Hall – now Alkerton Glove Works – for the opening ceremony.

Among those present were the chairman of the committee, the Rev. J.H. Morton, Lord Edmund Fitzmaurice, chairman of the Wilts County Council, Viscount Emlyn, chairman of the Great Western Railway Company, Lord Moreton, T.A. Butt Miller, MFH and many others. The secretary of the Committee was the late Mr A.T. Giles.

Now people are asking 'Will history be repeated and the Stoneyard plaque be put back at the place from which it was stolen?'

7 March 1953, *Wilts and Gloucester Standard*

Alas! we're still waiting to see!

Fairs and Markets

In the early eighteenth century there was a Saturday market and three fairs a year, held on the third Wednesday in both April and July, and the third one on the 21 September (St Matthew's Day[1]), when there was also a sale of chapmen's goods. There was a sheep, cow and calves fair on the second Tuesday in April.

The town's stocks were said to have been at one time in Thames Lane, 165 feet from the Calcutt Street entrance. They were removed into Calcutt Street and remained there until as late as 1837, when the Market Committee proposed to have them removed. A Blind House was situated near the stocks, with a reference to it in the Minutes of the Waylands Estates of 29 March 1838.

It appears that there is now only one of the old turnpike cottages left, that at Latton Wharf, thought to have been known as Weavers' Cottage, alongside the River Churn at Weavers Bridge. This is thought to be where a highwayman was killed while attempting to escape his pursuers, when his horse struck the bridge. Two other cottages, one at The Forty to the south and the other at the bend in the Malmesbury Road, were there as recently as the 1950s.

Notes

1. The feast of St Michael and All Angels (Michaelmas) followed a few days later on 29 September, when farm workers offered themselves for new employment. In Cricklade it may have been convenient for these transactions to take place on 21 September.

17   A Strange, Eventful History

Shall we now contaminate our fingers with base bribes?
William Shakespeare, *The Merchant of Venice*

Dr Thomson opens his chapter on Cricklade's parliamentary history by referring to the *Report of the Committee on House of Commons Personnel and Politics 1264–1832*, published in 1932, in which reference is made to the histories of the Institution 'but of the men who gave the institution life, who shaped it and in so doing shaped our history and even our minds, no record has been attempted'. His work is an attempt to provide such a record for the Borough of Cricklade.

There can have been few parliamentary histories of any borough that have been more unusual and certainly more notable than has been that of eighteenth-century Cricklade. Much of this is highlighted in what came to be known as 'Petrie's Cricklade Case' (see chapter eighteen) when Samuel Petrie, a candidate for parliamentary election, sued John Bristow, of Broadleaze, Cricklade, agent for the candidate John MacPherson, for giving or receiving bribes with others in a case that began at the Lent assizes in Salisbury in March 1781.

We should remind ourselves that this great upheaval in the quiet homes and streets of Cricklade, a little of which I will relate here, was then an unusual phenomenon in those eighteenth century years. However, there were others to follow, though of less importance, including the infamous Sudbury elections more than half a century later, and a young Charles Dickens, a newspaper reporter at the scene, immortalized this in the nicest possible way, telling of the chicanery and outright dishonesty of happenings in his fictitious Eatenswill, so lucidly and delightfully described in *Pickwick Papers*. Cricklade had its moments and, like Sudbury, made its evolutionary contribution towards the election processes we know today.

The Cricklade Constituency was in existence for 610 years from 1275, when it sent its first member, John le Hunter, to Parliament, until 1885 when M.H.W. Masakelyn was elected with a majority of 1,910 votes over those of Sir Daniel Gooch Bt.

After 1884 contested elections were the exception owing to the expense involved, which had to be borne by the candidate and without rivalry, very little excitement was engendered. Each contestant had to bear the cost of the hustings, fees to the officials, polling booths etc. In many cases, where county elections were involved, there was not only the cost of the conveyance of voters, at times over long distances, but often that of feeding them and sometimes even housing them overnight.

The Petrie Case was largely instrumental in highlighting the necessity of obstructing fraud and assuring that votes were accurately cast. With the Act of 1782 and the introduction of the secret ballot, many far reaching changes took place in our voting system. It became paramount that counting was to be free of outside influences and that there was to be protection against ballot-rigging and representatives of the contending parties associating with the officer supervising the proceedings (in England this was the Town Clerk). All of these combined to ensure against further malpractices.

How one voted in those days did not necessarily reflect any political views one might hold. Pressure could be brought to bear on voting for a certain candidate in all kinds of ways. In this way tradespeople, fearful of losing a valued customer, would cast their vote in his direction, tenants voted for landlords, shopkeepers for their wealthy customers, employees for their employers. It was just as disloyal to vote against the local squire as it would have been for a Yorkshireman to cheer for Lancashire in a county cricket match. It was ever a question of abiding by the old adage: 'God Bless the Squire and his relations/And keep us in our proper stations.' My maternal grandfather had no vote in this election, but his father, William Henry Stephens sen., is shown in the poll book to have voted for Sir Daniel Gooch. They knew each other well and no doubt his choice of candidate was made in gratitude for taking his son, my grandfather, as engineer on the historic voyage of the ill-fated *Great Eastern*. This was when the ship laid the first successful transatlantic cable from the north-west coast of Ireland to Hearts

Content in Newfoundland. Daniel Gooch, later to be knighted for his services in this project, was a director of the company.

Poll books were published from 1695 after every parliamentary election, and have now become a valuable source of information to the historian and genealogist. In these will be found listed all who were eligible to vote, where they lived and, as I have mentioned, the way they voted. The right to vote was first given in 1430 and was for all who held land and goods to the annual value of 40s, and for more than 400 years it remained the sole criterion for voting in county elections. Although, as years went by, land values rose out of all proportion, most people who held land were not enfranchised, because they held it either copyhold or leasehold. Local customs regulated the franchise after 1832. Such was the case with my paternal grandfather who, shortly before he was married in 1868, was given the right to vote in the election of that year as owning land, whereas it was actually owned by his mother who had recently been widowed. Women were not yet enfranchised.

The first Member of Parliament for Cricklade of any particular interest is that of Thomas Crickkelade, son of Nicholas Crickkelade MP for Gloucestershire 1351–3. Dr Thomson tells us:

> He was born *c*.1360 and died before 1458. He married Alice, daughter of John Stodleigh of Stodleigh, near Calne, Wiltshire. Alice Crickkelade before her death, about the year 1458, inherited the Wiltshire estates of the Stodleighs and manors in Somerset and Gloucestershire from her mother's family: Walsh of Longridge Somerset and Landdough, Glamorgan . . . Thomas was a lawyer; in November 1407 he was surety in a case of rape committed at Foxham, Wiltshire. A chancery writ was issued on 17 May 1414 ordering certification of the acceptance of Thomas Crickkelade as attorney for Thomas Fowler, who, in the previous reign (of Henry IV) had sued in the Court of Common Pleas touching the detaining of a horse by one William Wydecombe. On 16 July 1414 he was included on a Royal Commission of Inquiry in Gloucester into the estates of a tenant of Richard, late Lord Dispenser, whose property during his minority had been in the hands of the King . . . . In 1412 he had a holding of land in Cricklade and Chelworth worth 20 marks a year. He was MP for Calne 1427.

The MP for Cricklade elected in 1472 was one John Whittokesmede of Beanacre near Melksham. Dr Thomson writes:

> When he was elected he had already sat in seven parliaments, representing a different constituency each time! . . . He also served as J.P.

His daughter married Giles Gore of Alderton ... This man's remarkable career is a most striking example of a practice which was almost unknown during the fourteenth century, but which became common from Edward IV onwards, that of a man being elected for one constituency after another. While having a local association of land-ownership or public office, men of this type were usually in Parliament for ends other than the welfare of their electors. They were of knightly classes, and like Whittokesmede many had been returned for their counties.

The next MPs for Cricklade of interest were Sir Henry Poole 1604–11 (see chapter ten), Neville Maskelyne and Hungerford Dunch, who held the seat 1659–60. Dr Thomson goes on to say: 'Neville Maskelyn was the son of Edmund Maskelyn of Purton who bought the Borough of Cricklade about 1610. His mother, Catherine Davys of Little Mitten, Worcestershire, was kinswoman to Sir Neville Poole, both having descent from Neville of Wellwyn, Worcestershire.'

As the history of the town draws us closer to the present, accounts of its people and the events that have taken place there become more interesting. A brief account of the 1774 election introduces us to Petrie for the first time, and many of the family names brought into the limelight as a result of his presence still exist in Cricklade today (see appendix). The candidates for the vacant seat were John Dewar, son of a West Indian planter, and Samuel Peach, a merchant banker of Bread Street, London. There was some dispute as to where the poll should be held.

Dewar wanted it held in the Widhill Aisle of St Sampson's Church, to which Peach agreed (the earliest record of this rendezvous was in 1695). Dr Thomson again:

The poll was to start at 9 a.m. on the 27th December. The Bailiff would not open the poll at that time because Nesbitt, the outgoing candidate, had not put in an appearance. This delay lasted for two hours, during which time Dewar's counsel directed abusive and threatening words towards the Bailiff. The poll being eventually opened, polling continued at a leasurely pace until 4 p.m. by which time only 41 votes had been counted out of 200, 26 for Dewar and 15 for Peach.

That evening there was a meeting of Peach's council and agents at the White Swan Inn, which is now a fruiterer's shop on the corner opposite the Vale Hotel [No 31 High Street], which was attended by the Bailiff's counsel. The proceedings were overheard by one, Archer, a nephew of the landlord, and a Dewar supporter. Hiding himself in the room above, Archer, through a chink in the ceiling was able to hear the plot being hatched below, which was to close the poll as soon as Peach was leading. Archer hurried off to fetch Parker, Dewar's agent, who afterwards gave evidence . . . .

The entrance to the church was crowded with people. Mr Benson was attended by the Bailiff's council. The proceedings were overheard by London merchant and a supporter of Peach, who had been made a Special Constable for the occasion, pushed against Mr Herbert MP for Wilton, when the latter grabbed him by the collar and a scuffle took place. Whereupon Peach's supporters set up the cry 'Riot! Riot!' This so frightened the Bailiff and his counsel that they decided to close the poll. Members of Dewar's party tried to persuade them to open it but without success, and Mr Herbert suggested that he and Mr Benson be placed in custody until the election was over, but the Bailiff refused to reopen the poll. The electors for Dewar decided to follow a precedent set in 1689; They went to a constable and gave their votes to him. However, Peach's supporters were informed of this, but none came to vote. The Bailiff unable to carry out his original plan, returned both candidates.

Both Peach and Dewar petitioned against this double return. The petition was heard in the House of Commons three weeks later, on the 19th January. Peach accused the Bailiff of unjustly returning both candidates and that he closed the poll just as a number of his supporters were about to cast their votes, whilst Dewar requested that Peach's name be erased as he himself had the largest number of legal votes. The Parliamentary Committee, set up to hear the petition did not accept the constable's poll, 'because by a statute of George II every voter was liable to have the bribery oath tendered to him, which he is to take before the returning Officer, or others legally deputed by him'. The Act was more honoured in the breach than in the observance by the electors of Cricklade . . . . A fresh writ was issued.

The new election began on the 28th February 1775. It lasted five days. There were three candidates! Peach and Dewar again, and Samuel Petrie, linen merchant, of Tockenham Yard, made his first appearance in the borough. Peach was returned by the Bailiff as duly elected, the poll being Peach 54, Dewar 41 and Petrie 6.

This however, was by no means the end of the affair. The story that follows becomes an object lesson, together with Petrie's Cricklade Case, on the painfully slow, evolutionary changes in our democratic system of government that is now taken very much for granted. To Crickladians, many of the places described will be all too familiar. It was not surprising that petitions were made against Peach.

One was from Dewar, one from the electors requesting that the return be amended in favour of Dewar, and one from fourteen electors who accused the Bailiff of having acted with partiality towards Peach .... Owing to Parliament being prorogued, the committee did not meet until the following February. The several parties and their agents were called. In the meantime, Dewar had gone abroad and his agent Wallis, who was also agent for the six electors, asked leave to withdraw Dewar's petition. However, as he had not received authority from the six electors for this bequest, the committee decided to try this petition and, after pressure from Petrie, they heard Dewar's petition also. There were four main points on which the committee had to give a decision:

1. What were the precise boundaries of the Borough?[1]
2. Whether new houses on old sites or new houses on new sites gave a right to vote.
3. Whether holders of a leasehold property were required to have a lease or sub-lease of at least three years not dependent upon a life or lives, or whether a three-year lessor whose lease was dependent upon lives could vote.
4. Whether forty days residence by a leaseholder before an election was the only prerequisite to the right to vote, or whether a legal settlement in one of the parishes was necessary for each type of voter. Council on both sides agreed to allow the issue to depend upon the decision of these disputed points without offering evidence upon individual cases. Both parties further agreed to accept the following as basic premises of the case:

   (a)   That the Bailiff was the proper returning officer and that he and the constables were elected before the steward of the manor of Cricklade.

   (b)   That the smaller manor of Abingdon Court, held under the Dean and Chapter of Salisbury, was within the borough and was subordinate to the manor of Cricklade.

   (c)   That the property was held on leases depending upon the lives and also on leases of three years or more, held from those who held long leases determinable upon lives.

   (d)   That Mr Nesbitt, MP for Cricklade and lord of the manor, was the avowed friend of Mr Peach, and that the appointment of the Bailiff was almost completely in his hands.

The reason for the boundary dispute was a property consisting of seven houses in Calcutt Street that stood between what is now the Cricklade Museum and the boundary stone at the bottom of the lane.[2] Peach's counsel held that as far as Calcutt Lane is concerned the old embankment (i.e. the line of the town wall) was the limit. Council for Dewar held that the borough was coextensive with the manor and that all houses were all side by side (terraced) and in possession of Thomas Pound (died 1784), Thomas Kilminster sen., Richard Liddel (died 1789), John Pound (died 1786), Robert Strange (died 1788), William Wakefield and William Matson.

William Archer, aged 65, was the first witness called. He stated that he had been born in Cricklade and had always lived there. His father, who died in 1736, had told him that the limits were: east, the meer stone at the bottom of Calcott Lane (now Calcutt Street); west, a similar stone at Horsey Down; south, the Meerstone at Stephen's West Gate; north, Weaver's Bridge. He had been constable in 1761. Thomas Bound's house was built in 1732; it had always belonged to his family. He believed it was inside the boundary and persons had voted for it. The same applied to the other six. In 1741 Thomas had gone to canvass with Welbore Ellis who said there had been a procession round the boundary once or twice in his time, but that he had never taken part. Asked if he had known the owners of the new houses vote before, Thomas replied that he had never known their votes rejected before the last election.

Oliver Adam's house in the middle of the town, William Fry's built in 1720, Mark Pyke's 1744, Edward Snell's 1720 and Nevill Simmond's (site now occupied by 90 High Street) 1755. None of these houses had been debarred before. William Archer stated that the voter must have forty days' residence; his own vote had been rejected on this ground in 1722, because he lived in the parish outside the boundary.

The second witness was John Skilling, who lived at a house that is now 39 Calcutt Street. He stated that he was appointed by the constable as a watchman in 1735. His duties were those of a London watchman and he was instructed that Thomas Kilminster's, which was the outside house, was within the boundary. He had never known new houses being objected to before. There had been a fire in 1723, and new houses built afterwards had been given a right to vote. There was no distinction between ancient and modern sites. He remembered votes being rejected for want of forty days' residence, or because the person was a pensioner. (A parishioner was a person entitled to a settlement at birth, or who had served an apprenticeship, was a servant or in covenanted service. John Crewe, born in Cricklade, gave similar evidence to Skilling.)

Other witnesses called by the petitioners were: John Hayes, baptized Cricklade 1713, who said he had lived all his life there, that he had once been bailiff, twice constable and also a watchman, he stated that sub-lessors for three years had always had a right to vote; William Giles (baptized St Sampson's 1701, son of Zachariah Giles) could remember the elections in 1720. He said that the holders of leases for three years under those who held them for ninety-nine years determinable on lives, either of feoffee lands or under Dr Heberden (lessee of Abingdon Court) had a right to vote; George Simmonds, Morgan Byrt and John Strange, gave similar evidence.

The first witness for Peach was William Saunders, born Cricklade 1702. He had known Richard Byrt (grandfather of Morgan Byrt) intimately. Old Mr Byrt had great influence in Cricklade. He knew a lot about the borough. He had given the witness the following account of the boundaries. On the south, by the Causeway leading to Purton Stoke, the boundary stone is a stone called the Borough Stone. Eastwards from that stone the boundary crosses the lane into what is called Paul's Croft and is distinguished by a bank called the Borough Bank, then turning to the north including Townsend's house it crosses Calcutt Lane (Street) into Dennis's ground where the bank appears again and runs to Abingdon Court. From Calcutt Lane the boundary leaves the bank, crosses over to Hatchett's Green, then to New Bridge, thence to Horsey Down. From Horsey Down it extends south about a furlong down the lane to the Parson's Ground, which is within the borough, and then eastward across a green or common to the Borough Stone. Old Mr Byrt had always told him that the disputed houses were outside the borough. He himself had never known any of them to serve on juries. The houses were built since the 1721 elections: he believed they were built to create votes.

A freeholder had a right to vote for a house in which he did not live, if it was his property. Thomas Hinder had voted without opposition, although he had been absent twenty years. He believed that residence was necessary in the case of a copyholder or a lease-holder.

1. The only evidence that the bank was the boundary on the east had come from two men who had long been absent from Cricklade. If the bank were taken as the borough boundary it would exclude eleven of Peach's votes, so when it suited them they extended the boundary beyond the bank.
2. If the distinction between old and new sites were well grounded, the number of electors would remain constant. This was not so.
3. On the question of leases, Peach's council had produced no evidence.

4. It was clear that forty days residence was necessary, but not so clear that a parochial settlement was necessary in the case of voters who paid less than £10 per annum.

Counsel for Peach said:

1. If the bank was acknowledged as the remains of a Roman encampment that did not disprove it also being the boundary.
2. Cricklade had probably been a burgage tenure borough, and though the franchise had been extended to leaseholders the right of voting would only rest in ancient houses.
3. Holders of at least three years' leases, though depending on life or lives, as well as freeholders and copyholders, had a right to vote if they had been in residence forty days before the election.
4. They came to no decision about parochial settlement.

The name of S. Peach was erased and that of J. Dewar substituted on the 20 February.

Dewar returned from abroad to take his seat; his name appears on a division list in 1780 when Messrs MacPherson and Dewar, and also Walboro Ellis Esq, the ex-MP for Cricklade voted to a minority of 215 against 238 in opposition to Mr Dunning's motion for amending the abuses in the public expenditure.

Notes

1. The boundaries of the borough expanded for two reasons, the first was to include as many houses as possible that carried a parliamentary vote, and the second was to extend the right to free pasture in the North Meadow. The borough was originally enclosed in the line of the walls. Its expansion in the eighteenth century is shown by Byrt's map in the Cricklade Museum, and by the semi-legal description of its limits given in the nineteenth-century document of uncertain origin, also in the Museum. One of the meer stones of the enlarged boundary was at the Town Bridge, which was removed when the feoffees built the present bridge.
2. This must mean the street – Calcutt Street – and the bottom would presumably have been Spittals Lane, which is on the other side. To the best of my recollection there are seven houses there still. I heard somewhere the lane was called Spittals because a hospital was once there.

18   Petrie's Cricklade Case

> They wouldn't be sufficiently degraded in their own estima-
> tion unless they were insulted by a very substantial bribe.
> Sir William Schwenk Gilbert (1836–1911)

Petrie's Cricklade Case was one that made history and that
Cricklade has never quite forgotten. After no fewer than nineteen
trials, of which only one will be reproduced here, the following Act,
(George III, XXII, *c*. 31) received royal assent on 17 May 1782, and
nothing of note that could compare with these outstanding events
has ever happened in Cricklade since that time.

I. An Act for preventing of bribery and corruption in the election of
members to serve in Parliament for the Borough of Cricklade in the
County of Wilts. Whereas there was the most notorious bribery and
corruption at the last election of Burgesses to serve in Parliament
for the Borough of Cricklade, in the County of Wilts., and whereas
such bribery and corruption is likely to continue, and be practised in
the said Borough in the future, unless some means are taken to
prevent the same and in order therefore to prevent such unlawful
practices for the future and that the said Borough may, from henceforth, be duly represented in Parliament, be it enacted by the King's
most excellent majesty by and with the advice and consent of the
Lords, spiritual and temporal, and Commons in this present
Parliament assembled, and by the authority of the same – That from
henceforth it may and shall be lawful, to and for every freeholder,
being above the age of 21 years, who shall have within the hundreds
of Highworth, Cricklade, Staple, Kingsbridge and Malmesbury, or
one or more of them in the County of Wilts, a freehold of the clear
duty yearly of forty shillings to give his vote at every election of a
Burgess or Burgesses to serve in Parliament for the said Borough of
Cricklade.

II. And be it further enacted by the Authority aforesaid that the right of election of a member or members to serve in Parliament for the said Borough of Cricklade; shall be and is hereby declared to be in such freeholders as aforesaid, and in the persons who by the custom and usage of the said Borough have or shall have hereafter a right to vote at such an election; and the proper Officer for the time being to whom the return of every writ or process does belong, is hereby required to return the person or persons to serve in Parliament for the said Borough who shall have the major number of votes of such freeholders and other persons having a right to vote at such an election, any law or usage to the contrary not withstanding.

III. Provided always that such freeholders only shall be entitled to vote as shall be duly qualified to vote at elections for Knights of the Shire for the said County of Wilts. according to the laws now in being for regulating County elections.

IV. And he is further enacted by the authority aforesaid, that every such freeholder before he be admitted to poll at any election for the said Borough shall, if required by the Candidates or any of them, or any person having a right to vote at the said election, first take the oath, or being one of the people called Quakers, the Solemn affirmation following, viz, 'I do swear, (or being a Quaker, solemnly affirm) that I as a freeholder in the hundred and division of Highworth, Cricklade, Staple, Malmesbury and Kingsbridge, or any or more of them in the County of Wilts and have a freehold estate consisting of specifying the nature thereof, and if it contained messuages, lands, tenements or tithes in whose occupation the same are, and if in rent, the names of the owner or possessors of the tenements out of which rent is issuing or of some of them situate or being — in the aforesaid hundred or dim visions, or in one or more of them, if the clear value of forty shillings over and above all rents and charges payable out of or in respect of the same, and that I have been in actual possession or receipt of rents and profits thereof for my own use, above twelve calendar months, (or that the same came to me within the time aforesaid by descent, marriage settlement, devise, or promotion to a benefice in the Church, or by promotion to an office) and that such freehold estate has not been granted or made to me fraudulently on purpose to qualify me to give my vote, and that the place of abode is at, in, and that I am 21 years of age, as I believe, and that I have not been polled before at this election. Which oath or solemn affirmation the proper officer to whom the return of every writ or precept for such an election shall belong, is hereby required to administer, and in case any freeholder, or other person taking the said oath or affirmation, hereby appointed, shall thereby commit wilful perjury, and be thereof convicted, or if any shall unlawfully and corruptly procure or suborn any freeholder or other person to take the said oath or affirmation in order to be polled, whereby he shall commit such wilful perjury, and shall be convicted thereof, he and they, for every such offence respectively, shall incur such penalties by two Acts of Parliament, first made in the fifth year of the reign of Queen Elizabeth, intitled, etc, and the other made in the second year of the reign of his late Majesty, King George the Second.

V. And be it further enacted by the authority aforesaid, that such proper officer, to which any writ to precept shall be directed for making any election for the said borough, shall upon receipt of such writ or precept, endorse upon the back thereof the day of the receipt thereof, in the presence of the party from whom he received such precept and shall forthwith cause public notice to be given within the said borough of Cricklade and the several towns of Highworth, Staple, Malmesbury and Wootton Bassett by affixing up a notice thereof in writing on the market houses, or on the doors of the Churches of the said towns of the day of the election, and shall proceed to election thereupon within the space of 12 days and not less than eight days, next after his receipt of the said precept.

VI. And be it further enacted by the authority aforesaid, that the Act shall be publicly read at every election for the said borough of Cricklade immediately after the Acts directed by the Act of Parliament to be read thereat, and before the persons present shall proceed to make such election.

The trial (out of nineteen enacted) and the preparations for the 1780 election at Cricklade are described as follows:

1780   *21 George III*
Paul Benfield, John MacPherson, Hon. George Richard St John (vice MacPherson)

The preparations for this election began in January 1780. MacPherson was the first candidate to start preparing the ground. His agent, a farmer named Bristow (of whom we shall be hearing a great deal more later) lived at Broadleaze Farm, a mile from the centre of Cricklade on the Purton road. On the 4 January, Bristow went to Thomas Mann Gunn, landlord of the White Swan and ordered him to light a fire in the bar parlour for Mr Adams his brother in law (postmaster and cattle dealer) and himself, as they were 'going to pay the voters their fives'. When the room was ready a large number of the electors of Cricklade came into the room singly and Bristow gave each of them five guineas. He told them that the money was given on behalf of Col. Herbert. Each had to sign a note of hand payable to Col. Herbert. Those who demurred were told, either that it was necessary in order to make the payment appear as a loan and not a gift, but that if they voted for MacPherson they would hear no more of it, or that the note was merely a kind of receipt so that Bristow might not be suspected of pocketing the money, a habit which was apparently popular among agents at that time.

The distribution of 'fives' went on for nights without any attempt at concealment by donor or recipients. Gunn, the landlord into whose pockets most of the money found its way, named 126 of the Cricklade electorate who had acknowledged Col. Herbert's beneficence in his presence. Seventy-five had been heard by others to admit receipt of the money. Thomas Hayward, being a lunatic, was not paid in cash, but Bristow told Gunn he had bought him clothes, which Hayward confirmed. William Pinnock and William Cuss received five guineas between them as each lived half the year in the same house. At the poll Cuss's vote was rejected. Gunn himself received the money. The distribution was held up at times for lack of change; at one time a draft for £40 had to be sent to Cirencester to be cashed.

Col. Herbert arrived in Cricklade on the 8 January, which was a Sunday, John Skillin went round the town inviting certain people to meet Col. Herbert at the Swan. After the glasses had been refilled several times, Skillin rose and addressed the company. He hoped that all present would support Col. Herbert or his friend at the next election. The suggestion was well received. Col. Herbert, however, was not satisfied; he went outside with Skillin and asked him to make the suggestion that he would nominate both candidates. Skillin returned to the room alone and put this before the company, who were definitely against it, considering that five guineas was not enough to cover nomination of more than one candidate. On hearing of this decision the Colonel tried to appear content, but he could not conceal his anger and he left the town the following day.

The distribution of money continued for another two weeks, stopped until other candidates appeared, and then carried on until a few weeks before the election. Those who had not had money were regarded by their less scrupulous fellows with scorn. They were known as 'Gridiron Men'.[1] Gridirons were chalked on the doors of their houses. The number of gridirons diminished from the original one hundred to about thirty or forty as the election date approached. Thomas Hunt, a supporter of a candidate named

Grant, sketched eighty gridirons and some time afterwards was asked by Saunders to make a wooden one with ten bars, symbolic of the ten guineas that were promised to Grant's supporters.

Hunt, who seems to have been a painstaking craftsman, made the gridiron and covered it with gold leaf. Myers, Grant's agent, was so pleased with the gridiron that he purchased ribbons from Tombs the draper, bedecked the gridiron, and formed a procession around the town. This was previous to Grant's canvass of the town. The gridiron was then hung from the signpost by the White Hart, kept by Hollister Forrester. Bristow asked Forrester to take it down. Forrester's reply was that it was a peculiar lock and to open it required a golden key with five wards. This key was obtained from the Swan and the gridiron was taken down.

Col. Herbert returned to Cricklade about ten days before the election to introduce his nominee, MacPherson. He stayed with Morgan Byrt, who lived at the house 23 High Street (occupied by Dr T.R. Thomson in Cricklade until his death). Byrt, Herbert and the Revd Edward Campbell, curate of both parishes and schoolmaster, canvassed the borough on MacPherson's behalf, after which Herbert again left Cricklade.

Paul Benfield and Samuel Petrie arrived about this time. Benfield soon became the favourite candidate. His cousin, Crook Godby, landlord of the White Horse Inn, arranged with the bellringers that each time Benfield visited the town they would ring a peal. His local connections, coupled with his seemingly unlimited funds, were responsible for his popularity. In order to obtain the necessary qualification he had bought property from William Packer, another relation. Godby is reputed to have made over to him some of his houses in the town, and he was negotiating for the purchase of the town manor from the late Arnold Nesbitt's trustees. All Nesbitt's tenants were informed of this imminent change of landlord and requested to vote for him.

Benfield, Packer and Godby acted as agents, also Jonathan White, who was notoriously corrupt and therefore esteemed by the Cricklade electors. White did not have anything to do with payments or promissory notes. In his canvass for Benfield he told voters that 'all was right', and they need not fear 'that everything would be as they wished'. No amount was mentioned, White simply tapped the ground with his stick a certain number of times. The electors knew this language perfectly. Benfield engaged every public house in Cricklade except the Swan and ordered them to keep open houses. Benfield and MacPherson soon joined forces and carried out a joint canvass.

Petrie's arrival on the 7 November 1780 caused a rift between Gunn and Bristow, because Gunn took Petrie into his house. This so incensed Col. Herbert that he withdrew his patronage from the Swan and opened the Kings Head in opposition. Many attempts were made during the subsequent lawsuits to paint Petrie as black as his two opponents, but without success. Petrie seems to have confined his canvass to reminding electors of his behaviour in the last election when he had been responsible for the successful petition against the return of Samuel Peach. This form of approach was not much appreciated by the Crickladians, accustomed as they were to more concrete reasons for their support. Grant, the only other candidate who had attempted to compete, left the town soon after Petrie's arrival.

The election took place on the 11 September. It lasted six hours. The state of the poll was Benfield 202, MacPherson 172 and Petrie 21. The bill paid by Bristow for the election dinner and ribbons was £300.

If Petrie, because of moral scruples or lack of money, could not compete with his nabob opponents before the election, the grim determination with which he set about them after the election proved him a redoubtable opponent in a court of law.

The verbatim account of the nineteen trials that compose the 'Cricklade Case', collected by Samuel Petrie and published in 1785, consisted of 488 pages of small, closely-spaced print.

Petrie versus Bristow, Townsend and others

Petrie began his attack on the 13 March 1781 at the last Assizes at Salisbury, before Sir Richard Perryn, when he sued anyone convicted of having given or received a bribe for election purposes, as well as depriving them of the right to vote or hold public office subsequently.

The first witness called Richard Townsend, returning officer (bailiff, draper and grocer), stated that Col. Herbert had some old houses in Cricklade, bought about 1777. He said that all the inhabitants of Cricklade frequented public houses at times. He was obviously determined not to remember anything prejudicial to the members who had been returned.

Morgan Byrt, Captain of Militia, living at what is now 23 High Street, equally reluctant, admitted that he had 'lent' money for Col. Herbert.

Richard Adams, postmaster, mentioned many persons who he

knew had received money. He stated that some of the gridirons were still visible on doors of those who had not received any money from Bristow.

Thomas Townsend (sen.) admitted having received £5 5s. Mr Bristow did not explain what the money was for. They knew that before. His son Thomas received money at the same time but his other son George had not got any.

Charles Robins said he borrowed £1 1s from Bristow to pay his debts; he afterwards had £4 4s from Mr Byrt. He had not repaid the money. He expected to be called on to pay it. His vote was rejected at the election.

At this juncture in the proceedings there was a change. Witnesses, realizing that Petrie's counsel was content with an acknowledgement that a loan had been received, suddenly lost their memory.

Charles Simmonds knew nothing of other people's business. Charles Smith said he had no money and knew nothing of anyone else. Francis Pocock and Henry Garlick knew nothing of themselves or anyone else and Thomas Tombs would not answer.

The following witnesses all used the same reply. Thomas Horne, William Lucas, George Powell, Edward Little, John Smith, Stephen Slatter and Stephen Hopkins all said: 'I know nothing of Mr Bristow's concerns.' Thomas Davis, who voted for Petrie and Benfield, said he had gone to the White Swan with John Carter and that as they sat drinking, Bristow called them in and gave them five guineas each. He signed a note; Bristow said he would never be asked for the money.

Thomas Mann Gunn, who was to be the most-called witness of the succeeding lawsuits, said he had kept the White Swan for seven years. Bristow had paid bills for the meetings that Col. Herbert had held in his house. Gunn gave evidence of systematic corruption by Bristow. Mrs Gunn gave evidence similar to her husband.

A verdict was given for Petrie against Bristow for £5,000, being £500 each in the case of T. Townsend, C. Smith, H. Burchell, T. James, C. Boulton, F. Fitcher, H. Haywood, W. Strange, R. Eyles and W. Beale.

An unsuccessful application for a new trial was made by Bristow on 1 May 1781. Judgement was signed against him on 19 May 1781 and Petrie proceeded to take possession of his property near Cricklade. On 29 May a jury was sworn in the premises to decide to whom they belonged. George Adams (see above) claimed the stock as his and claimed the freehold to belong to Mr Charles Meadows from whom he said he rented it. After two days the jury decided the whole property, valued at £180 per annum, belonged to Bristow, and handed it over, together with the stock, valued at £326, to Petrie's agent. A few days after, the people left in charge on Petrie's behalf were forcibly ejected by George Adams and others. Petrie brought an action for recovery in the King's Bench, and filed a bill in Chancery to test the alleged sale to Meadows. Petrie did not bring the action to trial, and in July 1783 he executed a release to Bristow and closed all proceedings against him. John Bristow was buried in St Sampson's in 1788. His memorial plaque is on the east wall of the Widhill Aisle.

Petrie's second and main attack was his famous action against the voters of Cricklade who had accepted bribes, which was tried at Salisbury on the day following the Porchester Case, 1 August 1781. The defendants numbered 113: all pleaded not guilty. In order to facilitate the trial Barron Perryn, who had finished the business of the Crown Court on the previous day, helped his colleague, Judge Buller. The defendants were tried twelve at a time, six in one court and six in the other. The outcome of the trial was that judgement was given against 83 of the defendants tried, out of 105.

Towards the end of the proceedings, Petrie's counsel consented to withdraw his case against the remaining eight. The main witness for the plaintiff was Thomas Mann Gunn, who was so much in demand that the trial in one court was often held up until he had finished giving his evidence in the other. Judge Buller, in his summing up, stated that if he had found Gunn prevaricating in the slightest particular he would have rejected his evidence completely, but he failed to find any grounds for setting it aside, especially as it was confirmed by George Townsend, who seemed a credible witness. As well as being a very able witness, Gunn must have been a brave man. He was in Cricklade in 1791. The 83 verdicts, each for £500 represent a total of £41,000. That Petrie never expected to be paid a penny of this sum was evident from the opening words of his counsel, who said that there was never a case when the proverb 'Sue a beggar and catch a louse' was more applicable.

Notes

1. It is possible the gridiron was mindful of its association with the stage; the hanging ropes operated by the stagehands, or because of its historical significance as an instrument of torture, as opposed to a gridiron's usual function of the grilling over a fire. Fear therefore, may well have prevented these people from acceptance of bribes, hence the description attributed to them.

19 Latton, Wiltshire

Now have the abbeys their payment?
A new way they found to invent
Letting a dozen farms under one,
Which one of two rich Franklins
Occupying a dozen men's livings
Take all in their own hands alone.

It has been seen that the 1517 Domesday of Enclosures came to mean that tenant evictions were as common by ecclesiastical owners as from private estates 'while the average rental value of lands let by ecclesiastics are higher'.[1] Sir Thomas More accused the abbeys of creating pasture out of tillage and the general dissatisfaction resulted in popular rhymes like the above.

Henry de Hamtonel must have appreciated the richness of the meadows around the village when, in 1305 he made an agreement with John de Latton:

> We have granted John de Latton and Isobel his wife these several things hereafter specified, to receive each week so long as they shall jointly live: fourteen white loaves and nine gallons of beer, whereof five gallons shall be such as the convent uyseth, and the other four gallons shall be of the chaplians beer, and they shall receive one mess every day out of our kitchen, in like manner as our day-officers receive it out of our house.

If Isobel was left a widow she was to receive a half. For this John released his Latton lands to its church, held in lease by his father from Cirencester Abbey. The document is an early example of an annuity, and we cannot help wondering for how long the de Lattons, who it seems were childless, lived to enjoy this 'manna from Heaven' and such quantities of beer for which they sold their birthright. However, as Fred Thacker (op.cit.) has said 'it was only common sense to live as well as they could and to benefit the Church at their death'.

The origins of Latton are not at all clear. John de Latton's ancestry, if it was of Norman French origin, as seems to have been most likely, cannot now be traced; it is not a name in William of Normandy's Castle of Falaise, nor does it appear on the so-called Battle Abbey Rolls. The possibility, however, that his family name was given to the village, as for example was that of the de Keynes, cannot be ruled out, but that it was taken from it, as was that of Poole. Although Latton, Wilts., is not listed in *English Place-Names*, a Latton, Essex, is detailed, which might mean (in Old English) 'a leak enclosure', hence 'a herb garden', with no evidence for the more general meaning 'kitchen garden, vegetable garden' until later in Medieval English. The name is lost in the mists of time and, like so many others, open to many interpretations. It is not listed as a family name by either Bardsley or P.H. Reaney.

The Prior of the Hospital of John the Baptist in Cricklade held lands in Latton and at the time of the Confessor the Cricklade Hundred included lands in both Latton and Eisey.

Thacker called Latton a pleasant little village in the midst of orchards sitting astride the Ermin Way a mile or two north-west of Cricklade. 'I do not think I know,' he wrote, 'another village that so closely embowers itself in clumps of lofty trees; a soothing place if you have come hither from sun-smitten Cricklade.'

The headless village cross with its tapering octagonal shaft stands in the middle of the wide road leading down to the church of St John the Baptist and the track beyond, which runs through the park to Down Ampney. Its two lower steps are lost, it has been said, by continuous road surfacing, leaving it at its original level. The Ancient Monuments Branch of the then Ministry of Works, declared it a protected building, with a temporary sign which, on their behalf I, personally, attached to it in c.1958.[2]

Aubrey found nothing in Latton's lovely old church 'proper for the observation of the antiquary'. As has been mentioned in the case of Ashton Keynes and Kemble, this church too has suffered at the hands of its restorers. One writer has stated 'In passing I may say that a modern architect (c.1860) "restored" and cruelly mutilated this building and others about here; and in doing so threw away, as his evil habit was, all these little white marble memorials as rubbish; though happily they were remembered and rescued.' One he refers to reads: '*Juxta parentes Hic requiescit* MARIA DUNN, *Edvardi uxor Pia, Placens, Pudica, Proba: Puerperio taman in fefelix. Et in Sui Damnum faecunda Marti cessit to Sbris AD 1743'*

The headless village cross at Latton

It is known that a fourteenth century secular priest, who was continually at odds with his fellows in Cirencester, had a wall fresco painted showing a wolf dressed in a friar's robe preaching to his flock, while the vicar stood by. This was in existence until about 1870 when, like many other objects of great interest, it was intentionally destroyed to the sorrow of all those who loved the church. There is a corbel representing a wolf's head on the south wall of the nave. The timber to the roof is dated *c*.1400. I remember that a further sacrilege occurred in this church, at sometime in the 1960s, when a large framed painting in oils that had hung on the south wall of the nave went missing. I do not believe it has ever been found.

The registers date from April 1576,[3] when on the 14th of that month, 'John Ware, the sonne of Thomas Ware was baptised Anno Domini 1576', the Revd Randall Ashton being 'Vicker'. (Incidentally there is a field in the village known as Ware's Close.) Legend has it that the last squire of that name, who died about a century and a half ago, was reported to have been seen in the village street when he was in fact on his death-bed at home. After 1653 the Latin phrase *Anno Domini* ceased to be used in some registers, to be replaced by English, with a revival to the Latin after the Restoration.

Latton was called Latinelud by Leland; it was a rival with Lechlade for the Latin college that coexisted with the Greek School at Cricklade. When Thacker made what was possibly the last of his many visits to these parts very early in the twentieth century, he gave us an interesting story of the path that begins from Ermin Street. The first part of this is now a track leading to the modern Lake Louise Park housing estate after which it turns sharply left handed, and is very narrow for about a hundred metres between high stone walls, until terminating near the end of Gosditch Lane, almost opposite to the church. He writes:

> A little pathway in the village called the Mere, running parallel with the Gosditch and not wide enough for wheeled traffic is of curious interest in that by immemorial custom nothing but a coffin is allowed to be borne along it. It is thought to have been an old church path along the boundary of the Abbot of Cirencester's land; maintained dry and paved at the church's expense in case floods and mud should make Gosditch Lane (by which you come from the cross and which in living memory was lined with a wide ditch or pond) impossible for churchgoers.

Latton had two mills, both mentioned in Domesday. One has long since vanished whilst the other was still standing on the Churn near the canal bridge at the beginning of the twentieth century. A part of this is today known as the Old Mill House, and is occupied by Diana Holmes, a prominent local historian.[4]

A century ago there was a tale still circulating of a hare, put up by hounds, which when caught changed into an old woman sitting combing her grey locks. Her name was Barbara Hannah, and the locals suspected her of witchcraft. The mark of the hounds' teeth remained with her until her death, it was said. She was rather a character in the village and many tales circulated about her.

Coins found in the village were said to have been discovered in rather strange circumstances: a cottager came across a dog sniffing at a stone, which he raised to discover the coins. The dog vanished and was not seen again.

Thacker, who we have to thank for recording so much of the local history of the Upper Thames area that might otherwise have been lost for ever, writes of some poor fellow in the village (*c*.1907):

> who had fallen into rapid consumption. He took some of 'them things as you finds under sto-ans' as pills, and recovered but died of summat else dree months arter'. It would not be surprising if the pills turned out to be live woodlice. Odd local expressions are to a child: 'Don't yer get a-oondermenting with that there,' meaning don't meddle. 'Tis so burrow', that is to say, ''tis a nice hedge, it burrows the garden', 'in the burrow', on the sheltered side; 'I keeps some in ambush', in reserve, but these good old people have gone or are passing away and their delicious Anglo-Saxon with them. As one of them not long dead remarked; 'You don't hear a man say a lo-ad of hay now, but lode'.

Now, the best part of a century after Fred Thacker wrote the foregoing, he would have been surprised to learn that many of these terms are still widely used.

Thacker gives us a slightly different version of that part of Sergeant Foster's letter during the Civil War when he writes of the allusion to Latton: 'Saturday, September 16th [1643]: We advanced from Cicester five miles to a village called Letton; Where were ten cart load of cavaliers, who were sick and lame, and brought thither to be quartered, who when they heard we were marching to this place, they then found their legs and run away.' Thacker thought this was a little barrack-room joke, connected with the recapture of Cirencester by the Parliament forces that autumn.

Until 1820 Eisey had its own incumbents under the patronage of the Abbot of Cirencester and others after which the incumbency was jointly held with that of Latton. There are records of three of these: 1820, Henry James Barton MA, BNC Oxon Vicar of Latton cum Eisey; 1838, Hyde Wyndham Beadob, Vicar of Latton cum Eisey in plurality with other livings; 1893, William Philpot Andrews, BA, Jesus College, Cambridge; on the death of Canon Beadon.

At one time the darkly clad and slightly bent figure of the Revd Claude Tickell might once have been seen in all weathers leaving his Latton vicarage to take the Mere path towards Ermin Street and to walk parallel with the (by that time) derelict Thames and Severn Canal in the direction of Cricklade. He would leave it just short of Weavers Bridge which crosses the Churn, get over a stile to the canal tow path, which he would then follow to Eisey. Then his journey had to take him between the hamlet's few cottages and climb the Gastons to reach his little hilltop church up among its ancient elms. How did he feel, one might ask as he trudged his weary way home again on the many occasions when his little church had been found to be empty and deserted. By that time – the 1930s – the decline in church worship everywhere had already begun with the lowliest and smallest churches emptying first; it was a condition that rapidly accelerated when the Second World War was over.

After the Dissolution, hay from Latton was provided by Cirencester Abbey for sheep at Aldsworth all of eighteen miles away, and although the Roman roads of Ermin Street and the Fosse Way were in general use, it would have been quite a journey with a horse and wagon for such a distance at a time when roads – Roman roads notwithstanding – were still no more than very rough tracks.

Probably no person other than William Cobbett has ever brought home to us so vividly the conditions of the poor in his day, and it was when he was taking a part of this route on Ermin Street on his way to Gloucester that on 6 November 1821 he described what he saw:

> They are sewing wheat all the way from the Wiltshire Downs to Cirencester. The labourers are very poor indeed. In a group of women labourers who were attending the measurers to measure their recent work, presented such an assemblage of rags as I never saw even amongst the hoppers at Farnham, many of whom are common beggars, I never saw country people, and reapears too observe, so miserable in appearance as these. There are some pretty girls, but ragged as colts and as pale as ashes. The day and frost barely off the ground, and their blue arms and lips would have made any heart ache but that of a seat-seller or loan-jobber. A little after passing by these poor things whom I left cursing as I went, those who had brought them to this poor state.

He found conditions much improved as he approached Gloucester, after not trusting his horse enough to remain on its back down Birdlip Hill but walking by its side:

> 'All here is fine, fine farms, fine pastures; all enclosed fields, all divided by hedges and the labourers themselves pretty well as to dress and comliness. The girls at work in the fields (always my standard) are not in rags with bits of shoes tied on their feet and rags tied round their ankles, as they had in Wiltshire.'

Notes

1. *RHS Domesday of Enclosures*, pp. 48, 65.
2. For many years I had the pleasure of my firm, H.J. Cuss Ltd., carrying out numerous works for the ministry including the Cricklade Town Walls, the 1961 excavations at Knapp Hill and others in North Wiltshire and South Gloucestershire, *Vide*, chapter 11.
3. A decree in 1538 by Thomas Cromwell stated that the clergy of all parishes should keep a weekly record of all births, marriages and deaths, but through idleness or poor communications, not all parishes began to keep records at the appointed date.
4. Holmes, Diana, *Cricklade* (Alan Sutton Publishing, 1993) a beautifully illustrated book.

20 Down Ampney, Gloucestershire

Those villages of soft grey stone,
With churches, oh so old.
That nestle there among the trees,
And shelter from the wold.

They say that God's in Gloucestershire
And I've no doubt 'tis so,
For o'er the land both far and wide,
What better place to go?
Things Dear to the Country Heart
George Shipway (1914–88)

This pleasant Gloucestershire village, is not watered by Thames river itself but by its tributary the Ampney Brook, after which it is named, and joins the Thames by the historic Eisey Hill near Cricklade. Nevertheless, like one or two other villages included in this book, it has such a close affinity with the parent river, both geographically and with its people that perhaps it merits a chapter of its own. Down Ampney is what the name implies, a place lower down, and taken from the Ampney Brook which rises about a mile and a half east of Cirencester, near Norcote. Other Ampneys on this stream are Ampney Crucis, Ampney St Peter and Ampney St Mary. From whichever direction one enters this long straggling village, it becomes obvious that it belongs to the Cotswolds and not to the Thames valley. Its dwellings are of stone or imitation stone, locally known as Bradstone which is produced at South Cerney by E.H. Bradley & Sons and is found in buildings all along the valley. Brick-built dwellings or houses of stone with brick quoins or other admixtures of these materials (that planners but a short distance north of

181

the Thames and in this village would never readily permit) can be found everywhere near the river. Here the subsoil is the Oxford clay, about 100 feet deep, and brick manufacture was an important part of the area's economy for many hundreds of years until modern methods of production and improved road haulage gradually phased out the hand-made product, so that by the Second World War local manufacture of bricks had practically ceased.

Historians will associate Down Ampney with a meeting or meetings, of Augustine with the Welsh Bishops.[1] The evidence for such a meeting or meetings is very strong. On a spot where now stands only a large barn, marked on the *Landranger* Map No. 163 at GR109859, and on the older maps as 'The Oak', a meeting almost certainly took place. It was once known locally as Oak Barn.

Bishop Browne when speaking at a meeting in Bristol in May 1914 with the Workers Educational Association, told of his visit to The Oak and of finding there the roots of a great tree which, 'like the other had been shamefully destroyed'.[2] The good bishop's opinion was that it was here, near Down Ampney, that the original meeting took place and the second at Gospel Oak. An opinion, writes J. Lee Osborne, 'that was held by other authorities.'

There is a well at The Oak, known as Lertol's Well[3] having apparently existed for many years. This well was sealed with a plaque to commemorate its strongly believed historical association with St Augustine. When the airfield was constructed sadly this was, in its turn, covered in concrete, and so I believe it still remains. Bede tells us that the meetings with the bishops took place in order to plan the best means of teaching Christianity to the pagans, as well as to discuss the many ecclesiastical observances, in particular that of a date for keeping Easter. However, the story goes that there was a disagreement with the Welsh bishops who 'did not comply with the entreatism, exhortations and rebukes of Augustine', but proposed to settle the matter by performing a miracle stating that whoever carried out this successfully would be deemed to be right in his views. A blind man being brought forward, the prayers of the Welsh proved unavailing, but on Augustine beginning to pray, the man's sight was restored. In spite of this the meeting broke up without full accord. In conclusion J. Lee Osborne writes:

> It is impossible to visit Down Ampney or Gospel Oak Farm without calling up these scenes. We picture Augustine and his monks, with their silver cross and painted board; we can see the venerable men seated under the shade of that spreading tree in the forest clearing, with,

doubtless, some of the wild Saxons and their blind man – one wonders how he came to be there – gathered round. Then the appeal to a miracle, and the astonishing result; was it all right, we would like to know? Then the second meeting, the angry dispute and the parting. This story of Augustine, told here of necessity so briefly, is no more legend. It is a living parable today, as all history is, for those who read it.

Queen Elizabeth I passed through Cricklade on her way 'to Donameny one Friday night, being the first of September 1592', from Lydiard Tregoze, and Diana Holmes,[4] tells us her massive retinue consisted of '1,000 horses and perhaps 200 carts'. Her way would have been by the old route along the Pry Lane and across the Dance Forty into Cricklade. Here Dr Thomson (op.cit.) considers it reasonable to believe that she would have inspected the new tower of St Sampson's Church, then rebuilding, and so continued along the High Street and the causeway to Ermin Street where, in about half a mile she would have turned past the village cross through Latton. There the concourse, probably reaching a half way from Cricklade to Latton, would have lumbered slowly past the church and across what is now known as Down Ampney Park, a muddy track, as it still remains today. Never before and never since can this beautiful parkland have seen such a pageant of colour – but now with a locked gate at one end to prevent its use by vehicular traffic – and so to her destination, Down Ampney Manor at the near end by the village church.

The cross at Down Ampney

All Saints' Church at Down Ampney

The church of All Saints was consecrated in 1265, its handsome spire having been added in the fourteenth century. It seems that some restoration work and certain rebuilding took place in 1863, for this was the Victorian Age, and Britain found herself in a period of comparative peace and prosperity. All along our valley during the renaissance of the church in the 19th century, other churches, from Kemble down to Lechlade were at one time or another in this fever of restoration. In their order Poole Keynes was the first in 1845, followed by Latton and Kempsford in 1860; Castle Eaton, South Cerney and Cricklade St Mary's came next in 1862, Down Ampney in 1863, Cricklade St Sampson's, 1864, Somerford Keynes, 1875, Ashton Keynes, 1876 and Lechlade 1882.

One cannot do better than to quote Fred Thacker's enthusiasm for this beautiful church of Down Ampney, as he found it in the opening years of the twentieth century:

Externally the church favours Kemble, though the tower and spire are better proportioned to each other. Within it is wonderful, quite wonderful to behold and to dream in. There is the rood staircase and the screen, and on high the rood loft delicately carved in beautiful wood, crowned with a crucifix and the two Marys. The triple lancet windows at the east end are delightful in themselves, and their fascination is intensified by the tender colours of the glass, which glow so softly in the mystic half-light of the chancel. The church is a relic of Templar architecture, and a knight in chain armour with palmer's shells on his shield lies in the south transept: Sir Nicholas de Villers, who held the manor in 1287, and from whom the Villiers, Dukes of Buckingham descended. Beyond him a woman rests beneath a canopy, similar in shape to that of Maisey Hampton.[5] From the transept a hagioscope[6] looks through upon the altar. There is some fine wood carving; the old work, including the 'Sir Anthony Hungerford' of the carved wood screen across the north transept, is from the minstrels' gallery in the old banqueting hall of the House, now divided up, I hear, into smaller apartments. There is a fine old chest to be seen marked RKG W 1630 CW; and a splendid Bible on the reading desk, printed by the artist John Baskerville in 1763. It is very interesting to behold a quantity of the sculpture left unfinished on the Early English capitals . . . . Towards the west end is an inscription to Sir John Hungerford, who died in 1634, set up to the memory and as a *Memento Mori* for himself, by his son, Sir Anthony Hungerford, who married Elizabeth Lucy, daughter of Thomas Lucy of Charlcote.

There are two effigies kneeling, beneath a Renaissance canopy to Cesar Chandeler 1754 and his wife 1752. Of the church plate the chalice is 1578, there are two patons dated 1654 and 1717 and a flagon of 1727. The stained glass south-west window of the side aisle is dated 1962 and is by Christopher Webb.

Within the church there is a Roman sarcophagus, and it is believed that somewhere near at hand there exists a Roman cemetery; one such stone coffin was found at Driffield, two miles away to the north-west and is in the Corinium Museum in Cirencester.

The church has a window to the memory of Ralph Vaughan Williams, who composed the well-known hymn tune for 'Come down, oh Love Divine, seek thou this soul of mine . . .' and carries with it for evermore the name of his birthplace Down Ampney. He was born in 1872, the son of the incumbent parson, in the 'new vicarage' built fifteen years earlier in the middle of the village, which is now a private residence. The present incumbent lives in South Cerney. The 'old vicarage' nearer to the church, was north of Down Ampney House and has long since been pulled down.

'The Arnhem Window' in the church is dedicated to the men and women of the First and Sixth Airborne Division of the Royal Air Force who took part together with the Air Dispatch Groups, RASC, in the operations from the Down Ampney Airfield in 1944–5. Two other stained glass windows can now be seen on either side; these were restored after being discovered beneath a side altar having been placed there after the building of the new vestry.

Friends of the village, Mr and Mrs Martin Gibbs made a gift of ten thousand pounds to the church. The beautiful window of St Martin and St Anne was given in their memory by their family. Other gifts included the altar, the rood screen, a picture in the Lady Chapel and the priest's stalls.

The screen and roodloft mentioned by Thacker are among the finest, and are carved in oak, with little angels and vine borders as well as a fan-vaulted cnaopy, matching the canopied pulpit. Before 1640 the rood screen of Jacobean oak stood in Cirencester Parish Church. The figure of Sir Nicholas de Villers, which Thacker mentioned, is with a shield and sword, his legs crossed and feet resting upon his dog; the woman next to him in a paler stone is the serene figure of his daughter with her hands placed together. Sir Nicholas settled in Down Ampney, to assist the Knights Hospitallers in the building of the church, after fighting in the last crusade. A carving of the Holy Lamb is on the wall at the east end of the nave. Looking out from the fifteenth century porch are two little faces. Two scratch dials can be seen on the tower, one with three rays and the other with seven.

The Manor gardens are bordered with a fine, high yew hedge

against the churchyard, as if it was desirable to shut out day to day reminders of mortality from view.

The Down Ampney
Airfield memorial

There is another memorial to those who lost their lives in the Arnhem landings. It stands at the outer edge of the long since deserted perimeter track at Down Ampney Airfield. This is at a point at the end of the main runway, across which they flew in the American Dakotas, with their Horsa gliders in tow, packed with troops and equipment. It was just one small part of that great air armada in those memorable days of September 1944. I saw Dakotas flying down within a metre or two of the ground with towing hook dropped to lock on to the 300 foot-long nylon rope attached to the glider – itself too heavy to be lifted by one man and measuring three to four inches in girth – suspended between two slender poles, which fell to earth when hit by the glider's wings. The nose of this sturdy twin-engined aircraft, affectionately known as the RAF's workhorse, could be seen to dip momentarily earthwards as it took the enormous strain, before righting itself and taking its charge into the sky. The training was of course to enable gliders of this great operation, known as 'Market Garden', to be picked up from the battlefield and brought back home again. Needless to say, few ever made it.

Down Ampney airfield, like most of the others mentioned above in the south and west (with the exception of Fairford, Keevil and Brize Norton), is no more. In 1993, only portions of the perimeter track were left to remind those who were once familiar with the numerous buildings that stood there close to the edge of the village, from the administration block to the large, well-equipped hospital, that so much activity could ever have gone on there.

At the beginning of the twentieth century there remained two fields at Oak Barn that were still known as The Wicks, reputedly named after the Iron Age tribe the Hwicce that once dwelt in the area and inhabited one of the sub-kingdoms of Anglo-Saxon England, that included Gloucestershire, at its southern boundary. St Augustine himself would have heard them, where the ground crews will remember the songs of larks floating down out of the blue sky over the airfield, in the long hot days of those wartime summers. They were moments of magic, when the roar of aircraft engines were silent with a peace that seemed unreal in a wartime world.

Down Ampney House is possibly the best known and the most worthy of attention among the few great houses along the Upper Thames valley. Until partly destroyed by fire in 1961 when the manor was owned by the Marsh family, the beautiful and imposing Tudor Gatehouse stood tall and proudly to welcome callers. It was pulled down two years later and sadly never rebuilt. It was one of a few of its kind that remained in England up to that time. With its twin towers and turrets beneath which Queen Elizabeth herself would have passed, it stood as a reminder of medieval England's colourful history. The beautiful avenue of sycamores remains, that leads from where the gatehouse stood into the park.

Down Ampney House, as in many villages with a feudal history, was built close to where the church stands, for its earlier foundations would have been set down before those of the church itself. The story goes that many of the great stepping-stones from the Thames near Watereaton House were used in the foundations of an addition to the manor, probably in the fifteenth century. On entering the great hall of four bays, the most noticeable features are the beautifully carved queen posts and roof trusses. The hall itself is lit by two large mullioned windows flanked on either side by buttresses, and within are shields bearing the arms of the Hungerford family.

Down Ampney Manor and the estates were purchased by Sir Thomas Hungerford in 1374, his family having settled not far away in neighbouring Wiltshire in the twelfth century. He sat eleven times for Wiltshire and was the first House of Commons speaker. He was succeeded by his son Sir Walter, Lord Hungerford, who has been described as a warrior, a great statesman and a true Lancastrian, who took part in the Wars of the Roses and fought under Henry V in the wars against the French. It was he who is said to have uttered the famous words in Shakespeare's Henry V (and not the Duke of Northumberland): 'Oh that we now had here but one ten thousand of those men in England that do no work today.' Sir Walter died in 1449 leaving a son of the same name who, during his father's lifetime, was made a prisoner of war by the French but was later ransomed for three thousand marks. A beautifully bound and jewelled fifteenth century missal, preserved in the Bibliothèque Municipale of Tours in France is said to have been a part of the ransom. The Down Ampney line, however, flows through his younger brother Edmund on whom the property was settled. He was the first of the Hungerfords to reside at the manor, and is the forebear of the Hungerfords of the village and of Windrush and Black Bourton. The Sir Anthony Hungerford of the church monument was his great, great grandson and marked the end of the Down Ampney, Hungerford line when his second marriage was childless.

The manor came into the possession of the Dunch family through the marriage of Hungerford Dunch, son of Edmund Dunch (Baron Burnell) of Little Wittenham, Berkshire and Bridget, the only child of Sir Anthony Hungerford above. His estate was worth £2,000 per annum and at his death in 1680 he left land of the annual value at that time of £18 (by 1869 of £57) per annum, vested in the high bailiff and constables of Cricklade, to be divided among twenty-four of the town's poor. It was one of many charities bestowed on that town that space will not permit here of elucidation. His son Edmund Dunch was MP for Cricklade in 1701 and subsequently.

In the early years of the eighteenth century Down Ampney House had some additions made to it by James Craggs and it was remodelled in 1799 for Lord Eliot by Sir John Soane. Subsequently the interior has been given an elegant neo-Georgian character by Anthony Sanford.

Notes

1. *vi. et.* chapter 6, pp. 74–7.
2. Referring to the Gospel Oak in these same pages.

3. It is thought the name Lertoll is OW – *lorte* meaning dirt, a muddy place or mud, plus *wella* – a well, a spring, or *hol*, a hole or hollow (cf., Lertwell, Berks.) chapter 2, *vi. et.*
4. Holmes, Diana, *Cricklade* (Alan Sutton Publishing, 1993).
5. Margaret de Villiers, *c.* 1320.
6. More frequently termed a squint.

21 Eisey and Watereaton, Wiltshire

> I wandered by the brookside,
> I wandered by the mill,
> I could not hear the brook flow,
> The noisy wheel was still
> There was no burr of grasshopper,
> The chirp of any bird;
> But the beating of my own heart
> Was all the noise I heard.
> > *The Brookside* Richard Monkton Milnes,
> > Baron Houghton (1809–1885)

As will presently be seen, these age-old hamlets, on either side of the river were, for a long period, closely associated. The origin of the word Eisey is still rather obscure but it appears that it is of Anglo-Saxon origin. Remote though it is, one possible explanation has been suggested that it emanates from the Middle German *öse*, 'ring-shaped handle', from the loop in the river below the hill. We find some confusion in *English Place-name Elements*, it being Old English, but I gather it could mean 'island in the river', not an island in the modern sense, but used as high ground surrounded by a stream in a marshy area, which might be acceptable.

On the summit of the hill, probably for nearly a thousand years, stood a little church dedicated to St Mary, in use as stated by Dr Thomson (op.cit.) 'in 1195 and probably before'. The last building here was consecrated in 1844, coincidental with that nineteenth century restoration frenzy mentioned elsewhere. The ceremony

191

was attended by forty members of the local clergy, among whom
was the Revd N.G. Woodruff from Somerford Keynes. Sadly it was
pulled down as unsafe in 1953, and because there were no longer
any worshippers it was never rebuilt. I believe the last time it may
have been used was for a funeral service for a member of the
Horton family, at one time the long-term Earls of St Germans'
tenants of Eisey Manor. His wish had been to be interred in the
graveyard of his ancestors, but this gives cause for confusion and
the burial may have taken place subsequent to the building's
demolition.

Mentioned in a previous chapter is the incumbency of the Eisey
living with that of Latton and of how, in the fading years of the
history of 'the little church on the hill', a cleric used to walk from
Latton in all weathers to attend his dwindling flock. At last the time
arrived when they came no more to hear his sermons and, as far as
the church was concerned, like those that lay in its churchyard, the
hamlet too had died.

Between the site of the deserted graveyard and the river bend
below is the 'apparently systemless series of banks and ditches so
far unexamined by the archaeologist', as described by Dr
Thomson,[1] that can still be clearly identified. They are earthworks
thought by some to have been made by Parliamentary forces in the
Civil War for a battle that never actually took place. On the older
large-scale maps it is marked as Gaerston (Gastons), a name that is
of considerable interest, which Dr Thomson describes as a
'paddock' and the only ancient name at Eisey. However, the meaning would appear to be 'the place of a battle' (Gas; Lat. *chaos*, Gk
kha–os). A monk, when listing the names of those who died in the
battle of 1471 near Tewkesbury during the Wars of the Roses, refers
to '*bello Gastiensi prope Theokesbyri*', and the field near the town
where the battle took place is still called The Gastons. I believe this
is likely to dispel the Cromwell legend of Eisey Hill, for may not
such a word have been long since out of use by the seventeenth
century? It seems possible that a battle took place on this hilltop at
a much earlier date. The archaeologist of the future may one day
tell us more.

The area has been noted on maps, produced from aerial
photographs, made in 1971, 1981 and 1991, as 'Hamlet with
medieval origins'. The earthworks – erroneously I believe – are
considered to be the site of a medieval village.

Walter Jones was vicar during the Commonwealth. Did he, we
wonder, look down towards the river bend from the edge of his
churchyard and watch the activity of hundreds of Cromwell's army

digging the defences, and indeed, having to walk amongst them back to his vicarage? In view of the above it would appear to have been unlikely.

Eisey, (wrote Thacker) 'whose church I originally found locked, but gained admission on another visit and found the modern Norman within. I beheld with regret the cracks in the chancel arch. The building dates back, I believe, less than half a century, though I found a tombstone dated 1824.'[2]

The new church was consecrated on 4 September 1844 and was in turn pulled down as mentioned above. The inventory of church possessions (temp. Ed, VI) shows four bells and a chalice weighing six ounces. Thacker states ' ... under the chancel is said to be buried a Georgian font belonging to the old church.'

The inventory of 1928 lists a nineteen-ounce chalice, a 6½-inch round paten of five ounces and a square stone font. The chalice and paten are now at Latton and the one bell remaining is in the new church at Penhill, Swindon. The churchwardens' account books, the manuscript notebook of the church's inscriptions and a copy of the Tithe Award together with a map were in Latton, but by now may be at the Wiltshire Records Office. The registers date from 1571, when the first register entry was made. Many entries here refer to bodies 'buried in woollon', that arose out of an enactment of Charles II, first heard of in 1666, but having to be re-enacted in 1678 'in respect that there was not a sufficient remedy given for offences against the said law'. It laid down that no corpses should be buried in any stuff or thing other than wool, under a penalty of £5. The Act remained in force until 1815, considerably contributing to the growth of the wool trade, as was its intention.

See the facsimile copy of a deed of tenancy between Alice Cuss and the owner, written shortly after she was widowed. The first entry of this page in the same handwriting refers to an indenture of the date of Philip and Mary and would be pre-Elizabethan in age (*c*.1550), and by mention of Henry VIII the deed with Alice Cuss would have been endorsed at about the same time.

The Horton family of Eisey Manor were tenants of the Earl of St Germans, one of the great landowners in the area, whose ancestral recipient, Roger de St-German, has an entry on the memorial in Normandy's Castle of Falaise as having fought with 'William, sometimes known as William the Baatard' at Hastings. The entry for the parish in 1903 says 'The Earl of St Germans is lord of the manor and chief landowner' and was the eighth earl, Baron Eliot (see chapter twenty).

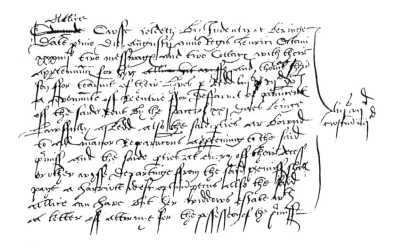

Edmund Allice Cuss holdeth by Indenture beringe date primeo die
Augusto anno Regis Henrici Octavi xxxxiiii two messuages and two
Cottages with their appert[enances] him Allice his wife and Thomas
their son for tearmes of their lyves & redd liii s, xi. d yearly . . . .
of re-entrie for default of paiment of the said rent by the parties xxi
being bound lawfully as[sesse?]ed also the said ptis are bound to all
manor reparacions appertaining to the said p[remiss] and the said
ptyes at th time of ther decease or other wise departing from the said
premises shall pay a Herriot . . . . . . wills the said Allice can have but
her widdows estate with a letter of attorney for the possession of the
premises.

A copy of a tenancy agreement with Alice Cuss, widow, from Eisey
manorial records

Fred Thacker says:

The *English Register* of Godstow Priory contains an account of a
little dispute at Latton in 1307, illuminating those old days, when the
priory was presented at the wiltshire assizes for having stopped 'a
course of water in temyse [not Isis, you will notice] called Morheued
within the liberteis' of Queen Margaret, '*florum Francorum*', consort
of Edward I; to the annoyance of the queen '& of all the cuntre &
cetera'. Godstow denied the charge and proved that there were of
old time 'certain stones placed at the Mereheued, with iron and lead
joined together to the ease and profit of the people'. I cannot hear of
any spot likelier to fit in with the old record than one just west of the
Horse Bridge at Water Eaton House, where to this very day [c.1906]

great stones remain in Thames; concerning which an old man only ten years dead is remembered to have said that there were once many more; which were removed within his memory upon a timber carriage and used for the foundation stones of an addition to Down Ampney House. The smallest of them weighing half a ton. If the water were unduly dammed here it would overflow into Latton territory west of Eisey Hill, the nearest outlet on the north bank [Ampney Brook]. The Queen's lands were probably just there, west of the Warlick Ditch, an ancient watercourse on the north bank almost opposite the Dance Brook, dividing Latton and Eisey.

Watereaton as it is known today, is now a manor house and farm buildings, belonging when I was young to Mr Douglas Gantlett, one of many carrying this name in the vicinity's farming community. Watereaton is bounded on the south by the river Thames and its tributary the Ray and to the north, in part, by Golden Rose Lane; this became known as Big Rose Lane, with the narrow macadam road leading to it from Blunsdon being Little Rose Lane. This last once continued as a track to the now demolished Port Farm, so named after the ancient Port Way, which was a part of Golden Rose Lane itself. The eastern boundary may well have been another ancient track, continuous with the road to Maisey Hampton, Ready Token and the Icknield Way. Undoubtedly the copse in the south-west corner where Big Rose Lane ends, is a remnant of ancient woodland.

In the mid-twentieth century there were five farms in Watereaton. Of these Port Farm was pulled down c.1960, the others being Seven Bridges, South Farm, formerly Watereaton Farm, North Farm, the other being the manor, which has been demolished and replaced by the present Watereaton House. Dr Thomson writes of this farm in 1958 when the remains of a fish pond could still be seen. A backwater of the Thames was a wharf serving the community in old times, which today is hardly noticeable.

In Domesday we read:

> Hermande Drewes holds *Etone* (Water Eaton) of the King. Edric held it in the time of king Edward and it paid geld for 2 hides. There is land for 2 ploughs. There is 1 plough in demesne and there are two and a *coscez*, and 1 villein with 1 plough. There are 2 acres of meadow. The woodland is 2 furlongs long and 1 furlong broad. It was worth 30s.

The woodland referred to would have been Watereaton Copse at the east end of Big Rose Lane mentioned above. The copse is now

twice that length; a bank can still be clearly made out between the
original portion and the new, which is nearest to the lane.

Nunne-Eiten was described by Leland as a small property
belonging to Godistow. In the *English Register* dated 1450 it is vari-
ously named as Water-eaton, West-eaton, Nunne-eaton and
Eatonmynchons, and is therefore considered to have been sited at
Watereaton and not at Eisey as some have described it. It was a
manor, at first of the 'Holi mynchons of Godstow'. Reginald, son of
the Earl of Hereford, granted it *c*.1142: 'to God our Ladi, & to saint
John Baptiste & the holi minchons . . . Well & worshipfull, frail &
quietli' to hold. In the charter it is stated that Reginald and
Emmelene his wife 'willed it to be known that both thei & his sonis,
Reinolde & Hammeline, and his too dowthters Anneis & Jiluen'
had given it for the 'remedi of their sinnis'. They were to enjoy it in
peace: 'In woods & in plains, in meade and pasture, in waters & in
millis & pondes, in waiis and pathis.' It was later decreed by Pope
Celistine III that it was to be subject to Eisey and the lesser tithes
to Godstow, and Eaton was to have its own churchyard. From the
foregoing, the importance of the stepping stones, bound together
with iron and lead, spanning the river in old times must have been
considerable. A wide bridge, known as the Horse Bridge has long
since spanned the river just below the site of the stepping stones.

Thacker says that the old manor house had a tradition that it
was 'a house of mercy' connected with Oxford. He mentions the
remains of the fishponds and also the dry stream bed that fed them.
Little is known of the chapel of St Lawrence at Watereaton. I
myself recall that the site was covered in cowsheds and other farm
buildings adjacent to Watereaton House. Thacker says, 'An old man
at Latton is remembered who, in his youth, saw the gravestone
lying about in heaps'. The former owner, Mr Douglas Gantlett,
mentioned that he had sometimes come across some of these
gravestones. There is a note of about 1750 in the Latton church safe
stating that the church at Watereaton was demolished '200 years
ago' and that the only remains are some gravestones in the farm
yard.

Sir John Brydges, afterwards Lord Chandon, whose father lived
for a time at Blunsdon House, bought Watereaton and the tithes
were bought later by Sir Thomas Seymour. In his will dated March
1500–01 he mentions 'the yeres of my farm at Eton'. His grandson
John Goddard's assessment at Watereaton in 1545 was the 'largest
in Water Yatton and Esye'. We next hear that Watereaton was
bought by Sir Stephen Fox (1627–1716). In 1600 some sixty acres of
Watereaton and Eisey were leased by deed at an annual charge of

£10 for the aid of an apprentice charity at Great Bedwyn near Marlborough. Port Farm, together with both North Farm and South Farm were sold in 1812 and the farm boundaries between all five holdings have since been changed.

A Thames and Severn canal milestone at Eisey. Posts were set at intervals of a quarter of a mile

Notes

1. *Wiltshire Archaeological Magazine*, vol. 57, pp. 34–9 (1958).
2. The crack referred to must have been the first sign of the weakening of the foundations. It was to last for about another forty years after Thacker's second visit.

22   Castle Eaton, Wiltshire

Why so headlong little stream,
Under wistful willows wending;
Why so swift to grasp the dream,
Mad to learn the story's ending?

Surely here is sweeter life
Here within the tender meadows;
Rest is here, beyond is strife
Here is light, beyond are shadows.

Anon.

Castle Eaton or Eton Meysi has been recorded many times.
Another early name for the village was Ettone, loosely interpreted
from the Anglo-Saxon, this could mean a place surrounded by
water, although how this was possible remains obscure. The
Thames now passes in a loop from its original course and has been
brought close to the church and the village at its back. Here there
is an exact parallel with the Thames at Cricklade, where the original course of the stream was across the meadows and is now only a
drainage ditch that still retains its original function as a boundary.
There the river was diverted to be brought close to one corner of
the Saxon defensive fortifications, both as an extra mural defence
and for a more readily available water supply. The Ettone residents
may have diverted the river for similar reasons, for the country
then was ever in a parlous state of flux and uncertainty, as it was to
remain for several centuries, and the Ettone residents might have
had much more in mind than a ready supply of water close at hand.
However, the change in the course could have been made at a
much later date when the commercial possibilities of the river as a
means of communication with London was beginning to be fully

appreciated and its wharf, as well as its water supply, brought as close as possible to the village.

Here it was in about 800, the year of Egbert's accession in Wessex, that the Thames boundary between Wessex and Mercia was probably considered by the latter to have been the weakest point for an invasion, and the Hwicce under their leader Ethelmund, Duke of the Hwicce, decided that somewhere in this area an attempt had to be made on it. But let us pause now for a moment and try to examine the picture at that critical time. Offa, King of the Mercians, had died in AD 796, his name made famous by the great earthwork he built from the estuary of the River Dee in the north to Chepstow in the south. Known as Offa's Dyke, this was to separate his kingdom from the troublesome Welsh tribes he realized he would never have the power to overcome. Mercian influence had extended from the Welsh borders to East Anglia and south to the Thames. The Hwicce had been absorbed and only Wessex remained to be conquered and Egbert's rule challenged. The Cricklade fortifications would be vital to success, but a direct onslaught was considered impossible because of the marshes north of the river and the extra-mural defence close beneath them – an attack therefore would have to be made in the east or south. It was yet to be many centuries before the Thames was bridged, and the Kempsford ford, not always fordable after a heavy rainfall and known sometimes to be hazardous, was on the well-used route between the settlements where Fairford and Highworth now stand. Here across the river the entire army made its way to assemble in the meadows before continuing south and west to Cricklade to make a flanking attack on its weakest side. However, the Wilsoeti (Wiltshiremen), under their leader Wroxtan, Duke of the Wilsoeti, were waiting for them and the peaceful meadows must have echoed that day to the sounds of the battle and the screams of the wounded and the dying. Both the leaders themselves were killed and the Mercians were defeated. Some heavy pieces of iron were found in the area in 1670, thought possibly to have been relics of this battle.

Castle Eaton is another of the handful or so of Cricklade's 'lesser churches', sometimes also known as 'daughter churches', and has always had a close affinity with the town for practical as well as theological purposes. Cricklade was once its postal town and, during the railway's heyday, milk from its farms was taken daily by horse and cart to the railway station to be loaded on the night train to London.

Castle Eaton and Kempsford are the last villages as we move

from one place to another along this lovely valley, that might truly be said to be on the bank of the Thames until we reach Lechlade. It is reasonable to believe that Saxons were not the first to settle in this spot. Iron Age artefacts along this part of the river, as well as photographs, have revealed signs of early occupation. A gold stater was found on the site of an Iron Age round house and is now in the Devizes Museum; a brooch of about this date, also found on a Castle Eaton site, is in the British Museum. However, there is no evidence that the Romans ever attempted to settle here. They probably showed little interest in members of the Dobuni, as long as they were quiescent when the tribe had been subjugated and absorbed. There is no doubt at all that the ubiquitous Saxons had settled here at Castle Eaton, just as may be seen in nearly every other place in this story, the cemeteries in Kemble, and in Lechlade but generally it is in the churches where proof of their living presence can be found.

Domesday 1086, states that:

> Earl Roger holds Castle Eaton. TRE paid geld for 15 hides. There is land for 12 ploughs. Of this land half is in demesne, and there are 3½ ploughs and six slaves. There are 8 villns and 2 cotsets and 5 ploughs. There is a mill rendering 15s. 6d., and 100 acres of meadow, [and] pasture 6 furlongs long and 3 furlongs broad. It was worth £15 TRE, now £12.

Butterfield, the Victorian ecclesiastical architect, appears to have been less unkind to this beautiful church than others which he 'restored'. An outstanding feature of its architecture is the unusual bell turret, seen in the sketch, to which special attention is invariably drawn by every church historian. E.C. Ponting refers to it (*WAM*, vol. xxx 1898) as dating from the second quarter of the thirteenth century. 'There is no bell', he says, 'but the gudgeons may be seen.' In this same article the Revd J.A. Harrison, vicar of Castle Eaton, says, (1968) 'Yet there is a bell hanging in the turret at Castle Eaton' but he had not been able to discover a reference in print ever having been made to it. Here also we learn that Dr George Forrest Brown, Bishop of Bristol, a Cambridge scholar and a Disney Professor of Archaeology before his accession to the Suffragen Bishopric of Stepney and subsequent to his transference to Bristol, made a visit to Castle Eaton and climbed into the tower to examine the bells. Apparently he scrutinized the ring of the six early eighteenth century bells, but his attention was particularly drawn to a seventh and smaller one used as a ting-tang, and after

The bell turret at Castle Eaton

careful examination, is said to have remarked to the incumbent, the Revd Luckman: 'I am convinced that this is the original sanctus bell, taken down from the turret as superstitious under the Elizabethan injunctions and re-hung here. You had better have it restored to its original position.' 'I assume then, my Lord, that it then may be restored to its original use,' Luckman replied. The bishop then snapped 'Don't draw unwarranted conclusions from what I say!' Eventually in July of 1990 the bell was restored to its original place in the turret, and a brass tablet was placed on the chancel wall to commemorate the occasion. The Revd Harrison stated that it had been used as a call-bell for Holy Communion and had indeed been rung at the consecration.

It had been discovered in 1961 that cracks were appearing in the stonework about the bell turret, at which time it was dismantled and completely rebuilt. The bell was examined by Mr Frank White of Appleton, a church bell hanger of the fourth generation, who thought it to have been cast in the early fourteenth century. It measures 19 inches in diameter and 16¾ inches in height and had been absent from its true home in the turret for more than 300 years. No inscription exists, merely a foundry mark in the shape of a tall cross, which could not be identified.

In Castle Eaton as elsewhere in every hamlet, village and town in England, the conquest by William of Normandy, was, by the dispersal of his family and followers from Normandy, to change the face of the land for ever. Everywhere the strange-sounding names of the new landowners must have come hard to the Anglo-Saxon tongue.

It is likely that one of the half-dozen Norman families of Mare (Marre), which included Guillaume de La Mare who first settled at Castle Eaton, already found the church within the grounds of the manor. Later we learn the Zouche (Souch), de la Zouch family, also had an ancestor among the 315 inscribed as 'Companions of the Conqueror' on the above mentioned tablet in Normandy's Castle of Falaise, William's birthplace. Their most famous descendant was Richard Zouche (1590–1661), who was born at Ansty, Wiltshire. He was a jurist and, as one might expect, a Royalist, and became a negotiator in the surrender of Oxford to the Parliamentary forces in 1646. He was said to be the first to place the law of peace before that of war. From this great name, through marriage, had come the Sancto Mauro, St Maur (Seymours), a family that was destined to become so memorable in England's history. In St John's College, Cambridge, there is a brass memorial, dated 1414, to an earlier descendant of the Norman family, Eudo (Edward) de La Zouche, a Doctor of Law during the reign of Henry IV (1399–1413) and directly descended from Nicholas Seymour at Castle Eaton. Audrey Tomlin mentions the fifteen generations dating back to the original owners of the manor, covering 550 years to 1870, a particularly wide generation gap to compare with the average twenty-nine years.

There is evidence that there was a church on this site before the Norman Conquest and it is believed that it was rebuilt or at least added to by Nicholas Seymour (*c.* 1300). The evidence of an earlier

Saxon building is apparently beneath the floor of the present vestry and in a part of the north wall.

One time owners of the manor at Castle Eaton were the Meysis who gave the name Eton Meysi to the village. It is possible they too originated with the Norman Conquest, similar names (Hugo de Masi and Massey etc.) appearing in the castle's list and on the abbey Rolls. The Seymours were the first in the county to obtain permission (1311) to fortify their manor, which overlooked the river, the reason for which is only a matter of surmise for little trust was placed in their dangerous neighbours, the Despensers at Hannington. In the most readable and enjoyable little book on Castle Eaton,[1] Audrey Tomlin gives us a brief insight into these precarious times for the village.

Almost nothing has changed along the river since the Revd W.H. Hutton (op.cit.) punted his way upstream from Kempsford to Castle Eaton; after leaving Kempsford he says:

> the river winds and turns, and is now shallow and broad, now swift, narrow, deep. The banks are never high, and there are few trees by them; but they are covered everywhere with flowers or fringed with reeds. You see no houses till you come to the quaint church of Castle Eaton, standing just above the stream. It is a strong building, well cared for, built at first when the Norman rulers used the waterway, and re-edified in the fifteenth century. The stone turret for the sanctus bell, in the shape of those wooden ones you often see, is its singular feature, and it gives the whole church an effect of quiet originality to which the green meadows, the swift stream and the solitude supply the perfect setting.

The church has a western tower nearest to the river and the open meadows beyond, with nave, chancel, south porch and north chapel, with a full crypt beneath, and is late Norman. The north aisle was added in the fifteenth century. In the entrance, where once must have been a beautiful memorial brass, (robbed, no doubt as happened so often elsewhere) is a stone slab, the only clue as to its identity is the impress of an outline of a knight in armour, his sword buckled to his left side. It has been said that the south porch also appears to have been in part built of stone from earlier use. The doorway is late Norman. The font, seen below, without its early base, was probably supported on pillars and is also late Norman. It was removed to its present position from the body of the church *c.* 1906.

St Mary the Virgin church at Castle Eaton

The font at Castle Eaton

The Revd John Sharpe, vicar 1847–60, in 1848 himself met the cost of rebuilding the chancel and, near the altar, he placed a memorial to his five children who sadly pre-deceased him, and prepared for his own burial beneath the chancel floor. In the 1862–3 restoration mentioned earlier, Mr Butterfield's work was not quite so despoiling as in some of the other churches. At that time the crypt was filled in and the chapel used as a vestry as well as to house the organ; a fourteenth century piscina remains. The restoration cost was about £1,000.

During his extensive wanderings, when he visited most of the churches along the Upper Thames valley, C.E. Ponting says of this church: 'The pulpit and the manor pew are curious specimens of carving of the 17th century . . . and of Elizabethan work on a modern base and around the lower part are mitred pieces of inserted carving from a 15th century screen.'

A memorial shield to those great benefactors of the church and village, the Goddard family, now stands by the north wall in the side chapel, returned inside in 1932 after Butterfield had it relegated to weather in the outside porch for nearly three-quarters of a century. C.E. Ponting remarked on it there in 1898. In the chapel is a memorial to three of the fallen who gave their lives in the First World War. The embattlemented tower is fourteenth century.

All that is left of the village cross stands forlorn, only about a metre high on its base, by the end of the path nearer the church. The Revd C.M.R. Luckman moved it there when the new lychgate was built. It was he whose preaching I heard in my youth at St Sampson's Church in Cricklade, the subject is lost to me now but a memory of the vibrant sermon has never been forgotten. He was an incumbent greatly loved for nearly half a century. The base of a second cross stands in a village garden.

Edmund Beaufort, second Duke of Somerset, who held lands at Cricklade was killed at the first battle of St Albans, but left a son, Sir John Wrythe, Garter King of Arms. In 1460 and thereafter, William Kemmel of Latton was sued with others by the Revd Richard Herman of Castle Eaton for carrying off Sir John Wrythe's money and goods from the Castle Eaton parsonage.

We see from earliest times in medieval England, how the vagaries of religious aspirations from one sovereign to the next, swung the pendulum and affected the fortunes of families both great and small. Of Castle Eaton, even the clergy in one instance were affected as were a few others in every English county. Humphrey Galimore, the incumbent who had been rector from 1550–54, unlike the Vicar of Bray, lost the living in the sad days of

'Bloody Mary's' reign to be replaced by a Catholic, Gilbert Bursley. However, after holding office for only three years his disentitlement was assured, and within the first year of Queen Elizabeth, Humphrey Galimore was reinstated and continued to hold office until his retirement in 1575.

The village cross at Castle Eaton, near the church

Notes

1. *Castle Eaton's St Mary the Virgin Church: A Brief History and Guide to the Ancient Building and Surrounding Grounds of Castle Eaton Parish Church in the County of Wiltshire* (1992).

23 Kempsford, Gloucestershire

If you would be known, and not know, vegetate in a village;
If you would know, and not be known, live in a city.
Charles Caleb Colton (1780?–1832)

Charles Colton's advice is as true today as it was two centuries ago. Kempsford (Old English) was first known as Kynemeresforde, the meaning having been described as The Ford of the Great Marsh. The precise significance of the compound is unclear, but it is possible that it was named after the owner who used the ford for access, or who had jurisdiction over it by ownership of the land on one or both sides of the river. There are others such as Aylesford, Daylesford, Pendeford, Snarlesford and Wandsford, all of which may have had their beginnings in this way, and they lend credence to this suggestion. Kempsford is of about 2,000 hectares, or nearly 5,000 acres, the boundaries are nearly all defined by watercourses within which are the hamlets of Whelford, Dunfield and Horcott. The southern boundary of the parish with that of Wiltshire is defined by the Thames and its western boundary is a watercourse once known as the county ditch. This continues almost due north, cutting in two the now well-known Fairford Airfield. Its long runway was extended to nearly two and a quarter miles by closing the unclassified Kempsford-Fairford road so that it passes out of Gloucestershire, across the strange shaped neck of land in Wiltshire for nearly three-quarters of a mile and ends on the far side in Gloucestershire once more. This main east–west runway was used for the trial flights of the first Concorde and for the giant B52 American bombers.

Before the Norman Conquest the Manor of Kempsford was in

the hands of Osgood from Earl Harold, and by 1085 it had passed to Ernulf of Hesden and was assessed at twenty-one hides. The succession passed to his son-in-law, Patrick de Chaworth, and was held by him until about 1133. Almost every village has some strange and unusual tale to tell so Kempsford is not alone in this, and legend, the natural successor to local gossip and hearsay, has also left its mark with this notable family.

The story has its contradictions and we are left to make our own assumptions. The last Patrick de Chaworth died leaving an only daughter, Maud, the heiress to the Kempsford estates, who was given by the King in marriage to Henry, Earl of Lancaster. Whilst Henry was away in Wales, Maud was said to have spurned the advances of a certain knight of the Earl's retinue. At that time she had given refuge to her brother with whom she walked at nights along the Green Walk down to the river and on the terrace alongside the water. On the Earl's return the rejected knight let it be known that she had a lover and if the Earl went down to the Green Walk at night he would surely see them. This the Earl did and in a fit of frenzied rage he stabbed her there on the terrace steps and threw her body into the Thames. On the discovery of his mistake it is said that he left the village and did not return until he was old and blind when, perhaps thinking to make amends he rebuilt the chancel of the church to his wife's memory and indeed also founded a hospital at Lancaster in the honour of God and Mary the Virgin. This was in the 1330s. Maud's ghost is said to haunt a path situated by the old vicarage and known to this day as Lady Maud's Walk. A man I met recently in the churchyard pointed out that the walk is an avenue of yew trees leading from the churchyard, but now blocked off from the river by a high stone wall.

Disaster again struck when Henry, the old Earl's grandson and heir, was drowned while playing on the river bank. The bereaved Earl inserted the large and colourful west window of the church to perpetuate the boy's memory, and the bereaved father, the Earl of Derby, who was made Duke of Lancaster in 1351, in his sorrow left the village, his horse casting a shoe as he left. The shoe was retained by the villagers, and to show their affection it was nailed to the church door where it may be seen today nailed beneath the latch on the north door.

The hospital was founded by the Duke's father, who extended and gave the estate to the Collegiate Church of the Annunciation, in whose possession it remained until 1548 with the Dissolution of the Monasteries. Blanche, one of his two daughters, married her cousin John of Gaunt. The present church tower was thought to have been erected by John of Gaunt to his wife's memory. Their son was to become Henry IV. It is not thought that John of Gaunt ever took up residence in Kempsford.

The church at Kempsford

The entrance to the church at Kempsford

In 1549 the manor was granted to Sir John Thynne and passed through succeeding generations until it came into the hands of Henry Frederick Thynne, created a baronet in 1641, for loyalty to the Royalist cause. It subsequently suffered severe sequestration when the war was over. Henry Thynne's son, Sir Thomas, was created Viscount Weymouth in 1682 and in that year succeeded to Longleat House, to be in turn succeeded by his great-nephew Thomas, who gave Kempsford to Henry Thynne, his second son. In 1707 the estate was sold to Gabriel Hanger, Lord Coleraine, and passed to his three sons. George Hanger was the youngest of the three sons. He was buried in St Mary's Church at Driffield. His epitaph reads:

Near this place lieth the body of
General George Hanger
Lord Coleraine
He lived and died a firm Believer

in one God and one only
He was
also a Practical Christian
as far as his frail nature did
allow him to be.

Fred Thacker (op.cit.) writes:

Beneath the wording of this plain dealing epitaph lies an enchanting history. George Hanger was the salt, the 'character' of this solid country family. He was the third and youngest son of Gabriel, and was born in 1751, just after the new Italian Church had got itself completed. In the beginning of that curious medley, the *Life and Adventures* put together for him by William Combe (a Thames historian, bye-the-bye, and a man much of Hanger's kidney, perhaps his fellow prisoner in the King's Bench prison) he writes of his father as 'one of those respectable, independent old English characters in the House of Commons called "Country Gentlemen" ... but in his father's seat at Gray near Windsor, "in the best bed in the stateroom, according to ancient custom", that I first saw the light. I am inclined to believe' he adds, 'from the length of my nose that at my birth the midwife committed some indignity to my person.' He went through the American War of Independence .... His affairs became terribly involved, and he got into the King's Bench prison for nearly a year.

It is from about this time we begin to see the manor broken up, and eventually the ownership passed to a nephew, Arthur Vansittart of Shottesbrook, Berkshire. He sold a part of the estate including the farms at Dudgrove to his brother Robert. He died in 1829 when the remainder of the estate passed to his son Arthur and in 1831 it was sold to Sir Gilbert East, Bt., who promptly bought back the Dudgrove farms, but it was not to remain intact again for very long. Sir Gilbert, who died in 1866, was suceeded by his son Sir Gilbert Augustus Clayton East, who in 1871 sold eight farms on the estate, 3,085 acres, to William Carey Faulkner. He died in 1883 and his three sons John, James and Thomas divided up the estate, John's share, which he held until his death in 1941, being his part of the land that included the manor. This covered 2,320 acres when his part was offered for sale by his trustees in 1953.

It was probably the large, moated manor house, much of which was demolished by the early eighteenth century that gave rise to the belief that there was once a castle at Kempsford. It stood alongside the river close to the church and in 1258 it is recorded as having a gatehouse, hall, kitchen and other rooms. Part of the moat could still be seen in 1976 when my source of information[1] was due to go into publication. There were buildings in the early sixteenth century that are said to have consisted of an inner and outer court; those of the inner court were known as the Provost's lodgings and were in use by an official of Leicester college, by whom the manor was administered. In 1705 one building of the home farm was known as the porter's lodge and was thought to be a part of the old manor.

A new manor house was built by Sir Thomas Thynne, which is thought to have been completed shortly before he died in 1639. During that period records of assessments of the hearth tax can give us a very good impression of the status and wealth of a property owner. From this we know that Kempsford Manor house was a very large property indeed, it having no fewer than forty-four hearths. By way of contrast we know that most dwellings were assessed for only one hearth although merchants, yeomen and the like might have had three or even four. The courtyard around which the houses were constructed had been the 'Provost's garden'.

A summer house once stood at either end, some part of one of these remained up to 1976.

As one might expect to find with such a wide level area, largely enclosed by the two rivers, Coln and Thames, the soil is mainly alluvium with a subsoil of Oxford clay. There is a neck of gravel near Horcott, but most of these gravel-bearing beds are to the north on the other side of the Coln boundary. Acres of meadowland between the Thames and Coln were once purposely subjected to winter flooding to enrich the soil for spring grazing. The old Thames and Severn Canal took its course through these meadows, seen on the *Landranger* Map No. 163. The boat-turning area, a warehouse and the agent's house in the middle of the village can still be seen. The land was enclosed in 1801 but much of it has been drained by a system of ditches and 'carries', a black dyke being mentioned in 1133 which may have been the Grand Drain that ran from Furzey Hill in the north west of the parish across to the Coln in the east.

The ford was, in ancient times, a part of an important route from Fairford to Castle Eaton, a short distance across the meadows, and there it was in 802 that the Hwicce made their way and were soon joined in battle with the Wessex defenders on the land towards nearby Castle Eaton, still known today as 'The Old Battlefield'. The ford's use was seriously limited by the depth of water after rainfall and was apparently never readily negotiable; the track that once led from it to Castle Eaton having long since disappeared. The wagons on the Cirencester–Highworth road (now severed by the airfield to the west) crossed the Thames a mile to the east at Hannington Bridge. The upkeep of the bridge was shared equally with the village of Hannington, which would have been important in the development of Kempsford. Hannington Bridge was destroyed during the Civil War and rebuilt in 1647; built and:

> ... pitched with stone upon the plankes. Horses and foot people go over the bridge. Carts, coaches goe through the water by ye bridge out of Wiltshier to Kempsford on Glocester shire. On Wiltshier side are 2 planks for footwoak yo pass in time of floods before they come to the Arche, Tis about 3 miles from Highworth town, Sanders Alehouse is in Wilts hard by the bridge.

In 1828 both Ireland and Westhall describe the bridge as of wood. It lasted for 200 years and was again rebuilt with three arches in 1841. In *c*.1906 Thacker (op.cit.) found the bridge:

> ... excessively awkward to get through: a skewwise structure of three arches, with a swift stream beneath it. It was built, according to Dredge in 1841, though Robertson about 1886 is still describing the bridge as of timber. Probably he merely copied older records. Ham weir was about half a mile below Hannington bridge. I know the pool, and saw no surviving stones. Taunt said the sill remained in 1871 'to place stepping stones on'. This was frequently done, perhaps under some degree of compulsion; immemorial footpaths often crossed these old weirs, which the Conservancy found it necessary to accommodate, in instances lower down with footbridges.

The Revd W.H. Hutton once described Kempsford '. . . as almost the most beautiful village on the Thames . . .'. The centuries can have changed it but very little; with its ancient main street, and houses of mellow Cotswold stone, that leads to the Parish Church of St Mary which dates from the eleventh century and retains some of its Norman features. The church, although not as large, or quite as lofty as St Sampson's in neighbouring Cricklade, is every bit as beautiful, and like one or two others in the area of about the same Perpendicular period. Like that of Fairford built by the Tames family of graziers, and those of Highworth and Cirencester, all just outside the scope of our story; each is the result of the prosperity created by the broad, heavy breed of Cotswold sheep and their 'good Cotteswolde woll'. One or two houses may be seen from the river with the great tower of the church behind them.

The nave is early twelfth century, there are four original deeply splayed windows, as are the north and south doorways. At the western end are pilaster buttresses with zig-zag mouldings. The chancel and the spacious south porch, which was the entrance from the castle, were added in the thirteenth century, the latter being now the vestry; its window is early English. The fourteenth century saw windows built into the west wall, while in the fifteenth century considerable reconstruction took place, including new windows in the side walls and at the east end. A new roof and clerestory lights were added to the nave during this period and the outstandingly beautiful tower with its buttressed quoins was rebuilt. It seems probable that the north entrance porch with its four-centred arch was an early sixteenth century addition; a facsimile rebuilding of the porch gable was carried out during the 1860 restoration. At the nineteenth century restoration a south chapel was added, and soon afterwards the music gallery was removed from the west wall. The pulpit is 1862 and a new font, carved by William Roseblade of Latton was made in 1868. In the chancel is a fifteenth century canopied tomb and on the altar floor is a brass of 1521 to Walter Hickman, his wife and two of their four sons; he was a wool merchant and lessor of the rectory and the manorial demesne. The church has a peal of six bells, one of which, the fifth, dated 1678, carries the arms of Sir Henry Frederick Thynne. A peculiarity of this church is a niche in the east interior wall of the north porch. With the exception of this group of late Perpendicular churches (at the three Ampneys, Aldsworth, Baunton, Barnsley, Eastleach and Bibury) the like are rarely found anywhere else in England. The beautiful choir stalls are by G.E. Street. There is a parclose screen of wrought iron in the sanctuary. The painted panel on the north wall is thought to have come from the seventeenth century music gallery. It is in memory of two churchwardens, Thomas Pope and Thomas Parker and is inscribed as 'The gift of Thomas Pope of London'.

The lychgate is dated 1865. There are several carved chest tombs in the churchyard of both the eighteenth and nineteenth centuries, the most noticeable of which is the group on the south side to the Arkells, still a well-known farming family.

The church living has been a vicarage since 1198. In 1677 the vicar's glebe comprised thirty-four acres of pasture and nine yards[2] of lot meadow. The seventeenth century vicarage has panelling believed to have once been in the church. The staircase is seventeenth century. The garden was once within the precincts of the castle. There is an oak beam in the Manor Farm house on the site of the castle dated 1574. It was rebuilt by Sir Gilbert East in 1846.

More than 2,000 acres of meadowland were enclosed by Act of Parliament and some large farms were created. By 1815 of these the manor estate covered nearly 1,300 acres, but by 1870 they were made into eight farms. Although there remained large acreages of meadowland, arable predominated but soon began to decline. I have mentioned the cheese and butter production all along the valley, and of how it was sent by river down to Lechlade and so, by larger vessels, to London. In 1826 Cobbett (op.cit.) wrote:

> In coming to Kempsford we got wet, and nearly to the skin. But our friends – he seemed to have friends in every village he visited – gave us coats to put on while ours were dried and while we ate our breakfast . . . . We got here about four o'clock, and at the house of Mr Iles where we slept, passed, amongst several friends, a very pleasant evening. This morning Mr Iles was so good as to ride with us as far as the house of another friend at Kempsford, which is the last Gloucestershire parish on our route. At this friend's, Mr Arkell, we saw a fine dairy of about 60 or 80 cows, and a cheese loft with, perhaps, more than two thousand cheeses in it; at least there were many hundreds.

There were 624 cattle recorded on the Kempsford farms in 1866 and 2,583 sheep. In 1926 there were 828 cattle. Kempsford parish had four mills at the Domesday count. The mill at Horcott on the Coln was recorded again in 1225 and is thought to have still been working in 1556. There had been a mill at Whelford since 1058 and in 1552 two mills were in operation under the tenant who, in 1732, was John Edmonds and whose descendants were there as millers until the Second World War. We learn that Henry the Walker, was drowned in one of the mill ponds at Kempsford in *c.*1286. We know that these ponds, everywhere, invariably claimed many lives. Although the following quote describes a lock, mill ponds were equally as dangerous before locks were invented.

> One farmer hath a lock in store
> That hath made many a Child to weepe
> Their mothers begg from dore to dore
> Their fathers drowned in the deepe.

In 1608 a weaver and three tailors were the only craftsmen recorded in Kempsford. There were 142 families of workers in agriculture and twenty-seven of workers in trade in 1831. The canal trade no doubt boosted the numbers of craftsmen and tradespeople, as for instance in 1856 there was a timber merchant, a coal merchant (his supplies coming off the barges from the Forest of Dean) and also a corn merchant.

From the Churchwardens' accounts in 1803, we learn that fifty-seven people were on permanent relief at the time, and in 1817 the numbers had gone up to seventy two. In 1836 Kempsford parish became a part of the Cirencester Union and was later to be included in the Cirencester Rural District. However, since the 1974 boundary changes it has become part of the Cotswold district.

If we look at the number of pupils at the Church of England school in Kempsford itself, it would appear that the permanent population had changed very little since the count in 1869 which showed there were fifty scholars. In 1904 the number was still about the same; in 1936 it had risen to eighty-one and eighty-nine were on the register in 1976. The stocks stood on the small village green until 1880. The village cross, now with only its base and part of its pillar remaining once stood in the road by the green until it was removed to the corner by Reevey Farm, and finally in 1890 to the new churchyard opposite the church. I was unable to find it on my first visit and even a resident living next door to the churchyard lych-gate was not aware of its existence. I discovered it in the middle of the churchyard when I went there again.

What was thought to have been a relic of the castle near the river by the church on the older maps is shown as the Castle Pillar, but I have been unable to discover what this was. The church house was rebuilt after a fire in 1791 and stood opposite the green. Most of the houses, now of stone, have been rebuilt since the seventeenth century when they were said to have been mainly of mud and thatch. In 1755 the village had two inns, which included The George on the west side of the street. In 1891 the Cross Tree stood by the village green and the Axe and Compass towards the westerly edge of the village where it still stands today. The village hall was built in 1932.

The airfield, known as RAF Fairford now takes up by far the largest area of the parish, and was opened in 1944 by the RAF as a transport base, its most momentous function being its use for transport of aircraft and gliders, personnel and equipment for the D-Day and Arnhem landings (see chapter twenty). It had a considerable influence on the lives and the economy of the community. The airfield base was taken over by the United States Air Force in 1950 and greatly enlarged as a bomber base.

Notes

1. 'The County of Gloucestershire' *Victoria County History*, vol. 7.
2. There appears to have been no hard and fast description of exactly what the area of one yard comprised, but it can be judged as being in the region of thirty acres.

24 Inglesham, Wiltshire

A cot that nestles 'neath a hill,
A garden plot for me to till,
With close beside a little rill,
And over all a peace so still.

Things Dear to the Country Heart
G.W. Shipway (1914–88)

My sources of English place-names, would seem to agree that we have in the name of Inglesham one of those inexplicable compounds. While 'ingle' may be of Scandinavian origin, for the other syllable I can discover no rational explanation; names like Melksham appear to have been studiously avoided in the guides.

A first time visitor to the hamlet of Inglesham will be disappointed to find that at the end of a long, narrow cul-de-sac off the Highworth to Lechlade road, apart from its famous little church, there are less than a handful of houses, and only the river across a couple of meadows out of sight. Whilst it is not at all unusual for an earlier church to be in virtual isolation from the place which it serves, here there are few other dwellings, from Lechlade in the north to Upper Highworth in the south, but there was indeed more habitation of old, with evidence, which can still be seen in the surrounding fields, of a medieval village. There are those who, when Inglesham is mentioned, will think of the river there and of those long ago who sweated and toiled upstream from Lechlade and Inglesham to Cricklade, and knew well all its bends and unexpected shallows. However, just here the river flows deep and wide, in one place the longest punt pole failing to plumb its depths. It shows no signs of shallows or the almost impassable reaches choked with weeds that were soon experienced as the intrepid punter set off for his hoped-for gentle voyage to Cricklade. His first village was Kempsford; strange in a sense how some of these village churches in the upper reaches are built so close to the river and here is no exception, as is also the case with Castle Eaton, a stone's throw or two across the meadows. So past Cowneck, that peculiar stretch of water for which there is no known reasonable or logical explanation, until the Horse Bridge and Watereaton is reached. Near the former are the shallows where once, before man was capable of making records, those gigantic stepping stones, bound together with iron and lead were first placed. Then soon one arrives at the loop in the river partially surrounding the base of Eisey Hill, and sees in the distance for the first time the great tower of St Sampson's Church, Cricklade, welcoming him to refreshment in one of its hotels or inns, or some pleasant teashop in the High Street. It may be that the Conservancy now keeps these upper reaches dredged and clear of weeds, as I saw at Cowneck one summer, where the river gently flowed with neither rush nor reed to block its way. In an earlier chapter the toil and heartbreak of reaching Cricklade by boat from Inglesham is eloquently described by writers like Thacker and Hutton. The poet Shelley tried it once and gave up the struggle to return to the boatyard at Lechlade. On the other hand Inglesham will best be thought of by so many for its famous roundhouse, one of five of similar design, built by the Thames and Severn Canal Company along its twenty-seven mile length, most of which are still in occupation sixty-five years after the canal was finally closed.

There are many who know of Inglesham because of its church of St John the Baptist, and scarcely ever give the river and the canal with its roundhouse a second thought. In the undated versions (?c.1890) of his work in two large volumes *The Thames, From its Rise to the Nore*, Walter Armstrong MA only mentions the unusual bas-relief built into the wall of the south aisle – which was on the exterior south wall when he saw it – saying 'Inglesham has an interesting old church, to which many visitors find their way, mainly on account of a curious bas-relief imbedded in the wall of the nave. The group seems intended to represent the Virgin Mary with the child Jesus and the hand of God blessing them from the sky.' To the antiquarian this feature is of the greatest interest, while the impression to the casual visitor is one of veneration for the age of the place, after having gone down a step inside the deep porch (made necessary, some have said, by burials raising the level of the churchyard without) the heavy oak door is opened to reveal the interesting interior. Mercifully, the nineteenth century restorers passed this by; it was saved by its isolation, for even a century or more ago few worshippers came to help maintain it.

The uneven flagstone floor and the high oak box pews at the west end of the nave, naturally darkened by age – a character with this wood that makes it so attractive and, to the trained eye easily dated – are the first of the scores of fascinating features to be seen on entering. The furnishings and the floor are as Cromwell's troopers saw them and, sitting in one of these high pews, it is not hard to imagine them there and hearing the clanking of their breast plates as they kneel in prayer.

Strangely, and rather unusually, where the family historian in particular finds frustrating gaps in parish records during much of the interregnum, entries here were uninterrupted throughout the period. The first entry of baptism, dated 21 December 1589, is of Anne, daughter of Edmonde Steward, the first marriage of 27 October 1589 of Thomas Tawney to Anne Stone and the first recorded burial of 3 January 1591 of Thomas Churche. Entries continued to be made for nearly 400 years when the last marriage took place in April 1972 between Philip Anthony Delaney of Fairford and Jacqueline Mary Beachey of Church Farm Cottage. The last baptism was in 1940 of Edward, son of William John Beachey of Church Farm Cottage and the last burial was of Thomas Nash of Inglesham in 1940, who was seventy-nine years old. Of the last nine burials eight were people over sixty and only one child of eleven.

Barbara Raw,[1] gives the church as Norman but to many the building is tenth century and the carving of the Virgin and Child is dated as the early eleventh century. Expert opinions differ as to whether the work was executed before or after the Norman conquest. Kendrick[2] believes it is early eleventh century, while Raw reminds us of the stone having once been built into the outer wall. There is a scratch dial carved into the lower left-hand corner of it, with an unusually large hole for the gnomen. It was brought inside in 1910 and may have originally belonged elsewhere as, some believe, were those curious pieces of sculpted Saxon stone in the churches of St Sampson in Cricklade and in Somerford, but in all cases this is unlikely; a more logical explanation is that they were parts of an earlier building on the site.

Talbot Rice says '. . . that a Byzantine model was followed at anything like first hand in this instance is most improbable, but that the ultimate prototype was Byzantine seems equally certain.'[3]

The thin walls of this building, such as may be said to be typical of Saxon construction, have subsequently had corner buttresses added to lend them support. Little appears to have been altered in the building since the late fifteenth century, but external repairs to the fabric are evident from about the seventeenth century.

Under the watchful eye of J.T. Micklethwaite, the Society for the Preservation of Ancient Buildings met all the costs of extensive roof repairs over the years 1886 to 1900. 'The scrupulous and exemplary quality of the work took place under the virtual daily supervision of the Revd B.H. Burchall of nearby Buscot who apparently acted daily as an honorary Clerk of the Works throughout these years.'

Although no major nineteenth century restoration was carried out, from time to time a few of a more minor nature have been necessary, none of which appears in any way to have masked the venerable delight of the building's unusual and unique interior. Some reconstruction took place in the chancel in the thirteenth century and the nave and arcades are thought to have been built in its earlier years when, in 1205, King John gave the church to the monks of Beaulieu. When the early fourteenth-century roof was constructed some damage was done to the lancet windows. On the chancel's north side, semi-circular arches can be seen and during the construction of the fourteenth century roof, remnants of the apparatus for raising the pyx were found; whether or not these were preserved I do not know.

Larger windows at the east end were provided in the fourteenth century and bigger windows added in the century following when at that time the aisles' roofs were raised and parapets built to protect them. Both entrance doors are of interest, particularly the presently unused north door. What to many visitors will be of considerable interest are the wall decorations dating over a period of 600 years. Here, in places, as many as seven layers of paint have left a confused and mostly unidentifiable hotchpotch; yet, through the fog of all the centuries each has been found to be represented. X-ray technology may one day reveal a little more of their true meanings. Supervised by the architect John Schofield of Bristol, the paintings are being stabilized to reveal what may be safe to be done by Jane Rutherford and John Dives. A 1934 refurbishment saw the reinstatement of the remains of a thirteenth century reredos.[4]

The screens in the aisles are thought to be the oldest timber fittings and the pulpit and many of the pews may be only as late as the fifteenth century. Some have been reduced in height as may be seen by the rear pew in the east bay. The altar rail dates from the eighteenth century, but the choir pews could possibly have been installed at about the end of the Civil War. The font is earlier.

Amidst all the sights and impressions of continuity of crafts-manship created as one century followed another, one's attention is certainly drawn to the huge fourteenth century slab of black marble, ten feet in length and three-and-a-half feet wide, which partially floors the chancel; the knight's brass has long since disappeared but its matrix is clearly seen with the borders for the inscriptions. Such features in modern construction would fail to give cause for comment, but we are left in wonderment as to how this gigantic slab of limestone was conveyed here and from whence it came. There are other interesting memorials that should not be overlooked, such as a brass on the floor of the chapel dated 1783.

The village cross at Inglesham

The handsomely designed bellcot, as a finial at the roof's west end, has two bells dated 1717. The 'preaching' cross stands in the churchyard but is likely, like the village cross, to have once been somewhere near by on the village green, which is now a wide open area with the church on one side, open pastures on the other and a large honey-coloured stone-built house facing the approach from the A361. The cross stands on three steps with a tall base and an octagonal tapering shaft with part of its finial missing. There are several well sculpted gravestones. The demise of the village is believed to have come about with the passing of that same wool trade that gave us so many of the beautiful Cotswold churches. The church has been vested in the Redundant Churches Fund since 1981, having been made redundant two years earlier; its preservation is therefore now assured. The church that was his inspiration holds its tribute within to William Morris, the founder of the Society for the Protection of Ancient Buildings, which reads: 'This church was repaired in 1888–9 through the energy and with the help of William Morris who loved it.'

> Forget six counties overhung with smoke,
> Forget the snorting steam and the piston stroke,
> Forget the spreading of the hideous town;
> Think rather of the pack-horse on the down,
> And dream of London, small and white and clean,
> The clear Thames bordered by its gardens green.
> Prologue, *The Wanderers*, William Morris (1834–96)

Notes

1. 'The Inglesham Virgin and Child', *Wiltshire Archaeological Magazine*, vol. 61, pp. 43–6.
2. Kendrick, T.D., *Late Saxon and Viking Art* (London, 1945).
3. Rice, T., *English Art*.
4. 'Inglesham Wall Paintings observed 1933, executed 1330', *Wiltshire Archaeological Magazine*, vol. 47, pp. 527–9.

25 Lechlade, Gloucestershire

Believe me, my young friend, there is *nothing* – absolutely *nothing* – half so much worth doing as simply messing about in boats.

The Wind in the Willows, Kenneth Grahame (1859–1932)

Lechlade, a name derived from the River Leach that enters the Thames below St John's Bridge, and 'lade' ('to load') signifying that it must have been of considerable importance as an inland port for traffic in Anglo-Saxon times. It is the last of the towns and villages in our story of the Upper Thames, above which it is the infant river, the callow stream, the 'Stripling Thames', call it what you will, and, like a wayward woman, has proved to be as unreliable as it is beautiful. But now, fed by the swift-flowing Coln, just above the town, and cheek by jowl with the famous roundhouse and the entrance to the Thames and Severn Canal itself, the assurance is given that from now on its waters can be relied upon for boats in any season of the year.

Once a river of commerce it is now used almost entirely for pleasure, confirmed by a glance at its busy boatyard. This can be seen as soon as the town is entered after crossing the narrow Halfpenny Bridge, built in 1792. Here a halfpenny toll was charged until 1839. It is now listed as an ancient building and cannot be widened. Heavy traffic therefore, particularly in summertime, is now controlled by lights at either end.

Stone used for the dome of St Paul's Cathedral was loaded on barges at Lechlade. The town was once particularly well known for the barge traffic during the heyday of the Thames and Severn Canal. As many as one hundred barges have been counted in its busy wharf and moored on the river all the way down to St John's Lock. It had brought to the little town a prosperity hitherto unknown during its 128 years of use, until this eastern end was closed in 1927. Motoring to Lechlade on the A361 and shortly before Halfpenny Bridge is reached, the first thing one sees is the beautiful steeple of Taynton stone belonging to the Parish Church of St Lawrence. (Taynton is a Cotswold village about forty miles to the west.) This spire of 'one of the six finest parish churches in Gloucestershire', according to the architectural historian, the late David Verey, is a landmark for many miles around. When seen from this direction it always appears to have some malformation near its apex, although I have heard no mention of this from any other source. Perhaps it looks at its best from half a mile downstream at St John's Bridge.

If any doubt had ever existed of the age of the Lechlade settlement, at least as far back as the Bronze Age, it was to be dispelled after the discovery (in Butlers Field west of the town soon after a 'rescue dig' had started there in late April 1985) of Bronze Age barrows and an exceptionally large Anglo-Saxon cemetery. I recall an earlier rescue dig on a minor scale that took place, under the direction of the Ancient Monuments Branch of the Ministry of Works, in the gravel terrace off the Burford road north of the town in the late 1950s.

Where Lechlade now stands the land has been proved to have been in continuous occupation from the Neolithic Age, a period that archaeologists have found impossible to define accurately. However, it can be said to have existed when the giant stone circle at Avebury was formed and at a time when stone implements shaped by polishing in the late Stone Age were in general use, long before the use of metal and the Bronze Age, and after the prehistoric age of chipped stone tools known as Paleolithic. After the Bronze Age came the Iron Age, and so to the invasion of the European races, to the Romans and the Anglo-Saxons, of which more is being learned by the discoveries of grave goods in the large cemetery.

Aerial photography has revealed the sites of round huts, such as at Cricklade and Ashton Keynes. Here at Lechlade it was the Dobuni, towards the more easterly extremity of their range, who were very probably in occupation, as they were all along the valley of the Upper Thames to well beyond its source. At another place, the foundations of an isolated house have been discovered, defined by posts set in a circle twenty feet in diameter. Internal post holes are thought to have supported hammocks or looms.

St John's Lock with Lechlade church spire in the distance

Lechlade itself is tucked away in Gloucestershire's south-west boundary, where the county's southern boundaries are the Thames with Wiltshire, and now, since the 1974 boundary changes, with Oxfordshire where once it was Berkshire. The town and parish cover an area of about 1,600 hectares. The main feature of the low, flat landscape is meadowland interspersed with willow-lined water-courses and drainage ditches, and only little copses and brakes in the way of woodland, with the possible exception of that near the old manor house east of the town, which is no longer defined on the modern map. In common with other areas as well as the part where was once Smerell Farm, defined earlier in these pages, gravel and sand extractions have transformed its appearance.

Near the confluence of the Leach with the Thames, known as the Lade, was once the wharf for river commerce. St John's bridge was built in 1229 by Peter FitzHerbert, the second husband of Isabel de Mortimer of Lechlade Manor, and it carried the main road to London on which converged 'the salt road' from Droitwich through the Cotswolds from the north, and the Welsh way through Gloucester. The bridge is said to be the oldest on the Thames above Teddington, and there are records for its repairs in the fourteenth century. Leland stated that it had 'three arches of stone'. Shortly after 1831 Peter Cox, who was contracted to rebuild it, removed its two pointed arches, using the foundations at either end to support his single arch. We learn that the bridge was altered again in 1884.

A nunnery there, founded in 1200, became a hospital for the sick and elderly, to which, in 1245, Isabel granted the bridge and some land adjacent, a chapel and the mill. When Richard, Duke of Cornwall, brother of Henry III, became Lord of the Manor in 1252, he enlarged the hospital into a Priory of the Order of St Augustine. It is said to have housed seven priests and lay brothers and sisters, who all wore russet habits and looked after the poor and the sick, and the prior received a royal grant to take tolls for the maintenance of the bridge, which had apparently fallen into disrepair. Records reveal that the monks did not always live up to their reputation and the ideals of the Priory's foundation for by 1291 services were being neglected and there was little discipline. In 1300 the Bishop of Worcester held an inquisition after it had been said that the prior had expelled a number of lay brothers and sisters.

The repairs to the bridge were the responsibility of the hospital and the prior was given grants of pontage in 1338, 1341 and 1388. In 1351 the Bishop sent a commissioner to punish certain brothers for violent treatment of their fellows. In the following year the monks celebrated mass for payment. The Black Death may have been a further cause of impoverishment in the countryside. By 1375 Prior Stephen was excommunicated for diminishing 'the services, wasted and defiled the goods of the Priory and led a dissolute life'. The description of the ceremony taken by the Dean of Fayreford with all the rectors, vicars and parish priests of the Fayreford Deanery, tells us that having put on their albs and rung the bells, 'they then extinguished the candles and threw them on the ground with other requisite solemnities to denounce Stephen as excommunicate'. By 1462 the hospital had become too impoverished to pay tithes and was exempted. In another ten years it had become so ruinous that Edward VI granted the advowson to his mother, the then Lady of the Manor, Cecily Duchess of York, and transferred a chantry of priests founded in the Chapel of the Virgin in Lechlade church, to be a corporation holding land, and by this same deed a licence was also granted to John Twynyho to found another chantry priest. The former said mass at Our Lady's altar and the latter at that of St Blaise. Three years later, and when the chapel and hospital had been put into repair, services were held there on the Vigil and Feast of St John the Baptist. In 1508 both chapel and priory were granted to the college of St Nicholas at Wallingford, and the chantries with the altars of St Mary and St Blaise 'passed away under Edward VI'. The next we hear of it is from Leland who describes the ruins of the chapel and priory when writing in 1543 on 'seeing a chapel and large enclosures and stone walls'. In 1763 an effort was made to preserve the foundations when the site was used for building a parish workhouse. Six years later the commissioners' report read thus:

P'ishe of Latcheladde houseling people, 220. S Blaise Chauntry founded by one John Twynyhoe by lycence by hym opteigned of King Edward the iiiith to fynd a preyste to celebrate in the seid P'ishe church for ever.

Sir John Leeche, incumbent then of the age of 51 yeares having no other living than in the said chauntry which ye yerely . . . £6 ye tenths allowed.

The dean and chapter of Wallingford was responsible for the stipend, but with the lands now forfeited the commissioners reported that no one was paid.

In 1770 the workhouse on the same site was made up into compartments 'in which the wretched pauper women sat spinning'. By 1794 the workhouse had gone and a pest house was built on the north of the town. The Trout Inn stands there now, well known to fishermen and tourists alike and in 1977 part of the land was designated a caravan park.

The five-day St John's Bridge Fair, established by charter in 1234 a few years after the bridge was built, was held in the meadow near by. It would have been an annual event of considerable importance to the welfare of the community, where people flocked from miles around to enjoy the old time fun. Local farmers brought their products, particularly cheese and butter, much of which found its way by barge from the warehouse at the roadside near by, no doubt to find a ready market for the Oxford colleges that were soon to greatly increase in number, and beyond to London. In 1692 Baskerville mentioned 'seeing six or eight boats together' loading goods and this commerce still continued into the nineteenth century.

Thacker wrote of a Lechlade bargemaster in 1793 that the chief goods be carried down to London were:

Iron, Copper, Tin, manufactured and pig iron, Brass, Spelter, Cannon, Cheese, Nails, all iron goods and Bemb shells. He took back Groceries, Deals, Foreign timber, Merchandise of every Kind, a few coals, and of late Raw Hides for Tewkesbury and Worcester and Gunpowder to Bristol and Liverpool: has been applied to last Time he was up, to take Sugars to be carried to Bristol, but did not take

them, for when they came to enquire the Price, they found they
could go cheaper by the Kennet to Newbury, and the rest of the way
by land carriage.

By this year of 1792, the foregoing tells us how much commerce on
the Thames must have increased, now that the Thames and Severn
Canal was in full operation. At this time St John's Lock was in the
capable hands of Sir T. Wheate. Here is a good place to quote
Baskerville again on the importance of the River Coln, which
enters the river just below the Canal entrance:

> Coln flu;
> Here conjunctions, famous prove,
> On the score of united love,
> ffor here about Cown River wends,
> Its water into little Temes,
> And so these pleasing Banks they wash,
> And help the Boats, down with a flash.

At the turn of the century, in *The Thames from its Rise to the Nore*,
Walter Armstrong describes Lechlade thus:

> St John's Bridge at Lechlade marks the extreme boundary of that
> section of the Thames with which so many have lately become famil-
> iar. Lechlade itself is a small place, hardly bigger than Fairford. Its
> pride is the Church of St Lawrence, a fine perpendicular structure
> dating from the reign of Henry VII. ... The town and manor of
> Lechlade formed part of the dower of Katherine of Aragon. It once
> possessed a small priory dedicated to St John the Baptist, the only
> relic of which is now St John's Bridge ... built and kept in repair
> with funds obtained by alienating part of the priory lands. The bridge
> is a peculiarly substantial piece of work, and according to tradition,
> at least, is one of the oldest on the Thames. For all who wish to have
> a good time on the river in a boat of comfortable size, the wharf at
> St John's Bridge is the best starting place. Above it the navigation
> presents many difficulties and the scenery few beauties; the river
> may indeed be followed almost to its source in a canoe, but it
> traverses few of those bosky dells and shady glens which the delight
> of such an exploration lies.... At St John's Bridge the navigation has
> been eased by a cut parallel with the main stream and in this cut
> occurs a lock.

Perhaps Armstrong was right. However, beauty as they say, is in the
eye of the beholder, but as a voyager beyond Inglesham, he might

have had few opportunities, nor indeed, been in any mood to behold beauty where 'was all labour and sorrow' as Hutton has described it. Neither have I ever heard of anyone making a serious attempt to traverse the river in a canoe beyond Cricklade, much less to get 'almost to its source' in such a vessel. Thacker goes on to tell us:

> Ireland sketches the scene at this time from below the bridge. He shows no weir tackle; but has a vessel on the weir stream being towed down-stream by men on the *Trout* meadow bank. Wm Wells was the first pound keeper, at 3s.6d weekly. He stayed till at least 1798; possibly much longer. In May 1792 complaint was made that the tolls were being evaded; the keepers especially when freshly installed at the new pound locks, were . . . no match for the truculent and hard swearing bargemen. In 1793 the pound toll was 2½d. per ton.

In that year, 'no barge can pass down with a proper cargo on board, unless the Flash at St John's Bridge runs three hours after the barge had gone thro' the Hook there, and the water cannot be raised back to proper flash mark in less than twelve hours.' In 1813 the keeper's wage was raised from 17s to 24s a month. In 1821 a Mrs Wells was the weir owner and the following year Richard Rodney was the keeper. The first lock house was built in 1830, when Benjamin Hodges was in charge there and, according to Thacker, he was thought to be living at the Trout close by. Thacker could not remove the possibility from his mind that Benjamin Hodges may have been a descendant of 'Dame Hodgson and her son' who, in 1692, was said by Baskerville to be the lessee of the St John the Baptist Head, the earlier name for the Trout Inn. Thacker says:

> Just before the first Conservancy Act in 1837 the lock was stated to be 'in a frightful state of dilapidation'; missing gates being replaced with hurdles and straw. Hall in 1859 shews the lockhouse in its original position on the left bank of the lock. Ravenstein in 1861 mentions a pleasure boat toll of sixpence: 'pay at Ousney'. The lock was repaired in 1867, the old lock owner being W. Prideaux. It was being rebuilt in 1905 when I passed through for the first time in much discomfort.

Thus Lechlade has had a very important past, with Father Thames, its life-blood and the reason for its existence, always dominating

Old Father Thames at Lechlade

the scene. As well as the river, road transport also began to play a vital part – from the saddle horse and the pack-horse at earlier times. The ungainly, springless stage-coach trundled slowly along the rough, deeply rutted tracks throughout the late seventeenth and eighteenth centuries. Gradually, when springs were invented, more handsome vehicles were used on the improved roads, the upkeep of which depended mainly on tolls. Shortly after the death of Oliver Cromwell, in the middle of the seventeenth century, we know the costs of travel by coach over certain routes, which was several years before the first mail coach managed to get from Bath to London at a speed of seven miles an hour, carrying four passengers. But it was the early nineteenth century before the art of coach building was to reach its highest state of perfection, and mail coaches in their red livery, as well as some private stagecoaches, drawn by teams of four horses, on the main trunk roads, began to impress and attract more and more travellers. Coaching inns sprang up at intervals convenient for the changing of horses along the main trunk routes, and always, unless the coach stopped at a refreshment stage or it was necessary for the passengers to stretch their legs, the whole operation was carried out with remarkable speed and efficiency. This was the age of romance in stagecoach travel, improving on the time when the 'flying coach' on the great London road, was able to get to London in summer in twenty hours and in winter in two days. Stage-coaches and mail-coaches continued to run in healthy competition until the advent of the railways, and a few were still running at the outbreak of the First World War.

Innkeepers must have flourished in the prosperous years of the eighteenth century, eleven were licensed in Lechlade alone in 1755. The Swan in Burford Street is believed to be one of the oldest. On the corner of Thames Street and High Street the Red Lion, once known as The Lion, is also very old and has been there since at least 1552. The New Inn was built on the south side of the market place in about the middle of the seventeenth century and is thought to have become the most important hostelry in the town, while the Bell is known to have been there in 1719.

With the fading years of the glory of the 'four in hand', many innkeepers began to experience harder times and it is known that some of them sought additional occupations in order to maintain their living standards. These substantial old coaching inns, including the Trout at St John's Bridge, lend credence to the importance once attached to them and to the town itself for travellers. In 1794 London coaches began making thrice-weekly calls and the Oxford mail-coach called twice daily. At about this time a considerable number of stage wagons began using the route, carrying cloth from the Stroud area. The parish registers give us some idea of the strolling players, vagrants, licensed hawkers and travelling people who found their way to Lechlade. Records also show that now that there was easier access by road to London, in addition to the river, there were many examples of natives of Lechlade leaving home to take up residence in the capital.

Once the Great Western Railway was opened in 1840 it was able to serve Lechlade by means of coaches and carriers from the Faringdon Road station at Challow. In 1873 the East Gloucestershire Railway, from Witney to Fairford, was opened with a station at Lechlade that was to serve it well for a great many years. By the early 1930s, when I sometimes cycled to Fairford from my home in Cricklade to take a train passing through Lechlade to Oxford, I recall the impression I had that the stations appeared to be doing very little business. Like so many others of the smaller railway companies they continued to be subsidized for a great number of years, as mentioned before in the case of the Midland and South Western Junction Railway, which served Cricklade. The Fairford–Witney line was closed in 1962.

There were still fifteen public houses in the parish at the beginning of the twentieth century, and soon, with the coming of the motor car, hoteliers and innkeepers alike began to feel a new surge of life. Although the number of inns has now been reduced, places like the Red Lion, the Crown, the New Inn and the Swan have prospered to survive into the 1990s.

26   Lechlade – Churches and Manor

The wind has swept from the wide atmosphere
Each vapour that obscured the sunset's ray;
And pallid evening twines its beaming hair
In duskier braids around the languid eyes of day;
Silence and twilight, unbeloved of men,
Creep hand in hand from yon obscurest glen.

They breathe their spells towards the departing day,
Encompassing the earth, air, stars and sea;
Light, sound and motion own the potent sway,
Responding in the charm with its own mystery.
The winds are still, or the dry church tower grass
Knows not their gentle motions as they pass.

Thou too, aeriel pile! whose pinnacles
Point from one shrine like pinnacles of fire
Obeyest in silence their sweet solemn spells
Clothing in hues of heaven thy dim and distant spire
Around whose lessening and inevitable height
Gather, among the stars, the clouds of night.

'A Summer Evening Churchyard',
Percy Bysshe Shelley (1792–1822)

The church and other places of Christian worship, as with every
other village and township, has always remained the true focal
point of the Lechlade community. The Parish Church of St
Lawrence, c.1470, on the site of a previous church, was built, like
many others along the valley, close to the river, emphasising the
considerable importance that has always been attached to the

waterway as a means of transport.

The present edifice, known as one of the Cotswold 'wool churches', was built mainly from the wealth engendered during those halcyon decades of the wool trade. At that time rich wool merchants were wont to ease the burdens of their consciences, or perhaps subscribe out of the inherent goodness of their hearts, to construct these beautiful buildings, some of which I have mentioned, for example the solid, beautifully proportioned pile at Kempsford. The graceful outlines of Lechlade's church and spire have been the subject of poets and Thacker described St Lawrence Church as a 'triumph of medieval inspiration'. Shelley particularly loved this building and his ode above to 'A summer evening churchyard' could scarcely describe it more delightfully.

The roof of the church was destroyed by fire in 1510, to be rebuilt at a lesser pitch and a higher level, clerestory lights were then installed. It was at this time that the tower was strengthened, the spire added, the large east window inserted and the beautiful porch built, it has been said, from stones in the chapel of the old priory. The chapel in the south aisle is dedicated to St Blaize, the patron saint of the wool combers and blazers, and here we see that wool combs are depicted on the reredos. One of the benefactors of the church was John Townsend, wool merchant, who died in 1485, and in the floor of the north aisle, with his feet on the woolsack, is a brass dedicated to him and to his wife Ellen. There is another brass to John Twynyhoe. There is a memorial brass to Robert Hitchman, wool merchant who died in 1510, but his wife's effigy is said to have been missing for more than 200 years. Robert died in 1510. There is also apparently a tribute to an organist who played there for sixty-three years and for forty of these was sexton also. A symbol of Katherine of Aragon, who held the manor from 1501 to 1535, is in the form of a pomegranate, which may be seen carved on the fourteenth century door in the chancel's south aisle leading to the sacristy.

The corbelling of the oak-panelled chancel roof is of angels and the four evangelists, and there are forty carved bosses, which were repainted in 1934 by Patrick Philips, and have possibly since been refurbished. Here and there are relics of a church that once stood on the site such as the piscina, a badly damaged stone picture on the wall of the south aisle, and near the organ, a statuette of St Agatha. The priest's door is beautifully and delicately carved with oak tracery, and where once was the Lady Chapel, is now occupied by the late nineteenth-century organ.

In a canopy above the fifteenth-century font, on which traces of colour can still be seen, is a damaged figure, thought to be 'a casualty of the Civil War'. As in Lechlade, and so many other places in this Upper Thames area, war has left its mark. The font has an eighteenth-century cover. Holy oil for the font was stored in a canopied niche in one of the piers of the nave.

The nineteenth century pulpit, sculpted by local craftsmen, stands on a fourteenth-century base recovered from a nearby garden. The brass lectern is also nineteenth century, as are most of the stained glass windows together with a few of the twentieth century, one of which is thought to be among the finest in Gloucestershire. The windows contain a little medieval glass. Hanging in the nave is a fine brass chandelier, a tribute by Richard Ainge, one of a line of wharfingers who occupied Church House south of the churchyard and traded from Old Wharf at the bottom of their garden. John Ainge had lived there to be followed by his son Richard and his grandson Richard (d. 1878). Their seventeenth-century house was refronted early in the following century and was extended to both east and west in the twentieth century. In the formal garden there is a canal, a summer house of brick and a gazebo built into the churchyard wall.

The church clock (*c.* 1780, and known as a 'four poster') is by Thomas Reynolds of Oxford. A brief history of the six bells can be seen in the useful church guide on sale in the church itself. Externally the Perpendicular east chancel window has a niche above it in which is St Lawrence with the gridiron on which he was martyred. The beautiful north porch, mentioned above, has a battlemented parapet with castellated pinnacles and the flat stone ceiling is finished with lierne ribs.

The names and dates of all the vicars are known as far back as 1255. That of Conrad Nye was the first to come into prominence for promoting considerable rebuilding of the edifice, soon after his appointment in 1468. Thereafter, for the next hundred years or more we seem to find a number of incumbents with characteristics that might be said not to have been, for one reason or another, a credit to their cloth. In 1551 the vicar Adam Russell 'was found to be ignorant of the commandments', and deprived of the living 'for being married in 1554'. In 1662, John Golshill, a pluralist, neglected quarter sermons. John Dormer, his successor in 1572, although described as zealous in religion, employed an illiterate parish clerk in 1576 who omitted some of the prescribed readings. In 1579, it was said that he was tricked into resigning by a man who had obtained from him a lease of the vicarage, after being in trouble with the Commission for Ecclesiastical Causes.

There is a two-storey Baptist Chapel in Sherborne Street dated

1817, which was built with the assistance of the lord of the manor, William Fox. George Fox, who was the founder of the Society of Friends more than a century and a half earlier, does not appear to have been a forebear. In *c.* 1850, the chapel had a Sunday evening congregation of more than a hundred.

The Congregationalists did not fare so well in Lechlade. A chapel was built in the Burford road by the Revd H.J. Cramp in 1849, but his death, which occurred soon afterwards, left it 'heavily encumbered'. Its congregations apparently seldom reached a hundred and in 1851 it was closed, having passed into the hands of the mortgagees. However, sixteen years later it was reopened, but sadly closed again in 1888. Meanwhile a Wesleyan chapel had been built at the west end of the High Street, both it and the Baptist Chapel were closed in 1977.

Lechlade contains many fine eighteenth-century houses. Like Church House, both Sherborne House and Grey Gables in Wharf Lane also have gazebos. The former, built in the early seventeenth century, was associated with the Dutton family of Sherborne, but later became the home of a well-known Lechlade family, the Loders. In Burford Street is another fine old building, rebuilt by John Ward, a mercer, (d. *c.* 1721).

The manor, which was dismembered in the late seventeenth century, has such an interesting history as to be worthy of mention a little later. Most of the outlying farms date from this time. Claydon House on the Cirencester road is believed to have been built by Robert Bathurst (*d.* 1692), who was the son of the lord of the manor Sir Edward Bathurst, whose family lived there until the 1760s. The Bathurst pedigree is not easy to follow but we do know that Edward Bathurst, second eldest son of Robert (the elder Robert died a minor) was knighted in 1643. He narrowly avoided sequestration of his estates after the Civil War for his sympathies with the Royalist cause, by claiming that any help he gave them was given under duress. Although lying in debatable territory it appears that for the greater part of the Civil War, Lechlade was in Parliamentary hands. In 1645 a small force of Parliamentarians was sent to fortify it and successfully repulsed a Royalist attack.

On the subject of battles, I should mention here, although nothing whatever to do with the Civil War, but much earlier, of the place name in Lechlade, known as the Gastons, now a housing estate. At Eisey there is an area called on the earlier maps 'Gaerston' (Gastons), where I firmly believe a battle took place and where the evidence is in the mounds and ditches that can still be clearly seen on the hillside. We know that a battle during the Wars of the Roses took place near Tewkesbury and the field is still known as The Gastons. The argument is therefore strong, as at Eisey, that here, on this site in Lechlade, a battle once took place. Curiously nothing has been mentioned of this in the *Victoria County History*, and to this date the importance of the name has likewise been ignored at Eisey.

The Manor

As far as can be told, the interesting history of Lechlade Manor began with the Norman Conquest, as indeed did that of all manors as we know them. Parcelled up by William I, the land was taken from its Saxon owners and by 1085 only about one per cent of Saxon land-owners were left holding their land. Here at Lechlade it was given to Henri de Ferrieres, a name on the plaque in the Castle of Fallaise. Records in Domesday show that he was taxed on sixteen hides. The manor, with its watermill, a fishery that produced about 175 eels annually and the Meadow Ground, yielded £20 per annum.

By *c*. 1205 the manor was in the possession of Isabel de Ferrers (probably the daughter of Henri). She married Roger Mortimer, and after his death in 1216, was married to Peter Fitzherbert, who between them founded the Nunnery and the Priory hospital. Isabel was buried in the Nunnery.

Meanwhile the war with France saw the sequestration of many French estates belonging to the English and, in retaliation Henry III, deprived many Norman Barons of their estates, of which Lechlade was one, and granted it to his brother Richard, Duke of Cornwall. Richard had a gallows erected in Lechlade for public hanging. On his death and that of his wife Sanchia (they were both buried at Hailes Abbey) Henry III had the manor, including two mills, valued at £43 14¼d.

Richard's son Edmund inherited the estate and, being without issue, he gave the manor to the Abbey of Hailes to hold at a fee-farm rent of £100, which annual sum was ultimately to be settled on Queen Isabella and her two children. On Edmund's death Edward I granted the estate to Richard Talbot the Younger who exchanged interest in it with Hugh le Despenser the elder for that of the manor of Siddington, near Cirencester. Lechlade was then valued at £150, of which £100 was paid to the king.

After the execution of Hugh le Despenser at Hereford in 1326, the manor came into the hands of Edmund of Woodstock, Earl of Kent, the younger son of Edward I, whose execution is another story. For a brief period the manor then came into the possession of the Mortimer family, and Geoffrey de Mortimer held it until 1350.

For the next 200 years there were numerous owners, and first we learn that after the Mortimers it came into the possession of John, Earl of Kent, son of Edmund of Woodstock. On his (John's) death in 1353, the estate was bequeathed to his sister Joan, otherwise known as 'the Fair Maid of Kent', who married Sir Thomas Holland. After the death of Sir Thomas in 1361 she married Edward the Black Prince, also known as Edward of Woodstock, where he was born, and she became the mother of Richard II.

Meanwhile Elizabeth, John of Kent's widow, held the manor in dower until she died in 1409, when it passed to his great-nephew, Edmond Mortimer, Earl of March, son of Joan of Kent's daughter Elinor Holland. With his brother, Edmond was declared heir apparent to the English throne through Philipa of Clarence their paternal grandmother, grand-daughter of Edward III. Edmond and his brother both died without issue, and now the Wars of the Roses (1455–87) were to begin between the houses of York and Lancaster. With Henry VI, the Lancastrian claim to the throne was said to be stronger than that of Richard Duke of York, who considered that he had a better hereditary claim (though passing twice through a woman), and descended from the third (but second surviving) son of Edward III.

Richard was killed and the manor was then granted to his widow for her lifetime. St Lawrence Church as we know it today was built during this period of her widowhood. She died the mother of Edward IV and Richard III in 1495. The manor then passed into the hands of Henry VII, his wife being heiress of the House of York.

It was in 1501 that, as part of the dower of Catherine of Aragon, numerous manors in Gloucestershire, including that of Lechlade and the town itself, came into her hands. She died in 1535. It is thought possible that the manor may then have been granted to Katherine Parr, the six wife of Henry VIII. The youthful Edward VI conveyed it to Dennis Toppes in 1551, exchanging it for manors in Norfolk. In 1590, on the orders of Queen Elizabeth, his son, Thomas Toppes, lost the manor and it was handed to Edward Dodge and Peter Houghton.

A daughter of Edward Dodge, Mary, married John Bathurst, the elder son of Robert Bathurst. Edward Bathurst, Robert's second son, became lord of the manor in 1628. He it was who narrowly avoided sequestration of his estates after the Civil War mentioned earlier. He died in 1674 and is buried beneath the chancel in the church. His son having pre-deceased him, the manor passed to his grandson Edward, and now we get much nearer to the present.

Edward, who died young, left his two sisters, Mary and Anne, co-heiresses of the estate, and the baronetcy went to an uncle. The family eventually left England to settle in a recently formed colony in Georgia, USA. Anne married John Grenning and her share of the manor passed to a niece of her husband and was sold to Sir Francis Page in 1718 to be passed on to his widow Dame Francis Page. The Colston Trust bought Mary's share of the estate for a niece of Edward Colston. One of Mary's daughters married John Pullen of Lechlade. Sir Jacob Wheate, the brother of Dame Francis Page became owner of this part of the estate and Sir Jacob bought John Pullen's share in 1774.

By 1783 the vicar, Sir John Thomas Wheate, became Lord of the Manor with the ownership eventually passing to Dame Avis Wheate and the land began to be split up into smaller estates with the major part and manorial rights and privileges being bought from Sir Jacob Wheate's trustees by Samuel Churchill of Doddington, Oxon.

William Fox, mentioned earlier, who built the local Baptist chapel and was founder of the Sunday School Society, bought it in 1807. In 1819 it was sold to George Milward to remain in the Milward family until *c.* 1890. George Milward's grandson rebuilt the manor house and it was completed in 1873.

Since the Milwards the manor has changed ownership many times. First came the Prior-Wandesfords to be followed by James Jones and family. After Mrs Jones's death the estate was bought by the Hon. Algernon Mills, but he died before he was able to live there. The house became empty until 1923, after which the owners were Mr and Mrs Robert Grey, followed by Capt. Edgar Chester-Master who sold the house and the grounds to the Eltham Park, London-based Community of St Clotilde in 1939. The Community's day and boarding school for girls opened soon afterwards. As the school began to grow several additions were subsequently made to the building, including new dormitories, a chapel, gymnasium and so on. It presently holds some 200 pupils.

The Anglo-Saxon Cemetery

Mention has been made of the importance of archaeology in the dating – by artefacts – of excavations, helping to give us a clearer

insight into the lives of those ancient peoples who were our ancestors. It is fitting therefore to conclude these chapters about the
valley of the Upper Thames in general, and of Lechlade in particular, with a further mention of the most important discovery ever
made here. With the kind permission of the Oxford Archaeological
Unit, I quote in large measure from their fascinating account of the
first phase of their work taken from *Invested in Mother Earth*
published after initial excavations were completed, but before the
full results of their research are known.

In dating, for example, archaeologists generally accept that
whenever beads of amber are found with female remains, they
date after AD 500. Two hundred years later its use for personal
adornment is thought to have gone out of fashion. However, I
believe that by that time, this largely coniferous fossil had
become more difficult, if not impossible to obtain, and these
early personal adornments, usually found in graves of the wealth-
ier classes, were precious heirlooms, brought over by their invad-
ing ancestors. Many are believed to have emigrated from an area
in Jutland and around the Baltic where the largest finds of amber
in Europe are found.

At the outset of this most interesting and revealing booklet it is
said:

> The opportunity to excavate at Butler's Field arose from a proposal
> by the Cotswold District Council, the owners of the land, to
> construct houses. As the site was a Scheduled Ancient Monument it
> was agreed in consultation with English Heritage that the Council
> should fund the Oxford Archaeological Unit to investigate the
> archaeology of Butler's Field before any development took place.

Work began on Monday 22 April 1985 in this 'flat windy expanse of
grassland' where aerial photography had shown it to be in the
centre of 'a fascinating piece of ancient landscape'. David Miles
and Simon Palmer of the unit began with a three-week excavation
of the site, thought to be a prehistoric ceremonial area adjacent to
the grounds of a Romano–British villa.

An archaeologist should never dig, expecting to find something
in particular; by so doing invariably disappointment will follow, but
excavations should begin with an open mind, only then can the joys
of his or her calling be fulfilled. From the book by David Miles and
Simon Palmer, it is obvious they had borne this very much in mind
when some astonishing results were revealed. Within an hour or so

after excavations had begun they knew they had made an unexpected discovery – 'a major Anglo-Saxon cemetery' not revealed by aerial photography. The 'rescue dig' was consequently extended to twelve weeks and with the help of the Manpower Services Commission and support of the Cotswold District Council nearly 250 burials were revealed, out of an estimated total of more than 500, many of these being outside the area, within a Scheduled Ancient Monument, 217 inhumations and thirty-two cremations were revealed.

These were pagan burials: graves lay in disorganised positions and directions, and any found lying from west to east were probably coincidental. Christianity was yet a long way from the conversion of these savage but highly intelligent people. The cemetery had been in use for several centuries and so it is not surprising that grave dating varied very considerably:

> The Saxons indicated the status and sex of the dead person by their possessions in the afterlife. A few burials are austere and without grave goods, but most of the 6th century women had their characteristic ornaments, bronze saucer brooches or button brooches on the shoulders, amber and glass beads on a flax thread hung between brooches, bronze pins, iron knives (smaller than those of the men) ... Some of the richer grave goods had bronze bowls and small stave-built buckets. In some cases rich grave goods accompanied children of four or five years of age, indicating that an Anglo-Saxon society status was to some extent, inherent rather than simply being earned. One of the interesting aspects of the Lechlade cemetery is the way in which it was organised into coherent and distinctive zones at different times in its lifespan.
>
> In the north-western part of the cemetery almost all the 6th century burials were of females orientated around a north-south axis. A number of young children here were probably girls judging from the grave goods, amber and glass beads and brooches ... The number of 6th century male burials excavated was relatively small. Probably the nucleus of the male zone lies still below ground to the west. The 6th century burials were laid out in rows. Graves of the same period did not disturb each other.

Below is an illustration of what a young woman of about eighteen years of age belonging to a wealthy Anglo-Saxon family, may well have looked like. Her attire is based on the grave goods found with her skeleton.

The young lady . . . was laid out with her head to the south and her face turned to the west. Behind her skull a circlet of blue glass beads must have held back her hair. There was a large gilded saucer brooch on each shoulder with traces of a woollen dress adhering to the back. A massive gilded-bronze square-headed brooch held her cloak together. Amber beads and a string of tubular glass beads were thickly spread across her chest. A further heap of beads lay by her waist and had perhaps originally been in a bag [reticule]. The total of over 500 beads is an exceptionally large quantity. The young girl had even more jewellery – silver spiral rings on four fingers, bronze pins in her dress and a cosmetic brush. By her head a wooden or leather bottle was decorated with circular and triangular bronze plaques. Against this rested a bone spindle whorl and bone comb. A large ivory ring hung on the left side of her waist. This was the stiffener of a bag . . . Inside were various metal rings which were probably kept as protective amulets. An iron chatelain also hung from her waist – keys symbolic of her status as keeper of the house.

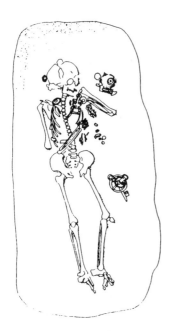

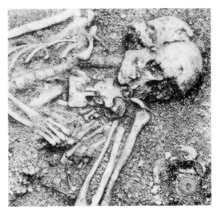

An 18-year-old girl buried with jewellery, brooches, rings, amber, glass beads and by her head a wooden bowl decorated with bronze discs and next to it a bone spindle whorl and bone comb

Below is dramatic proof of Christianity coming to pagan peoples. The seventh century grave lies east to west in the Anglo-Saxon graveyard of Lechlade's Butler's Field.

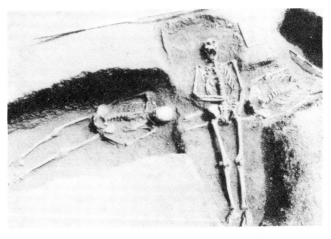

The stratigraphy of the dead: the early sixth-century burials lie north-south and are overlain by later seventh-century burials which lie east-west

The song that the river sang
Ere he merged in the infinite sea;
Like a brave life turned without pang
To the rest in eternity:
And ever he chanted and ever he ran,
And ended with joy and with joy he began;
And thus he sang to me.

I rise on a western hill
In a covert of dew and moss,
A murmuring musical rill
A maiden's leap will cross:
Small furry creatures and snakes that glide
Come stooping to drink in the hot noontide
And birds my waters toss.

By Lechlade I murmur and run,
Then linger with children at play
In meadows whose lover the sun
Has filled with the burden of May:
And love has not dimpled the face of a girl
More softly than mine as I eddy and whirl
Where islands check my way.

Mine ancient course I keep
Where Oxford sets her spires,
And out and away I sweep
Through far and leafy shires;
And clear and strong I hurry me down
By the old grey bridge at Henley town,
In a flight that never tires.

By eyot and wind-swept down,
With toll from many a rill,
I wind through the royal town,
And past sweet Cooper's Hill;
And broad and strong and full of the lips
I cradle at last the mighty ships
Whose sails the sea winds fill.

So Thames rejoiced and sang
As he drew to the sea and his rest;
His strong soul knew no pang,
Though he flung one sigh to the west;
And brave hearts end like the noble stream,
Having lived life full and 'followed the gleam';
Having sought and won the best.

Appendix

Cricklade surnames connected with its history within these pages and existing in the author's lifetime.

Abbreviations

C. Connected; D. Author descended from; LD. Likely descent; PD. Possible descent. NK. Not known by Author; NNK. Not now known by Author; NBC. Not believed to be connected; R. Related by marriage to Author; WK. Was known byAuthor.

A

ADAMS	Name extant. PD.
ALLAN (EN)	NK.
ANDREWS	NK.
ARCHER	Some were plasterers in the first half of the twentieth century LD.

B

BALDWIN	Craftsmen, Carpenters and Joiners.
BARNES	Builders living at The Forty. Moved to Lydiard Millicent.
BARRETT	Extant. PD. NK.
BOULTON	Extant. NBC.
BROOKS	A town doctor. Late grandson landlord of the Three Horseshoes.
BURGE	Extant. PD. NK.
BURGESS	Extant. NK.

C

CARTER	Butchers in the High Street. Extant. NK.
CHIVERS	Robert Chivers a bandmaster. Extant. PD. NNK.
CLARK (E)	Brothers, carriers early in twentieth century. Branch believed extinct.
CHAMPERNOUN	Farmers. Name extinct in district.

COWLEY   Carriers in the High Street early in twentieth century.
COOLE   Extant. D. Leading Congregationalists. Present J.P.
COOK   Farmer at Broadleaze *c*. 1920. Extant LD.
CULLERNE   Decorators until *c*. 1940. Branch extinct.
CUSS   Arrival late seventeenth century. Farmers, Masons, Carpenters & Joiners, Signalmen. Bakers. Engineers. Aircraft designers. Builders.

D

DAISH (DASH)   Farmed at Stones Farm, Stones Lane. LD.
DENNING   Town's M.D. WK. Extant NBC. NK.

E

ELDRIDGE   Bakers & Corn Merchants, 98 High Street (1925) D.
ELLIS   Extant. PD. NK.
ELLISON   Extant. NK.

F

FARMER   Extant. NK.
FRANKLIN   Builders in early twentieth century. Male line believed to be extinct.

G

GARLICK   Extant. NK. PD.
GILES   Domesday mention. One of oldest Cricklade surnames. Numerous. Well known. Many trades and occupations.
GINGELL   Extant. NK. PD.
GODDARD   Coal Merchants. D. WK. Extant. NK.
GODWIN   Extant. NK.
GRIFFIN   Extant. NK.
GUNNING   Saddlers & Harness Makers in High Street.

H

HAMMOND   Family came to town 1904. Motor Engineers. R.
HARVEY   Lane named after family: now Rectory Lane. Extant. NK.
HAINES   Extant. NK.
HAYWARD   High St Photographer/Tobacconist. Son killed WWI. Extant. NK.
HAYES   Horse dealers. Extant. PD. NK.
HICKS   Extant. NK.
HOBBS   Extant. NK. PD.
HOLLAND   Extant. NK.
HOPKINS   High Street Chemists early twentieth century. PD. NK.
HOUSE   High St family. Son's death on motor cycle.

J

JAMES   A High St Nurse after SWW. Extant. NK.
JONES   Extant. NK.

K

KILMINSTER	One of oldest sixteenth century Cricklade families. Extant. LD.

L

LANE	Extant. LD.
LARGE	Recall as farming family. Extant. NK.
LAWRENCE	Extant. NK.
LITTLE	One of oldest Cricklade surnames. W.J. Little, High Bailiff.
LOVETT	Solicitor's daughters: Danvers House private Girls School.
LUCAS	The Town Crier. High St Fishmonger.

M

MASLIN	A Printer living in Calcutt Street *c.* 1950. Extant. PD.
MESSENGER	Farm workers at Eisey late nineteenth century. Extant. NK. PD.
MILLARD	Coal Merchants early twentieth century. No. 1 High Street.
MILLER	Extant. No connections.
MILLS	A Gardener for Revd Wray at Rectory early twentieth century.
MUTLOW	WK. Extant. NK. PD.

N

NASH	Bandmaster early twentieth century and blacksmith High St. Extant. WK.
NEWMAN	Landlord Bear Inn. Car driver for L.O. Hammond & Sons.

O

OCKWELL	Builders. Founders of Chas Ockwell & Co., Glove Makers.
ORAM	Farmed Fiddle Farm *c.* 1828. WK. Extant. NKN.

P

PAINTER	Family at 24 or 25 High St in 1920s WK. Extant. NNK.
PALMER	Extant. NK.
PACKER	Thomas. Engineer with Town's water *c.* 1920. LD.
PARKER	Extant. NK.
PHILLIPS	High St. Off-License. 1920s LD.
PETRIE	Extant. NK. PD.
PEARE	Horse dealers, Dance House *c.* 1920s. Extant. NNK.
PINNOCK	Henry, Butcher: First WWI Volunteer. Killed in Action. Brother Jack a bricklayer. WK. Extant. NNK.
POOLE	Several families. WK. Extant. NNK.

R

RICHARDS	Revd S.W.L. Richards. Family gone away. Extant. NK.

S

SADDLER	Butchers early twentieth century. Old Cricklade family. Extant. PD.
SALMON	Farmers early twentieth century. Daughter kept Forty House School.
SAUNDERS	Farm workers Eisey late nineteenth-century, early twentieth century. LD.
SCOTT	A family owned White Hart early twentieth century.
SELBY	Plasterer craftsmen early twentieth century. Shopkeepers. LD.
SHIPWAY	Road worker early twentieth century of Calcutt St.
SMALL	Extant. NK. PD.
STEPHENS	W.H.S. 1 *c.* 1873. Bakers. Corn dealers. W.H.S. 11. Postmaster Chairman of Waylands Estates Feoffees. D.
STRANGE	Postman early 1920s. LD.
STRATFORD	Joseph a craftsman mason, early twentieth century.

T

TAYLOR	The Mss Taylor: Alkerton House: Branch extinct. Extant. NK.
TOWNSEND	Schoolmaster mixed school early twentieth century.
TRINDER	High Street butcher. Gone away. LD.
TURK	Landlord Bear Inn early twentieth century. Preceded Newman.

V

VINCENT	Police Sergeant High St. WK. Extant. C. NKK.

W

WAKEFIELD	Drapers High St early twentieth century. WK. Extant. NNK.
WEBB	Extant. NBC. NK.
WELLS	Extant. PD. NK.
WHEELER	Farmed Ashton Keynes crossroads *c.* 1946.
WHITE	Extant. NBC. NK.
WILKINS	Bros Charles & Noel; farmed Headlands Farm. Horse dealers.
WILKS	William a postman early twentieth century.
WISE	Extant. PD. NK.
WOODWARD	Farm worker families early twentieth century. PD.

All entries in this list have been made to the best of my knowledge and belief. I extend my apologies for any errors, incorrect statements or assumptions made herein, or for any names in the body of this book I may have failed to include.

Bibliography

Armstrong, W., *The Thames: From its Rise to the Nore*, 2 vols (*c.* 1890)

Baldwin, Mark., *Canals: A New Look*

Bateman, J., *The Great Landowners of Great Britain and Ireland*, 4th edn (1878)

Bennett, H.E., *Life in the English Manor* (Alan Sutton Publishing Co.)

Bindoff, S.T., *The Early Tudors* (1950)

Bond, Francis, *English Church Architecture*

Boydell, C., *History of the River Thames*

Brann, C., ed., *Kemble, Ewen and Poole Keynes: Three Villages by the Infant Thames* (Collectors Books Ltd., 1992)

Campbell, Mildred, *English Yeoman in the Stuart and Tudor Age* (1974)

Charlton, Bill, *A Year on the Thames*

Cobbett, William, *Rural Rides*, 2v (Dent, London)

Cornish, C.J., *A Naturalist on the Thames* (1908)

Cuss, H.W. John, *Enjoying Birds in Britain* (Merlin Books Ltd., 1994)

Davies, Gareth and Chorlton, Bill, *A Year on the Thames*

de Mare, Eric, *The Canals of England* (Architectural Press, 1950)

de Salis, H.R., *Chronology of Inland Navigation* (E. & F.N. Spon, 1897)

Dunlop, J. and Denham, R.D., *British Apprenticeship and Child Labour*

Feiling, Keith, *A History of England* (Book Club Associates)

Forbes, V.A. and Ashford, V.H.R., *Our Waterways* (John Murray, 1906)

Gardner, S.R., *History of the Great Civil War*, new edn, 4 vols (1893)

Genealogical Publications, Chicago. *English Ancestry and Homes of the Pilgrim Fathers* (Genealogical Publications, Chicago)

Gibbings, Robert, *Sweet Thames Run Softly* (J.M. Dent)

Gibbon, Geoffery, *Through the Saxon Door: A Story of Somerford Keynes* (1969)

Goodwin, D.D., *Pictorial History of Canals* (Batsford)

Gwynn, S., *Two in a Valley* (Rich & Cowan, London)

Hadfield, C.E.R., *The Story of British Canals* (Phoenix House)

Hadfield, Chas, *Canals between the English and the Bristol Channels*

Hadfield, Chas and Alice (eds), *The Cotswolds: A New Study* (David & Charles, 1973)

Hall, Mr and Mrs S.C., *The Book of the Thames* (1859)

Hanson, H., *Heyday of Coach Travel in Britain* (1983)

Highwaymen of Wiltshire, The (E & W Books)

Hole, Christina, *English Home Life* 2nd edn, (Batsford, 1949)

Hough, G.L., *Dictionary of Dates* (W. & R. Chambers Ltd., Edinburgh)

How to Read Local Archives 1550–1700 (Phillimore, 1967)

Hutton, Revd W.H., *By Thames and Cotswolds*

Hutton, Revd W.H., *Highways and Byways in Wiltshire* (Macmillan & Co. Ltd., 1917)

Jones, Sydney R., *English Village Homes* (Batsford, 1936 and 1947)

Kingsley, Nicholas, *The Country Houses of Gloucestershire*, 2 vols, (1989)

Krausse, L.L., *Pictorial History of the Thames* (1889)

List of Parishes in Boyd's Marriage Index, 6 edn (Society of Genealogists)

Local Historian's Encyclopedia, 2nd edn (Society of Genealogists, 1956)

Lund, *Middle English Surnames of Occupation* (1935)

Mackie, J.D., *The Early Tudors* (1952)

Miles, David and Palmer, Simon, *Invested in Mother Earth* (Oxford Archaeological Unit)

Mingay, G.H., *The Gentry: The Rise and Fall of the Ruling Class* (Longman Group)

Mortimer, R.E., *The Archives of the Society of Friends*

North, The Hon. Roger, *The Lives of the Norths* (1890)

Orwin, G.S., *The Open Fields* (1938)

Osborne, J. Lee, *Cricklade: The Meeting with Augustine and the British Bishops* (1921)

Parker, Roland, *The Common Stream*

Peterson, Madge and Ward, Ernie, *Ashton Keynes: A Village with no History* (Keith Cowley, 1986)

Pollard, A.F., *England Under Protector Somerset* (1900)

Priestly, Joseph, *Bradshaw's Canals and Navigable Rivers of England and Wales* (1831)

Rogers, Therold, *Six Centuries of Work and Wages* (1883)

Rolt, L.T.C., *Inland Waterways of England* (Allen & Unwin)

Rolt, L.T.C., *Narrow Boat* (Eyre & Spottiswoode, 1944)

Rolt, L.T.C., *The Thames from Mouth to Source* (1951)

Roots, I., *The Great Rebellion* (1966) [Brief and comprehensive]

Ruskin, Brian, *Lechlade from the Mists of Antiquity*, parts 1 and 2

Russell, R.L., *Lost Canals and Waterways*

Ryan, Cornelius, *A Bridge too Far* (Hamish Hamilton, 1974)

Simpson, A.W.B., *Introduction to the History of the Land Law* (Oxford, 1961)

Smith, A.H. (ed.), *English Place-name Elements*, 2 vols (Cambridge University Press, 1956)

Smith, F. and Gardner, D.H., *Genealogical Research in England and Wales*, 3 vols (Salt Lake City Bookcraft, 1958–9, 1964)

Smith, G., *Our Canal Populations: A Cry from the Boat Cabins* (Houghton, 1875)

A List of Parishes in Boyd's Marriage Index, 6th edn (Society of Genealogists)

Stephens, W.B., *Sources for English Local History* (1981)

Tate, W.C., *The Parish Chest*

Thacker, Frederick Samuel, *The Stripling Thames* (1908)

Thacker, Frederick Samuel, *The Thames Highway*

Thomson, Dr T.R., *Materials for a History of Cricklade* (Cricklade Historical Society)

Thomson, Michael, *English Landed Society in the 19th Century*

Thurston, Thomas, *The Flower of Gloster*

Trevelyan, G.M., *English Social History* (Longmans Green & Co., 1948)

Victoria County History, vol 7

Verey Walters, B., *Thirteen Rivers to the Thames* (1964)

Warren, C. Henry, *England is a Village* (Eyre & Spottiswoode)

Webster, R.G., *The Law Relating to Canals*

West, J., *Village Records* (Macmillan, 1962)

West, Michael, *Britain's Lost Waterways*

Williams, *Nonconformist Congregations in Britain* (Dr Williams Trust, London, 1973)

Leaves from the Journal of the Poor Wiltshire Vicar of Cricklade in 1764–5 (Wiltshire Archaeological Society)

Index

Abingdon Court, 18
Act of Toleration, 1689, effect on area, 137–8
Alfred the Great, King, 17, 105
Ampney Brook, 45, 47, 181
Ampney Crucis, 47, 181
Ampney St Peter, 47, 181
Anglo Saxons, 17, 72–3, 105–6, 135–8, 198–200, 225
   Butler's Field excavations, 241–4
Archer, William, 163
Arnhem landings, 186, 187, 216
Ashton Keynes, 42, 49, 104–13
   bridges, 109, 112
   Church of the Holy Cross, 105–8, 185
   Civil War, 108
   Cotswold Settlement, 104
   Neolithic remains, 104
   Roman remains, 104–5
   Saxon remains, 105–6
   village crosses, 109–11
Athelstan, King, 81
Atrebates, Iron Age tribe, 15
Augustine's Oak, 135–6, *137*, 182

Bagendon, 15
Bathurst Family, 237, 239–40
Benfield, Paul, 170
Bibury, 47
Bicknoller, 31
Big Rose Lane, 29–30, 195
bird life, 23–30, 130, 150
Black Death, 17–18
'black pits', 18
Blunsden Hill, 15–16
Boycott, Professor & William, 84
Braydon, Forest of, 18–19, 28, 60, 104, 136
Bristow, Mr, 168–73
Brunel, Isambard Kingdom, 78
Butler's Field excavations, 241–4
Butterfield, William, 106, 200

Cahaignes, William de, 89, 97, 104
Calcutt, 44
canals
   benefits of, 36–7
   development of, 32, 51

effect on bird life, 24
efficiency compared with railways, 33–4
Gloucester & Sharpness, 34
Inland Waterway Association, 37
Kennet & Avon, 33
milestones, 35, *197*
North Wilts., 12, 24, 33, 35, 38–40, 43, 51
objections to, 36–7
Sapperton Tunnel, 33, 34, 35, 78
Stroudwater, 34, 38, 40
Thames & Severn, 12, 24, 33, 34–5, 38, 40, 45, 61, 84, 123, 212
tunnels, 35–6
typical charges on, 39–40
Wilts. & Berks. Canal Co., 38, 39
Worsley, 32
Castle Eaton, 11, 45, 46, 55, 185, 198–206
   Anglo–Saxon remains, 199, 200
   Church of St Mary the Virgin, 200, 201–6, *204*
   village cross, 205, *206*
Cedwalla, King of Wessex, 72
Cerney Wick, 44
Chartist Riots, 101, 119, 120
cheese production, 61, 215
Chelworth, 19
Christianity, introduction of, 138
church restoration, 106, 185, 200
churchwardens, duties of, 142–3
Churn, River, 13, 43–4, 57, 115
Civil War, 18–21, 70, 92, 108–9, 116, 128, 139, 178, 192, 237–8
coach travel, 31–2, 231–2
Cobbett, William, 36, 61, 101, 112, 119, 125, 179, 215
Coln, River, 47
Corinium (Roman town), 15, 16
Cotswold Canal Trust, 38, 40
Cotswold Settlement (Roman site), 104
Cotswold Water Park, 25, 40, 57, 115
Cowneck, 45–6, 219
crayfish, 68–70
Crickkelade, Thomas, 159
Cricklade, 124–73
   August Bank Holiday Show, 147
   bird life in, 26–7, 130, 150

borough boundaries dispute, 162–5
Calcutt Forty, 130
Church of St Mary, 13, *127*, 128, 144–5, 185
Church of St Sampson, 21, 77, 96, *126*, 127–8, 136, 138, 139–43, *140*, 160, 185, 219
in Civil War, 20, 128, 139
coming of railways, 149–52
Common Hill, 130
Crown Inn, 131
Dance Forty, 129
early church, 138
Elizabeth I visits, 183
entertainments, 148
fairs & markets, 156
Hatchetts Bridge, 125, 138
importance of river transport, 60–2
industry, 154
King's Head, 131
land enclosures, 129–30
New Inn, 131
non-conformist churches, 146–7
North Meadow, 27, 43, 129
Parish Hall, 143, 148
parish registers, 144–5
parliamentary history, 157–73
Petrie's Cricklade Case, 130, 157, 158, 161, 166–73
population figures, 1676, 133
Priory Field, 57
Red Lion Inn, 131
roads, 150, 152–3
Roman remains, 16–17, 44
Saracen's Head, 132
Saxon times, 135–8
Stone Yard plaque, 151, 154–6
Sun Inn, 131
Three Horse Shoes, 130–1
Town Bridge, 43–4, 50
town crosses, 148
Town Hall, 130
town walls, 16, 44
university foundation, suggested, 124
Watkin's Corner, 153
West Mill, 42–3, 46, 50–1, 56, 128
wharf, 13, 43, 46
White Hart Inn, 125, 130, 170
White Horse Inn (The Vale), 128, 129, 131
White Swan Inn, 130, 160, 168
Cromwell, Oliver, 20–1
Cuss, Alice, 193–4
Cuss, Cecil Taylor, 58
Cuss, Joseph John, 142
Cuss, Nevil John, 62, 149

Dance Brook, 52
de Chaworth, Patrick, 208
de la Mare Family, 202

de la Zouche Family, 202
Derry Brook, 46
Dewar, John, 160–4
dialect, 178
Dickens, Charles, 125
Dobuni, Iron Age Tribe, 11, 12, 15–16, 73, 104, 225
Domesday Survey, 13
Down Ampney, 17, 29, 79, 181–9
Airfield, 186, 187–8
Arnhem Memorials, 186, 187
Church of All Saints, 185–6
Gospel Oak, 182
Lertol's Well, 182
Manor House, 183, 188
Roman remains, 186
village cross, *183*
visit by Elizabeth I, 183
Dudley, John, Duke of Northumberland, 141
Dunch Family, 189
Dyrham, Battle of, AD 577, 73, 94, 105

Edwards, Mrs Anne, 118–19
eels, 70
Egbert, Saxon King, 199
Eisey, 35, 44, 178, 191–4
Bridge, 52
Church of St Mary, 179, 191–2, 193
Civil War, 192
Gastons, 178, 192, 237–8
Eisey Hill, 42, 45, 191
'Eleven Years Tyranny', 18–19
Elizabeth I, 18, 183
elm trees, loss of, 28–9
Ermin St, 16, 17, 18, 34, 46, 179
Ewen, 80–5
Bittenham Springs, 82
chapel; of ease, 74, 84
mill, 11, 49, 81, 84
Old Monk's Pond, 82
Parker's Bridge, 81, 85
Roman remains, 82
wharf, 84
Wild Duck Inn, 84–5

Fairford, 47
Fairford Airfield, 207, 216
Falaise, Castle of, Normandy, 87, 89
fish, 67–71
'flashing', 54, 64
floods, 1928, 43
Foyle Family, 112–13

Galimore, Humphrey, 205–6
Godstow Priory, 50, 55
Gordon, Anna, 78, 92
Gordon, Sir Robert, 78, 92
Grey, Revd William, 115, 119, 120
Gunn, Thomas Mann, 168–9, 173

Hanger, George, 210–11
Hannington Bridge, 55, 62, 213
Herbert, Col., 169–73
Horton Family, 193
Hungerford Family, 188–9
    Sir Anthony, 98, 99, 185, 189
    Edmund, 189
    Sir Thomas, 188–9
    Sir Walter, 189
Hutton, Revd W.H., 63, 80, 105–6, 203,
    213
Hwicce (Iron Age Tribe), 17, 135, 188,
    199

illegitimacy, 122–3
illiteracy, 122
Inglesham, 34, 40, 218–23
    Church of St John the Baptist,
        219–23
    Round House, 47, 66, 219
    village cross, *222*
Iron Age Settlements, 11, 15
Isis, derivation of name, 47–8

Kemble, 72–9
    airfield, 79
    ancient yew tree, 73–4
    Church of All Saints, 74–7, 84
    railway construction, 77–9
    Roman remains, 72–3
    Saxon remains, 73
Kempsford, 55, 185, 199, 207–17
    Church of St Mary, *209, 210*, 213–14
    Fairford Airfield, 207, 216
    ford, 212
    inns, 216
    Lady Maud's Walk, 208
    Manor, history of, 207–12
    mills, 215
    population & trades, 215–16
    village cross, 216
Keynes Family, 87, 89–90
Key, River, 26, 44, 46
    Sir Geoffrey de, 89
    John Maynard, 90
    Ralph de, 97
    William de, 97–8

Lancaster, Henry, Earl of, 208
land enclosures, 17th C., 18–19, 129
    19th C., 101
Latton, 34, 39, 174–9
    Church of St John the Baptist,
        175–6, 185
    Civil War, 178
    dialect, 178
    Mere path, 177
    mills, 44, 177
    mysterious tales, 177
    origins, 174–5
    Roman remains, 16

    village cross, 175, *176*
Latton, John & Isabel de, 174–5
Lechlade, 12, 34, 43, 185, 224–44
    Bronze Age remains, 225
    Church of St Lawrence, 225, 229,
        234–6, 239
    Civil War, 237–8
    fair, 228
    Gastons, 237–8
    Halfpenny Bridge, 224
    inns, 228, 233
    Manor, 238–40
    medieval priory, 227–8, 238
    non–conformists, 237
    railways, coming of, 232–3
    river traffic, 224–5, 228–9
    road traffic, 231
    St John's Bridge, 224, 226–7, 229
    St John's Lock, *226*, 229, 230, 232
    Saxon remains, 225, 240–4
    Trout Inn, 228
    workhouse, 228
life expectancy, improvements in, 122

MacPherson, John, 168–71
Malmesbury Abbey, 94, 95
Maskelyne Family, 19, 160
Meysi Family, 203
Mortimer Family, 238, 239
Moseley Weir, 68
Muttleford Stream, 18

Newbury, Battle of, 108–9
non-conformists, 145–7, 237
Normans
    land-holding system, 17
    powerful families, 89–90, 104, 202,
        238
Nott, Lieut Col., 21

Oaksey, 78
oxbow lakes, 45–6

packhorse trains, 31, 36
Panda of Mercia, 124
parish registers, 144–5
parliamentary elections, 158–73
Peach, Samuel, 160–4
Petrie's Cricklade Case, 130, 157, 161,
    166–73
pike, 71
plague, bubonic, 21
Poole Family, 76, 86–9
    Edward, 88–9
    Sir Henry (15th C.), 87
    Sir Henry (17th C.), 88, 160
    Sir Neville, 19, 88
Poole Keynes, 86–92
    Church of St Michael & All Angels,
        90–2, 185
    Manor House, 92

palaeolithic remains, 86
poor, conditions of, 101–2, 119–23, 179
punting & canoeing, 63–4

railways
    effect on bird life, 24–5
    efficiency compared with canals,
        33–4
    Great Western (GWR), 12, 77–9,
        149
    at Kemble, 77–9
    at Lechlade, 232
    Midland & South Western Junction,
        12, 36
    Swindon railway works, 34, 47, 58
Ray, River, 47, 52
Richmond Family, 108–9
roads, early, 31–2, 231
Roman occupation & remains, 12–13,
    15–17, 44, 60, 72–3, 82, 186
    Cotswold Settlement, 104–5

St Aldhelm, 94–5
St Augustine, 135–6, 138, 182–3
salmon, 67–8
    Thames Salmon Trust, 68
Seven Springs, 47
Seymour Family, 202–3
Shelley, Percy Bysshe, 62, 219, 235
Skilling, John, 163
Smerrill, 85
Somerford Keynes, 94–103
    Church of All Saints, 95–8, 100–1,
        185
    conditions, 19th C., 101–2
    Manor House, 99, 103
    watermills, 102
South Cerney, 114–23
    Church of All Hallows, 115–18, 185
    The College, 118, *119*
    condition of poor, 19th C., 119–20,
        122–3
    gravel excavation, 115
    illiteracy in, 122
    life expectancy in, 122
    village cross, 120, *121*
Stoner, Sir Walter, 55
Strange Family, 99–100
Swill Brook, 46
Swindon, GWR works, 34, 47, 58

'Swing Riots', 1830, 101

Thacker, Fred S.
    on Aston Keynes, 107, 112
    on Castle Eaton mill, 55
    on Cowneck, 45
    on Cricklade, 125, 146
    on Down Ampney, 185
    on Eisey, 52, 193
    on Ewen, 80, 82
    on George Hanger, 211
    on Hannington Bridge, 62
    on Latton, 175, 177–8
    on navigation problems, 64
    on South Cerney, 115–16
    on Thames Head, 59
    on watermills, 92
    on weirs, 53, 54, 56
Thames
    source of, 57–60, 81–2
    navigability, 60–6
Thames Conservancy, 62, 65
Thames Head, 13, 57–8
    pumping station, 34, 58
Thynne Family, 210, 212
tithes, disputes concerning, 44
Token Ton (shallow draught boat), 65,
    66
tracks & lanes, ancient, 29, 195
transport, *see* canals; railways; roads
Trewsbury Mead, 81
trout, 70–1

Uffington White Horse, 15

Vaughan Williams, Ralph, 186
Vespasian, Emperor, 12
Villiers, Sir Nicholas de, 186

Wallingford, 12
Watereaton, 50, 195–7
    Chapel of St Lawrence, 196
    Horse Bridge, 196, 219
    House 45, 188, 195, 196
    weir, 55
weirs, problems caused by, 53–6
Weobstan (Saxon leader), 17
Wesley, John & Charles, 111
Whittokesmede, John, 159–60
Withington, 47
Woodruffe, Nathaniel, 101–2